THE SECRET GUAM STUDY

Frist published in 2004.
Re-published with a new cover and foreword in 2024 by University of Guam Press.

University of Guam Press
Micronesian Area Research Center
303 University Drive, UOG Station
Mangilao, Guam 96923-9000
(671) 735-2153/4
www.uogpress.com

ISBN: 9781878453662 (hardback)
ISBN: 9781878453778 (paperback)
ISBN: 9781878453952 (library ebook)
ISBN: 9781878453945 (trade ebook)

Library of Congress Catalog Number: 2023951080

This publication was originally made possible by financial support from the U.S. National Park
Service, CNMI Division of Historic Preservation (Historic Preservation Office), Department of
Community and Cultural Affairs, and the Micronesian Area Research Center (MARC), UOG.
The views expressed in this book, however, do not necessarily reflect those of the U.S. National
Park Service, U.S. Department of the Interior, Division of Historic Preservation, Department of
Community and Cultural Affairs, or MARC, UOG.

This publication was part of The Occasional Historical Papers Series produced by the CNMI
Division of Historic Preservation (Historic Preservation Office). The series was intended to make the
results of historical research conducted within Micronesia available to a wide readership.

Book design by Ashley Smith
Original (2004) cover design by Parke Gregg
Second (2024) cover design by Ralph Eurich Patacsil
Second (2024) cover photos courtesy of the Senator Antonio M. Palomo Guam Museum and
CHamoru Educational Facility; the Micronesian Area Research Center; and Gerald R. Ford
Presidential Library & Museum

The Secret Guam Study

How President Ford's 1975 Approval of
Commonwealth Was Blocked by Federal Officials

Howard P. Willens

With
Dirk A. Ballendorf

To the People of Guam

Contents

Foreword

The Death of Dreams on Distant Desks

As an unincorporated territory of the United States, Guam is indisputably a U.S. colony. Many of us in Guam understand some of the ramifications of being a territory, particularly as it relates to our exclusion from American democracy. We often say that we are second-class citizens who do not have voting representation in U.S. Congress and who cannot elect the president. These critiques are correct and are the easier points of contention that we coalesce around. There is a clear democratic deficiency experienced by the territories. Unfortunately, many of us believe that resolving these narrow issues will remedy territorial flaws. Comments such as "If only we voted for President," or "If the territories just had one Senator in the U.S. Senate," are often used to express our collective frustrations with the political status quo. Yet, these attempts to fix our democratic deficiency are highly deficient themselves as they do not tackle the root of what being a territory means for the people of Guam. Something far more impactful to our daily lives serves as the foundation of territorial status: the usurping of our agency and power. There is an inherent powerlessness to being a U.S. territory, and as a result, the dreams and needs of the territories fall low on the federal government's priority list. Frequently, our desires are placed at the back of the line if they do not benefit the federal government or military. We are rarely put first. This is why when discussing unfavorable federal policies related to Guam, we often say that decisions for the island are made thousands of miles away, both literally and figuratively.

The authors of *The Secret Guam Study* chronicle an illuminating example of how territories are viewed and treated. Like explorers in search of lost political treasure, Willens and Ballendorf trace the life and death of President Gerald Ford's decision that the United States "should seek agreement with Guamanian representatives on a commonwealth relationship no less favorable" than that which the United States was negotiating with the Northern Mariana Islands at the time. The study that ultimately informed President Ford's decision recommended that the United States be ready to accept a commonwealth arrangement for Guam, permit the people of Guam to draft their own constitution, establish a mutually agreeable Joint Status Commission, and let Guam's leaders know that the president was ready to proceed with status negotiations. The authors of *The Secret Guam Study* rightfully point out that this agreement would have helped resolve many of the struggles the island's people were experiencing with Guam's governance, including limitations on federal authority with respect to local self-government and limitations on the applicability of especially oppressive federal laws. Yet, it was not until almost thirty years later, in the early 2000s, that this study or the president's directive were widely known to have existed.

i

In chronicling this history of that which did not occur, Willens and Ballendorf reveal a fundamental truth of the federal-territorial relationship that we must keep in mind today: **dreams can die neglected on distant desks**. There does not have to be some insidious intention or elaborate plan to keep territories like Guam subdued and powerless. This powerlessness is already hardened into the hierarchical system that dictates our relationship to the federal government. As the quest for self-determination and decolonization continues, we would be remiss to forget this important lesson that *The Secret Guam Study* imparts. In outlining the contours of the malign neglect that occurred in this case, Willens and Ballendorf show how neglect can operate through the labyrinth of US government bureaucracy. The protagonists (or antagonists) of neglect in this story include the National Security Council, the Department of Defense, the State Department, the United States Congress and most importantly, the Department of the Interior (DOI).

DOI was the federal agency responsible for implementing President Ford's directive approving the Guam study. However, as the authors of the book write, "Rather than initiating an effort to begin meaningful negotiations with informed Guam representatives, Interior embarked on a dilatory and indefensible deliberative process, internally and with the other federal agencies, about how to deal with the presidential directive." Interior did this through blatant neglect and bureaucratic delay. Most importantly, they did this through a common technique we still see in Guam's quest for self-determination today: disproportionately placing the onus of change on the local government and people of Guam. It is not unusual to hear that Guam could achieve decolonization if only the community was united in the effort. While this is certainly true, this should not absolve the federal government and its respective agencies for their role in stalling all efforts until such unity occurs. In the non-implementation of the study, DOI unilaterally decided to place the burden on Guam's leaders to form a negotiating team that represented the executive and legislative branches. The onus of beginning the discussion with the federal government was placed on Guam's shoulders.

The most shocking of these revelations was that this negotiation approach by DOI "would be done without telling any Guam official about the existence or substance of the president's directive." We are often told that we should enter negotiating tables "in good faith," or in an honest manner. DOI did not act in good faith with Guam, this much is clear. It is not in good faith to simultaneously avoid the president's directive and not even inform Guam's leaders of its existence. Furthermore, there was certainly a level of disregard and disrespect for Guam in this process. Leaders in Guam sent repeated letters to the White House asking for the appointment of a special representative to engage with Guam on territorial issues. Due to confusion in the federal bureaucracy and individuals such as Congressman Philip Burton and Fred Zeder from the Office of Territorial Affairs, these inquiries were long ignored, with only interim responses being provided. To be fair, there were those who challenged the DOI's perversion of the presidential directive. The State Department, for example, did not agree with DOI's negotiating approach, arguing that "presidential guidance directs us to seek agreement with the Guamanians on political status, not to wait for them to request discussions." In advocating for this more active approach, the State Department was essentially telling DOI that its approach was not in line with the president's directive. Yet, the sludge of bureaucracy made it so that DOI continued to stall despite this State Department input.

In traversing the deliberate ignoring of the President's directive, the authors also lay bare another facet of the federal-territorial relationship: Is Guam domestic or foreign? The bureaucratic delay was, in part, enabled by disagreements of jurisdiction. To put it another way, different agencies of the federal government were playing a game of jurisdictional hot potato when it came to dealing with the island's political status. As the authors note, "Confusion in the White House as to whether Guam was a domestic or national security question served only to highlight the lack of White House leadership necessary to ensure that President Ford's directive was faithfully implemented." For example, in considering a response to Governor Ricardo Bordallo's letters, one Domestic Council staffer asked whether Guam fell within their intergovernmental relations duties. The overall result of the Domestic Council and the National Security Council passing the buck of jurisdiction and responsibility to one another was that there was lack of meaningful engagement. This resulted in White House staff essentially taking DOI's lead and delaying the presidential directive. This episode provides an illustration of the ambiguity of U.S. territories in the general American imagination.

In this regard the death of the Guam study reveals another important component of life as a territory; namely, how disproportionate the impact of federal decisions can be. For players such as DOI, impeding the Guam study's implementation may have helped them hold on to political power and advance the career of particular individuals. The DOI and Congressman Burton used bureaucracy to ignore the president's directive. As a result, they essentially killed what would have been significant and much-needed political progress for Guam. While commonwealth would not have been a political status where Guam reached a "full measure of self-government," the island today would arguably have been better than our being stuck in unincorporated territory status. Federal policy on the territories is inherently affected by politics, as federal policy on the states certainly is. In this case, Congress did not want a process they did not have primary control over, which contributed to how easily the administration's initiative was placed out of focus. However, because of our inherent powerlessness, the stakes of paying attention to the needs of the territories are much lower.

Another lesson to learn from the Guam study requires looking at the justifications for the U.S. government accepting a commonwealth-like arrangement for Guam; namely continuing to use Guam as a strategically located military base. In knowing this, we can understand the source of our inherent powerlessness' persistence. This ultimately gets at the heart of what was allowable and what was off-limits when it comes to adjusting Guam's political status. The federal government needed to ensure that any adjustment would be "within manageable bounds" and "no less favorable than the Northern Marianas." Thus, while it is true that the commonwealth arrangement would have been an improvement, the United States would not allow anything that would fundamentally threaten its military interests. Examining the Guam study, one can break down the basic ingredients of Guam's importance. As National Security Advisor Henry Kissinger wrote in his memorandum of the presidential decision, "Our essential needs in our political relationship with Guam are control over Guam's defenses and foreign affairs and continued military basing rights." Control over Guam's foreign affairs and military basing is what truly matters to the United States. Utilizing Guam's geography for American statecraft is the most fundamental reason the United States cares about Guam.

A large impetus for considering a change in Guam's status in line with commonwealth was the growing discontent of Guam's people with the island's political status, and how this might affect the future of the U.S. military in the island. Per the report, "if the Guamanians perceive themselves as a people whose interests have been denied, U.S. military forces could hardly expect to enjoy the same spirit of friendly cooperation which they have had in the past." To be clear, there was not a fear that the U.S. military would be ejected from the island. As a territory, Guam did not possess the power to do this. Rather, the fear was that ignoring Guam's demands would lead to a less favorable socio-economic environment characterized by political friction with Guam's residents. This should sober us in the continuing quest for self-determination. Rhetoric surrounding Guam's relationship with the United States means close to nothing if it does not consider the United States securing its perpetual military use of the island. This is the most important factor in considering the past, present, or future of the Guam-U.S. relationship. Other factors such as being a part of the American family, serving together in the armed forces, or being loyal to the United States during World War II are confetti on the cake of our relationship with the United States. They are an ingredient, but by no means the entire recipe nor the most important part.

One of the most striking portions of the study was the emphasis on removing "unnecessary friction between the military and civilian communities." While one could easily read right past this phrase, there is one word that should spur critical thought: unnecessary. The use of the phrase, "unnecessary friction," implicitly points to the existence of its counterpart: "necessary friction." There exist recurring sources of friction with the United States, with most involving keeping us under the sovereignty of the United States so that U.S. military usage and access is not impeded. Such constraints create and sustain a political status glass ceiling. Political status alternatives such as free association or independence that will severely decrease the ability of the U.S. military to operate unimpeded are threatening and will cause friction. Yet, this friction will be deemed necessary to protect U.S. interests. For example, in the study, they write, "significant increase in the level of military activity…is conceivably a source of friction with Guamanians. It need not be. Guamanians are strong patriots and will accept additional burdens readily if they understand the reasons…" Our acceptance of military projects is taken for granted as can be seen in the modern push for the placement of anti-missile systems and the relocation of the Marine Corps here in Guam.

We have to ask ourselves if we are willing to be eroded by the sources of our necessary frictions with the military and federal government. Guam's future leaders, who will continue to fight for decolonization of the island, must similarly decide on what Guam's fundamental interests are in our relationship with the United States. The United States has repeatedly lifted the veil of what matters for them. Similarly, we need to make sure we know what matters for us and ardently defend our interests.

Lastly, there is a clear lesson to be learned from the history surrounding *the secret Guam study*. In the legislative finding that created the second Guam Political Status Commission, it was stated that "a resolution of some of Guam's basic economic, social, and political questions should be sought within the framework of political status negotiations with the federal government with all due speed." This is wisdom that should serve as the permanent blueprint for Guam's leaders to follow. There are primary lessons to learn from this wisdom. First, there is a tendency here in Guam to over-demonize local governance. It is common to hear that the answer to all of Guam's problems should be more federal intervention. For federal intervention advocates, the island's leaders are simply far too corrupt to effectively run a government. They are too bogged down in self-interest and nepotism to be objective. While there is truth that elements of corruption are present in Guam, many in Guam act as if the federal government is immune from political sins.

In an opinion column I write for *The Guam Daily Post*, I labeled this the problem of the "unquestioned answer." Critics of a change in Guam's political status often say there are just too many unanswered questions when it comes to decolonization. From the economy to defense to citizenship, critics are quick to use the "unanswered questions" card as a way to polemically make the case against political status change. To be fair, there truly are many unanswered questions. However, we should take issue with those who play the "unquestioned answers" card as a way to stall any progress or to place unreasonable expectations of "crystal ball standards" of prediction on advocates of political status change. While being concerned with "unanswered questions" let us at the same time be similarly critical and skeptical of "unquestioned answers" such as the need for never-ending federal intervention or asserting that Guam is a place that is incompetent in every regard. I describe these "unquestioned answers" as the prepackaged script many in Guam tend to use when it comes to reacting to or proposing solutions to the more uncomfortable parts of our reality here. For example, we often ask, "How did (fill in the blank with a problem) happen in Guam?" Unquestioned answers: "Because only on Guam do these types of things happen. This is why we need the federal government." There are elements of truth in these answers, but too often do we seem to default to them without a serious consideration of alternatives or the logic behind these prepackaged answers. Yet, as *The Secret Guam Study* shows us, there are multiple ways in which neglect and individuals craving power can deprioritize territories to such an extent that should make us second guess placing all our faith in the federal government. Doing so does not mean we become apologists of our own problems. Willens and Ballendorf are correct that the local government (and our delegate in Congress) should not let partisan politics obstruct the progress and momentum of self-determination. We have agency in moving this issue forward, even if we are working against federal, bureaucratic sludge and foot-dragging. Contributing to this is not the best path. As Robert Underwood once remarked regarding political development in Guam, "failure can have many fathers." We, the people of Guam, must no longer be forefathers and foremothers of our political demise.

Overall, the answers and proposed solutions to many of Guam's problems are more nuanced than we tend to treat them. As *The Secret Guam Study* helps show, it is bad strategy to try and resolve our multiple grievances with the United States in a piecemeal fashion. We must not advocate for better Band-Aids to cover the festering wound of colonialism. Initiatives such as seeking amendments to the Organic Act; the drafting of a constitution that ultimately must stay under the federal-territorial relationship; voting rights in U.S. presidential elections; or electing a non-voting U.S. senator for the territories are all Band-Aids. While Band-Aids are not useless for shallow wounds, colonialism demands more serious intervention. The generations of political leaders before us understood the magnitude of the colonial wound. While Band-Aids may cover the wound from view, they do not heal. In this manner, Band-Aid political initiatives for Guam contribute to "well-dressed colonialism," with the political hierarchy untouched. Guam needs to understand its seemingly disparate problems as having a territorial root that is need of resolution. An approach rooted in this orientation acknowledges local culpability in our problems but sees the resolution of our political status issue as a way to address our problems comprehensively. Even if the Guam study and the subsequent presidential directive were not implemented, the authors of this book show us the importance of not diverging from the political status framework. In moving forward with a political status framework to address the root of our issues, *The Secret Guam Study* should also make us think deeply about how to begin a political status conversation with the federal government.

To conclude, *The Secret Guam Study* should be required reading for every person who calls Guam home and cares about the future of this island. Engaging with this historical episode shows the incredible difference in priorities that emerge from the current federal-territorial relationship. While the proposals in the Guam study would have fulfilled many of the political desires Guam's leaders fought for, it was never implemented and withered away. The importance of understanding the Guam study's story is in comprehending how pervasive this treatment is, and how this episode reveals a larger pattern in how we are viewed by the federal government. At the end of the day, it is not only the study that is shrouded in secrecy. Our territorial status, powerlessness, military importance, and physical distance has made Guam a largely unknown entity in the general American imagination. As a territory, we are inherently lesser than. As a territory, our dreams can die on faraway desks, just another federal casualty.

Kenneth Gofigan Kuper, Ph.D.
November 2023

Kenneth Gofigan Kuper, Ph.D. is a CHamoru born and raised in Guåhan (Guam). He is an associate professor of political science, CHamoru studies, and Micronesian studies at the Micronesian Area Research Center (MARC) of the University of Guam where he focuses on issues of geopolitics and international relations in the region. He is also a founder of the Guam-based think tank, the Pacific Center for Island Security, which examines security issues from an island and islander perspective.

Preface

This book had its origins in a visit that my friends, Howard Willens and Deanne Siemer, from Washington, DC paid to the Micronesian Area Research Center (MARC) in 2000. They had just published their first book about United States policy in Micronesia and were in the process of completing their second book about the status negotiations between the Northern Mariana Islands and the United States. They had discovered a few previously classified documents that seemed to indicate that the U.S. government had been prepared in 1975, at the direction of President Ford, to give Guam a political status at least as advantageous as that of the Northern Marianas. Their question to me was whether anyone in Guam knew anything about this.

We convened a small discussion group including Robert Rogers, a Guam historian and author, and my colleagues at MARC, Professors Don Shuster and Don Rubenstein. We all concluded that we had never heard of any such undertaking by the federal government, and surely not at the presidential level.

Howard and Deanne suggested that we could probably unearth the Guam study and the presidential approval, if it existed, by filing a request for documents under the Freedom of Information Act (FOIA). I agreed to do so, and Deanne agreed to serve as my lawyer. The FOIA requests—to the Department of State, the Department of the Interior, and the Department of Defense—were submitted in late 2000. In short, they requested all the agency documents pertaining to the preparation of any such study of Guam's political status during 1973–74, its review by President Ford, and its implementation during the Ford Administration ending in January 1977.

Nothing happened for ten months. The agencies acknowledged receipt of my requests but gave us no indication whether any documents relating to the study existed and might be provided. Deanne contacted the agencies in 2001 in an effort to learn when, if ever, they intended to respond to my

FOIA requests. She was given no definitive information from any of the agencies.

In an effort to improve the situation, Deanne and Howard in the fall of 2001 visited the Ford Presidential Library in Ann Arbor, Michigan, to ascertain if the study did in fact exist and had been approved by President Ford. They learned from the archivist that such a study had been completed by the federal government in 1974 and forwarded to the president for his review and decision. Although the Ford Library supplied some of the relevant documents, Deanne and Howard were informed that the study itself and other significant documents were still classified and could not be released. Requests seeking declassification of the study and other documents were submitted in late 2001, but only a few insignificant documents were released; the study itself was not declassified.

Deanne and Howard visited MARC again in January 2002 and reported on their findings from the Ford Library. Howard presented his tentative conclusions about the documents he had discovered to a seminar at MARC attended by graduate students, faculty, and the press. No one in that room had any knowledge of any presidential directive on Guam's political status as early as 1975 or any offer to give Guam what had been granted to the Northern Marianas. The *Pacific Daily News* wrote an editorial about the study and asked that the Interior Department release the documents reportedly held in a long unopened safe. Still no documents were produced by any of the agencies.

Finally, in May 2003, some thirty months after the FOIA requests had been submitted, Deanne and Howard recommended that we go to court to require the agencies to comply with the Freedom of Information Act. I authorized them to file complaints against the Departments of Defense, State, and Interior in federal court in Washington, DC to see if we could pry the relevant documents from the government's cold, hard grasp.

I took this action because I believe Guam has spent an enormous amount of time and resources over the past three decades seeking improvements in its political status, and Guamanians deserved to know the truth about what the federal government had done. Guam had a political status commission in 1975, headed by Frank Blas, that was ready and willing to discuss an improved status with the federal agencies. But the federal government ignored the commission and did not respond to its letter of August 1975 for more than twelve months.

Then in 1977, Guam's constitutional convention produced a draft constitution, which in 1979 was rejected by the voters. This resulted in part from the widespread public frustration at being asked to adopt a constitution before having Guam's relationship with the federal government improved through status negotiations. This led in turn to the creation in 1980 of a Commission on Self-Determination, two polls of public opinion in 1982, and a new Commission on Self-Determination in 1984. After several years of effort, a draft commonwealth act was drafted and approved by the voters in 1987. Beginning in 1989, four years of negotiations with the Bush Administration yielded no forward progress. The same was true with respect to the Clinton Administration, notwithstanding major commitments of time and effort by Guamanian and federal representatives. Hearings before Congress in 1997 on a draft commonwealth bill resulted in no congressional action.

All of this was costly, both in resources and in human terms, as Guamanians became more and more discouraged with their status problems. I thought it was important to find out what really happened in 1975 and whether the frustration of the last thirty years could have been avoided.

Almost immediately after the complaints were filed, each of the three agencies produced documents. It seemed obvious to us that the agencies had assembled the documents months before and were hoping that this pesky professor from Guam would lose interest in his FOIA requests. After reviewing these documents, Howard and Deanne told me that they thought the agencies had additional documents that should have been produced. I authorized them to file motions to compel production of additional documents against the Department of State and the Department of the Interior, whose searches of their files seemed superficial. Miraculously, each department found even more documents, and produced affidavits confirming that they had actually located and declassified Guam documents within months after my FOIA requests had been submitted. They did not explain why they had not produced the documents until I filed my lawsuits. At my request, Deanne and Howard are continuing to urge the federal courts to conclude that these three agencies have violated the Freedom of Information Act by requiring me to file lawsuits after thirty months of delay to obtain these documents

And now, after more than three years of time, effort, and expense, we have the more than 300 documents relating to the Guam study, its approval by President Ford, and its non-implementation by the federal agencies. All of these documents are available to the public through the Micronesian Area Research Center library. This book is the story of what we found. It is a story that is both profoundly important and incredibly sad. Guam deserved better.

Dirk A. Ballendorf
Professor of Micronesian History
University of Guam

October 1, 2004

Acknowledgments

The authors would like to express thanks and appreciation to Joseph Ada, Frank Blas, Kurt Moylan, Thomas Tanaka, and Robert Underwood who gave their time for interviews with the authors with respect to their recollections of the events recounted in this book. Professor Robert Rogers generously provided valuable suggestions regarding an earlier draft of this book. We are also grateful for the efforts of Dr. Richard H.J. Wyttenbach-Santos, Captain USN (Ret.), a retired vice president and associate professor at the University of Guam, who assisted in gathering materials and arranging interviews on Guam in support of the book; Carmen Qunitenilla at the MARC Library who located relevant materials in the collections of the documents of Ricardo Bordallo and Antonio Borja Won Pat; Don Shuster, Marjorie Driver, Omaira Brunal-Perry, and La Vonne C. Guerrero-Meno at the Micronesian Area Research Center who also helped us get this work done; and Ruth Tighe for her editing assistance. The authors would like to express their special appreciation for the assistance of Deanne Siemer, who represented Professor Ballendorf in his efforts to obtain documents under the Freedom of Information Act and provided essential editing and other support to bring this project to successful completion.

About the Authors

HOWARD P. WILLENS is a managing director of Wilsie Company. Mr. Willens has practiced law in Washington, DC in both the public and private sectors. He served as deputy assistant attorney general in the Department of Justice, assistant counsel to the Warren Commission, and executive director of the President's Commission on Crime in the District of Columbia. Mr. Willens was retained by the Marianas Political Status Commission to represent it in negotiations with the United States regarding their future political status (1972–1976) and served as counsel to the First Marianas Constitutional Convention (1976) and the Third Marianas Constitutional Convention (1995–1996). Mr. Willens has co-authored two books about United States policy in Micronesia and the negotiations between the Northern Mariana Islands and the United States that resulted in the Covenant. He is a fellow of the Micronesian Area Research Center.

DIRK A. BALLENDORF is a tenured professor of History and Micronesian Area Studies at the University of Guam. Dr. Ballendorf first came to Guam in 1961 on his way to serve as a Peace Corps volunteer in the Philippines. He served as the Director of the Peace Corps program in Palau and as President of the Community College in Pohnpei (now the College of Micronesia). Dr. Ballendorf earned his doctoral degree at Harvard. He has been a member of the faculty of the University of Guam since 1979, and is currently also the Acting Director of the Micronesian Area Research Center. Dr. Ballendorf has authored two books and a number of articles and monographs on the history of Guam and Micronesia, and he supervises graduate student research in these areas.

Introduction

On February 1, 1975, National Security Adviser Henry A. Kissinger advised the Departments of Defense, Interior, and State that President Gerald R. Ford, after reviewing a year-long classified study of Guam's political status, had decided that the United States "should seek agreement with Guamanian representatives on a commonwealth arrangement no less favorable than that which we are negotiating with the Northern Marianas." If such an agreement had been achieved pursuant to the president's directive and approved by Congress, Guam might have able to replace the Organic Act of 1950 under which it was governed by Congress with provisions comparable to those accepted by the United States with respect to the Northern Mariana Islands. Such an agreement would have provided a clear legal basis for developing Guam's institutions of government in accord with a locally drafted constitution; limitations on federal authority with respect to local self-government; multi-year financing arrangements; limitations on the applicability of especially oppressive federal laws; and an opportunity for serious discussion regarding United States military needs and usage of Guamanian land.[1]

Two years later, when President Ford left office in January 1977, this directive remained unimplemented and unknown to Guam's elected officials. If, in the years that followed, Guam had achieved most of its political status goals, the fate of this presidential directive would have been relegated to a footnote in this history of forward progress. But as Guam's leaders and citizens know all too well, this was not the case. To the contrary, Guam's wholly frustrating experience in trying to develop commonwealth

---

1.   Memorandum, February 1, 1975, Kissinger to Chairman, Under Secretaries Committee, 1 (Appendix 1).

legislation during the 1980s and 1990s encountered seemingly intractable opposition from both the executive and legislative branches of the United States government.

This book explores the origin and fate of this important and previously undisclosed study of Guam's political status. The study's summary chapter, the president's action, and other important documents are set out in appendices so that the reader can see the original source material. The book provides a detailed story of the way in which the federal bureaucracy, led by the Department of the Interior, successfully thwarted President Ford's directive and, to this extent, helps to explain some of the resistance that Guam encountered from federal officials during its status discussions years later. The lessons gleaned from this sad encounter with the federal bureaucracy should be useful in guiding future efforts to address Guam's still unfulfilled political status aspirations. It provides new documentation for claims that Guam's contribution to the national security and defense of the United States entitles it, at the very least, to be treated now with the candor and sense of justice that these United States citizens were denied in the 1970s.

Chapter One

Origin of the Study

When the Northern Mariana Islands began status negotiations with the United States in December 1972, Guam watched with keen interest. The southernmost island in the Mariana chain of islands, Guam had been part of the United States since 1898. The other Mariana islands, after being sold by Spain, had been ruled by Germany (until 1914), Japan (until 1945), and then by the United States under a trusteeship agreement with the United Nations. Notwithstanding this separation for more than seventy years, Guam and the Northern Marianas were linked by family and their shared history under Spanish rule, their common Chamorro culture, and their physical proximity.

During World War II, Guam was retaken and the Northern Mariana Islands were seized from the Japanese and occupied by U.S. armed forces. After the war, Guam's political status was upgraded through an organic act, passed by the U.S. Congress in 1950; and the United States governed the Northern Marianas, together with the Caroline and Marshall Islands in the Pacific Ocean north of the equator, as the Trust Territory of the Pacific Islands. Under the organic act, the governance of Guam was transferred from military to civilian officials, its institutions of government (including an appointed governor) were prescribed by Congress, and most of the local residents became U.S. citizens. Concurrently, in the 1950s the Northern Marianas began a long campaign to become a part of the United States. This desire for a future political status separate from the other districts in the Trust Territory of the Pacific Islands was prompted in large measure by their perception of the political and economic advantages enjoyed by Guam as a U.S. territory.

During the 1950s and 1960s, political leaders in Guam and the Northern Marianas pursued reunification of the islands under United States sovereignty. Two political parties had been organized on Guam before the war and were revived with the advent of the post-war elected legislature. The public position of Guam's leaders seemed to favor reunification. Two political parties were organized in 1957 on Saipan, the most populous of the Northern Mariana Islands. Both of these parties favored affiliation with the United States after termination of the trusteeship agreement; the Popular (later Democratic) Party sought to do so through reunification with Guam whereas the Progressive (later Territorial and then Republican) Party advocated a direct relationship with the United States. Opinion polls on Saipan showed strong support for the reunification movement and Guam's elected officials anticipated equally strong support among Guam's voters.

When the reunification proposal was put before the Guamanian voters in November 1969, however, it was rejected. Notwithstanding this unexpected outcome, Saipan's voters a few days later expressed their strong support for reunification. Many reasons were offered to explain the Guam result, including inadequate political education, low voter turnout, political rivalries arising from a concurrent campaign for Guam's first elected governor, and concerns about the economic costs of reintegration. Not as extensively discussed, however, was the likelihood that the outcome may have been influenced by residual resentment among Guamanians about the role played by Northern Marianas Chamorros working for the Japanese in Guam during World War II. Some Chamorros from Saipan and Rota were used by the Japanese as informants and spies to assist in their invasion of Guam. Others served as interpreters, messengers, and administrators during the Japanese occupation of Guam and, in some instances, were perceived by Guamanians as hostile participants in the Japanese effort to control the island and to defeat Guamanian resistance efforts.

After this rejection by Guam's voters, which many in the Northern Marianas still recall vividly, the Northern Marianas developed a new strategy for seeking affiliation with the United States. An opportunity was provided when the United States began political status negotiations in 1969 with representatives of the Congress of Micronesia, in which Northern Marianas leaders participated. Once it became clear during those negotiations that the other Trust Territory districts did not share the Northern Marianas goal of U.S. citizenship, the United States ultimately agreed to conduct separate status negotiations with the Northern Marianas.[2]

Guamanian interest in these negotiations was evident from their formal opening in December 1972. Bishop Felixberto Flores of Guam was asked to deliver the invocation as a "symbolic gesture" that recognized Guam's historic linkage to the Northern Marianas. Governor Carlos G. Camacho of Guam attended in a "strictly ceremonial role." The Northern Marianas negotiators made it clear to the U.S. delegation that they did not want formal Guamanian participation in the negotiations. Although Guam's non-voting delegate in the U.S. Congress, Antonio B. Won Pat, would have preferred some formal involvement in the discussions, he recognized the political implications and accepted the Northern Marianas decision. There was no doubt, however, that the negotiations—which "caught everybody by surprise"— were of great interest to Guamanians, who reacted initially with a mixture of pride in their neighbor's opportunity, regret about the defeat of the reintegration proposal, and apprehension that the Northern Marianas would achieve a more advantageous political status than Guam's.[3]

---

2. The pursuit of affiliation with the United States by the Northern Mariana Islands and the efforts to reunify these islands with Guam are discussed in Howard P. Willens and Deanne C. Siemer, *National Security and Self-Determination: United States Policy in Micronesia (1961-1972)*(Westport, CT: Praeger, 2000)[hereafter *National Security*], 19-25, 35-36, 93-95, 187-92, 241-47. United States agreement to these separate status talks and their successful conclusion were important factors in the further fragmentation in later years of the Trust Territory of the Pacific Islands. *Id.*, 257-58.

3. Howard P. Willens and Deanne C. Siemer, *An Honorable Accord: The Covenant between the Northern Mariana Islands and the United States* (Honolulu, HI: University of Hawaii, 2001)[hereafter *An Honorable Accord*], 52-53; Howard P. Willens and Deanne C. Siemer, *Oral Histories of the Northern Mariana Islands: Political Life and Developments* (1945-1995) (Saipan, MP: CNMI Division of Historic Preservation, 2004)[hereafter *Oral Histories*], Interviews of Edward DLG Pangelinan, Vicente N. Santos, and Roger Stillwell; *Pacific Daily News* (September 13, December 8 and 14, 1972).

Notwithstanding the 1969 rejection, the possible reunification of the Mariana islands in the future affected the agendas of both parties in the Marianas status negotiations—albeit with very different effects. Even before they agreed to separate negotiations with the Northern Marianas, U. S. representatives advised Marianas leaders that it was very unlikely that the United States would authorize a political status for the Northern Marianas that was different from Guam's. United States officials continued to nurture the goal of reintegration in early 1972, but conversations with knowledgeable Guamanian officials dashed American hopes that reintegration would offer a simple and expeditious solution to the Northern Marianas status question. Throughout this period, Northern Marianas representatives asserted that their constituents no longer desired reintegration with Guam. They made it abundantly clear that they would be looking at Guam and other insular areas "to see if the political and economic development in those areas suggests any problems or difficulties which the Marianas should avoid." Based on such an examination, Edward DLG Pangelinan, the chairman of the Marianas Political Status Commission, advised the U.S. delegation (and the world at large) in December 1972 that "it might well be necessary to develop a totally new political status for the Marianas."[4]

The Northern Marianas representatives naturally looked to Guam for advice and guidance throughout the negotiations in order to achieve a status that was as advantageous as possible. Guam's political leaders, despite their ambivalence about the negotiations, were eager to give the novice negotiators the benefit of their years of experience in dealing with the United States. At a meeting in November 1972, several members of the Marianas Political Status Commission met with Guam's first elected governor and other officials to discuss the anticipated U.S. land requests for military purposes in the Northern Marianas and the problems that Guam had encountered in dealing with the U.S. military on Guam. Well aware that Guam's government

---

4. *National Security*, 224-25, 233; *An Honorable Accord*, 49-50; Memorandum, February 16, 1972, Williams to Holdridge, 2; *Oral Histories*, Interview of Herman Q. Guerrero; Department of the Interior, Minutes of Interagency Group Meeting (March 2, 1972), March 7, 1972, 2; Department of Defense, Airgram, March 4, 1972, McCain to Moorer, 1; Department of Defense, Airgram, March 4, 1972, Pugh to McCain, 2.

was entirely a creature of the U.S. Congress, the Northern Marianas were insistent on seeking some formal limitation on the authority of Congress so that, among other reasons, Congress could not unilaterally force reintegration with Guam over the opposition of the Northern Marianas. The Northern Marianas negotiators were very familiar with Guam's difficulties in developing a diversified economy under the constraints imposed by various U.S. laws; this led to extensive negotiations regarding the applicability of federal laws generally and specific provisions relating to coastwise laws, immigration, and minimum wage. As the negotiations progressed, the Marianas Political Status Commission continued to consult with Guam's leaders about the negotiations and their possible beneficial affects on Guam's own political status.[5]

After the second round of status negotiations in early June 1973, the broad outlines of the future political relationship between the United States and the Northern Mariana Islands were detailed in a joint communiqué. It described preliminary agreements about such matters as mutual consent, provision for a locally drafted constitution, and assurances about maximum local self-government. Such attractive provisions—with promises of more to come—— prompted outspoken complaints from Guamanian political leaders. Guam Senator Paul Calvo expressed "grave concern about Guam's total lack of involvement in the negotiations that are being held to decide the political future of the Mariana Islands" and announced plans to go to Washington to complain about the situation.[6]

---

5.   Land Report, April 1973, prepared by James E. White for the Commission, 36-50; *An Honorable Accord*, 61-62, 81-90, 103-09, 119-25, 138, 160-62, 178-81; *Oral Histories*, Interviews of Adrian L. DeGraffenried, Daniel T. Muna, Edward DLG Pangelinan, Vicente N. Santos, James E. White, and James M. Wilson Jr.

6.   After a subsequent trip to Washington, Calvo predicted that the Northern Marianas could expect substantial opposition in the U.S. Congress to their commonwealth aspirations. He reported that the congressmen with whom he talked were generally aware of the negotiations and wanted Guam and the Northern Marianas to work out some common future political destiny. *An Honorable Accord*, 89-90, 130; *Pacific Daily News* (June 8 and July 8, 1973); *Oral Histories*, Interviews of Joseph C. Murphy and Roger Stillwell.

The U.S. delegation that conducted the Northern Marianas negotiations was headed by F. Haydn Williams, the president of the Asia Foundation in San Francisco. Williams had been appointed by President Nixon in 1971 to serve as his personal representative with the rank of ambassador to represent the United States in the Micronesian—and then Northern Marianas—status negotiations. His appointment was a result of the impasse reached in the Micronesian negotiations in 1970 and the long-overdue recognition by the White House that the national interest in these negotiations required someone of stature to lead and mediate the different views of the Departments of State, Defense, and Interior regarding these negotiations.

Williams had served in the 1950s as a member of the faculty and assistant dean of the Fletcher School of Law and Diplomacy at Tufts University in Massachusetts, where earlier he had earned his master's degree and doctorate. He had been deputy to the assistant secretary of defense (international security affairs) from 1958 to 1962, where he worked for John N. Irwin II. Irwin was Under Secretary of State in the Nixon Administration and recommended Williams for this new position as status negotiator in 1971. Williams had a good overview of the Pacific region as well as Washington politics and understood that Guam could be an important factor in the approval of the agreement he was negotiating in the Marianas. After Calvo expressed his concerns about the Northern Marianas negotiations, Williams met with the media and effectively answered their questions about the separate negotiations. But the influential editorials of Joseph C. Murphy in the *Pacific Daily News* remained extremely critical of the disparate treatment of Guam and the Northern Marianas.[7]

Ambassador Williams wrote to President Richard M. Nixon in June 1973 urging that Guam's political status needed attention. He reported that Guamanian officials expressed "considerable chagrin" that the Northern Marianas were being offered a commonwealth relationship with the United States while Guam, a U.S. territory since 1898, remained in what they labeled "inferior status." He passed on reports that Guamanian officials

---

7. *National Security*, 211-12; *An Honorable Accord*, 130, 168.

might initiate discussions in Washington about a change in Guam's status and that there was a growing interest in Guam regarding a possible union with the Northern Marianas. Williams took this initiative regarding Guam in part because of his concern that Guamanian leaders might use their influence to derail the Northern Marianas negotiations. But he was motivated to a greater extent because "he felt a strong sense of loyalty to the fact that they were a long-time member of the American political family" and "they should not be treated with less dignity than the Marianas."[8]

The Department of Defense moved promptly to support Williams and advocated U.S. action on Guam's political status. The joint chiefs of staff reported to the secretary of defense on July 20, 1973, regarding "the growing sense of alienation among the inhabitants of Guam" and recommended that the National Security Council prepare a study "with some urgency to review the political, security, economic, and social aspects of Guam." A few weeks later, the deputy secretary of defense echoed this sense of "urgency" in recommending that a study be undertaken to address "the growing ferment on Guam regarding its political status." [9]

The Defense Department emphasized the thoroughly predictable impact of the ongoing negotiations in the Northern Marianas (and the other Trust Territory districts) on Guam's desire to address deficiencies in its status. As evidence of the "growing alienation among the Guamanians," the deputy secretary pointed out the limited political outlets for Guamanians for affecting policies of the federal government and their concern about being treated as second-class citizens with respect to the extensive use of Guam's land by the U.S. military and outside (primarily Japanese) investors. From a strictly strategic standpoint, he emphasized that "US forward basing in the Western Pacific is becoming a matter of increasing concern" due to developments in Okinawa, Japan, Vietnam, and the Philippines. According

---

8. *Oral Histories,* Interviews of James D. Berg and Adrian L. DeGraffenried; Letter, June 29, 1973, Williams to the President, 2-3.

9. Memorandum, July 20, 1973, Colladay to Secretary of Defense; Memorandum, August 14, 1973, Clements to Chairman, NSC Under Secretaries Committee.

to the Defense Department, the proposed study should be undertaken "with a view towards assisting Guam in planning and achieving the goals and aspirations of the local community." In order to protect U.S. relationships and military posture in Guam, "action must be initiated now to preclude unfulfilled expectations of the inhabitants of Guam from jeopardizing future US national interests in that area."[10]

The National Security Council took up the Guam issues through its Under Secretaries Committee, composed of the officials who held the second-in-command posts in the Departments of State, Defense, and Treasury, the primary agencies concerned with national security, augmented by officials from other departments as specific issues required. On September 12, 1973, the Under Secretaries Committee directed that "a study of US national objectives, policies, and programs in Guam be undertaken to identify prospective course of action by which US interest may most effectively be fostered." Attaching the letter from the deputy secretary of defense, the chairman of the Under Secretaries Committee directed that the study effort be staffed by an interagency group made up of low-level officials from the interested agencies and chaired by the Department of the Interior. The study was to be completed by December 17, 1973.[11]

The interagency group was headed by Stanley S. Carpenter, deputy assistant secretary for territorial affairs at Interior. Carpenter was a career foreign service officer who came to Interior in late 1971 for a three-year tour of duty as part of an effort to upgrade the quality of the personnel at Interior dealing with the territories. Even before the Under Secretaries Committee had officially acted, Carpenter advised Secretary of the Interior Morton of its anticipated action, the lead role to be assumed by Interior, and the corresponding need for additional funds and manpower within Interior. Shortly after the committee issued its directive, Carpenter solicited the participation

---

10. Memorandum, August 14, 1973, Clements to Chairman, NSC Under Secretaries Committee.

11. Memorandum, September 12, 1973, Staff Director Grove to Members of Under Secretaries Committee.

of representatives from several agencies and circulated a draft "terms of reference" sheet regarding the study. His draft proposed that the study consider three major areas: military-security (involving control and use of land by the U.S. military and general relations with the government of Guam); relationship with the federal government (involving relations with federal agencies and Guamanian concerns regarding their current political status); and socioeconomic (including participation by foreign investors in Guam's economy and its need for increased federal financial assistance).[12]

Also in 1973, Guam created a Political Status Commission, which invited the Northern Marianas negotiators to visit in early July of that year. The Northern Marianas leaders were concerned with keeping the Guamanian officials advised about their status negotiations; they wanted to defuse any possible opposition from Guam and to assure the status commission that the Northern Marianas effort, if successful, would not operate to Guam's disadvantage. However, the chair of the Marianas Political Status Commission, Edward DLG Pangelinan, was sensitive to the powerful sentiment in the Northern Marianas that no deal could include reintegration with Guam. Pangelinan, the only Chamorro lawyer in the Northern Marianas at the time, had been elected to the Congress of Micronesia shortly after he finished law school. During his initial term in office, he had led the effort to separate the Northern Marianas from the rest of the Trust Territory. He made it clear in advance of the meeting with the Guam Political Status Commission that reintegration was not going to be discussed at the meeting. After the session, the Northern Marianas participants reported that they had explored the probable consequences of opening up their islands to foreign investment based on Guam's experience and had discussed the relationship between the military and civilian communities on Guam. Pangelinan declared publicly

---

12. Memorandum, August 27, 1973, Carpenter to the Secretary of the Interior; Letter, September 26, 1973, Carpenter to Hummel (State), enclosing the "Terms of Reference for Guam Study."

that it was definitely in Guam's interest to support the Northern Marianas in its search for an improved political status.[13]

Having served as Guam's representative in Washington for many years before he was elected in 1972 as its first non-voting delegate to the House, Antonio B. Won Pat generally shared the view that it was unfair for the United States to open up status negotiations with the Northern Mariana and not with Guam. According to Roger Stillwell, who worked for Won Pat for many years, he also recognized that it "wasn't helpful to his own political image." Won Pat was a skilled politician and central figure in the Democratic Party on Guam. Born on Guam and educated to become a teacher, he began his political career in 1937 when he was elected to the lower house of the then-bicameral Guam Congress. He was reelected to two subsequent terms until the Congress ceased functioning with the Japanese invasion in December 1941. After the war, Won Pat became a leader of the party that later became the Popular Party, and then the Democratic Party, which dominated local politics for the next twenty years. He served as speaker in the lower house for several terms, campaigned for the enactment of the Organic Act of 1950, and was elected to, and became speaker of, the unicameral legislature formed in compliance with that legislation. He served as Guam's first Washington Representative from 1965 to 1972 and then as Guam's non-voting delegate in the House of Representatives from 1973 to 1985 after this position was authorized by Congress and approved by President Nixon.[14]

In the fall of 1973, Won Pat introduced a resolution in the House of Representatives which asserted Guam's inherent right to choose its own political status and requested President Nixon to form a special commission to work with Guam's status commission. Meanwhile Won Pat embarked

---

13. Telegram, July 3, 1973, Trent to Washington; *I Gaseta* (July 5, 1973); *Marianas Variety* (July 13, 1973); *Oral Histories,* Interviews of Edward DLG Pangelinan, Vicente N. Santos, and James E. White.

14. Micronesian Area Research Center, University of Guam, MARC Working Papers #66: Inventory of the Papers of Antonio Borja Won Pat, 2-6 (1996); *Oral Histories,* Interview of Roger Stillwell.

on polling his constituents to ascertain their status preferences; his sample (of unknown size) revealed that 86.2 percent believed that the Northern Marianas should be united with Guam. Won Pat had not made any attempt with the Nixon Administration to advance Guam's cause, because "he understood that it was useless." Although his efforts in Congress in 1973 went nowhere, Won Pat was repeatedly assured by Congressman Phillip Burton, chairman of the House of Representatives Subcommittee on Territorial and Insular Affairs, on which Won Pat served, that "we'll get to [Guam] after we take care of [the Northern Marianas]"[15]

Guamanian concerns were expressed with increased force as the Northern Marianas negotiations appeared almost certain to reach a successful conclusion. After the third round in December 1973, the discussions relating to military land requirements were publicized, as well as the initial American offer of financial assistance for the Northern Marianas. Guamanian observers pointed out some of the key differences between the proposed relationship and Guam's status. By this time in the negotiations, it was clear that the Northern Marianas was going to be able to draft its own constitution, limit federal authority through a mutual consent provision, enjoy multi-year guaranteed federal funding for government operations and capital improvement projects, and carve out certain exceptions to important federal laws. In his editorials, Joe Murphy expressed respect "for the skillful way the Marianas negotiators are handling the talks" and suggested that, if he were one of Guam's political leaders, he "would ask for another referendum on the reintegration issue." Like other Guamanians, however, he still believed that Guam—a loyal territory for decades—should have "a better deal" than the Northern Marianas and that many in the U.S. Congress would object to the establishment of two separate governments in the small Mariana Islands chain.[16]

---

15. *Oral Histories,* Interview of Roger Stillwell; *Pacific Daily News* (October 29, 1973).

16. *Oral Histories,* Interview of Joseph C. Murphy; *Pacific Daily News* (December 20, 1973); *Marianas Variety* (December 21, 1973).

Congressman Burton heard these complaints personally when he visited Guam in January 1974. Elected to Congress from San Francisco in a special election in 1964, Burton had previously served in the California Assembly and earned a reputation as "a hard-charging urban liberal interested in labor, welfare, and civil rights." His assignment to the Committee on Interior and Insular Affairs seemed a strange one to some observers; but others speculated that he chose it "because he could gain seniority there faster than any place else." He took a leading role in reforming the committee to limit the power of its chairman over its subcommittees and was successful in adding reform-minded liberals to join him in this effort. As he became familiar with the Micronesians, Burton became their advocate, ensuring that they were treated fairly and generously by the legislative branch and that their political status aspirations were taken seriously by the executive branch. His success in reforming the Committee on Interior and Insular Affairs, and later the entire House of Representatives, and his growing potential for leadership in that body made him a critical player on all issues relating to the Interior Department and most issues of concern to the liberal wing of the Democratic Party.[17]

Burton realized that he had a fundamental problem developing in Guam as the political leaders there saw a far superior status emerging from the negotiations for the Northern Marianas. In a three-hour meeting with Guam's legislature, Burton heard Guam's status described as a "political dilemma" and Congress blamed for Guam's slow political development. He responded that Congress had been more responsive in recent years and that he and Won Pat were preparing legislation that would amend or repeal the Organic Act of 1950 so that Guamanians could prepare their own constitution. When asked to assist Guam's leaders to achieve reunification with the Northern Marianas, Burton responded that the Guam leadership had to take the initiative. Burton's frequent endorsement of the goal of reunification was clearly part of his overall strategy to assure Won Pat, his good

---

17. *National Security*, 220-21; John Jacobs, *A Rage for Justice: The Passion and Politics of Phillip Burton* (Berkeley: University of California Press, 1995) [hereafter *A Rage for Justice*], 131, 140-41, 220-21.

friend and colleague, that Guam eventually would benefit from the successful conclusion of the Northern Marianas negotiations. According to Jim
Berg, an astute staffer on the U.S. delegation, Burton and Won Pat "held
out to Guamanians the possibility of an ultimate unification" in which the
Guamanians "would clearly be the dominant players" and "this promise of
unity or the promise that unity is not foreclosed within the Marianas . . .
was enough to keep the Guamanians at bay."[18]

---

18. *An Honorable Accord,* 134-35; *Oral Histories,* Interviews of James D. Berg, Stephen D.
Sander, Roger Stillwell, and Pedro A. Tenorio.

Chapter Two

Preparation of the Study

By the time the Under Secretaries Committee acted to approve a full policy review of Guam's political status, Interior officials were well aware of the growing agitation on Guam for more self-government and improved relations with the federal government. In May 1973 Governor Carlos G. Camacho advised Carpenter that both he and the Guam Legislature had recently taken action to address the status issue. Governor Camacho, a founder of Guam's Republican Party in 1966, was appointed governor by President Nixon in 1969 and then won the first election for the position in 1970 after Congress amended the organic act to permit such elections. He and his running mate, Kurt S. Moylan, prevailed by a large margin over the Democratic ticket headed by Ricardo J. Bordallo, which had earned the right to run in the general election after a very contentious three-way race in the Democratic primary. But the Democrats won fifteen of the twenty-one seats in the legislature. Governor Camacho approved the legislature's creation of a nine-person commission composed of current legislators (six from the Democratic majority and three from the Republican minority) chaired by Senator Frank G. Lujan to study and make recommendations regarding Guam's future political status. In addition, the governor had created his own advisory council to advise him about political status issues and alternatives. In acknowledging receipt of this information, Carpenter expressed the hope that his office might "be involved, if only in an observer capacity, from time to time as opportunity may permit."[19]

---

19. Robert F. Rogers, *Destiny's Landfall: A History of Guam* (Honolulu, HI: University of Hawaii Press, 1995) [hereafter *Destiny's Landfall*], 242, 244, 250; Letter, May 4, 1973, Camacho to Carpenter; Guam Public Law 12-17, Twelfth Guam Legislature, First Regular Session (April 19, 1973); Executive Order 73-16 (April 19, 1973); Letter, May 30, 1973, Carpenter to Camacho.

Shortly thereafter, Interior officials became aware of another initiative regarding Guam's political status—this time proposed by Won Pat. He advised Interior of his intention to introduce a resolution in the House of Representatives stating that Congress believed the people of Guam needed a greater degree of self-government and that Congress would give serious consideration to the recommendations of a duly constituted Guam constitutional convention ratified by popular vote. In a subsequent letter to President Nixon, he sent a copy of the resolution and requested that the president appoint a special committee to consult with Guamanian officials and to recommend improvements in its political status. The letter was acknowledged by the White House staff and referred to the State Department, which quickly sent it on to Interior.[20]

From the outset of its work on the Guam policy study, the interagency group contemplated consultation with Guamanian officials. After its first meeting, Carpenter requested an extension of the deadline for this purpose. He asked the chairman of the Under Secretaries Committee to approve a division of the study into two segments: the first would focus on U.S. interests and objectives with the original deadline of December 17, 1973, and the second "would consider Guamanian concerns and would include consultation with Guamanian leaders" and be finished by February 1, 1974. The working group's proposal was accepted by the Under Secretaries Committee. In late October 1973 Secretary of the Interior Rogers C.B. Morton advised Governor Camacho of the planned review of the Guam-federal government relationship and invited him to "designate two or three key members of your government to participate in the effort." Secretary Morton suggested that this matter be kept "in strict confidence" until arrangements

---

20. Letter, July 23, 1973, Eustaquio to Morton; Letter, August 7, 1973, Carpenter to Won Pat; Letter, September 17, 1973, Won Pat to President Nixon; Letter, September 20, 1973, Friedersdorf to Won Pat. As a precursor of future Guamanian differences on status questions, Senator Lujan on behalf of his status commission promptly took issue with Won Pat's assumptions that the people of Guam "desire closer ties with their fellow citizens on the American mainland" and that only the U.S. Congress "has the right to determine Guam's status." Letter, September 27, 1973, Lujan to Won Pat.

had been made for a joint press release on the proposed review to be made simultaneously in Guam and Washington.[21]

Interior's efforts to consult in a timely fashion with Guamanian leaders were frustrated by Guam's internal politics. The joint press release about the review of Guam's relationship with the United States, carefully negotiated by Secretary Morton and Governor Camacho, was leaked before its release and portrayed inaccurately in the press. Senator Paul J. Bordallo, a Democrat and one of the governor's most determined critics, described the proposed study in the Guamanian press as intended to focus on long-term U.S. strategic military interests in Guam. Although the governor still agreed to the issuance of the press release, he requested that Lt. Governor Moylan discuss the matter further during his visit to Washington in early November.[22]

Under the circumstances, it was not surprising that any proposed discussion with the federal government would become a political issue. For more than two years, Senator Bordallo had been leading the opposition to a U.S. Navy plan to move its Guam ammunition wharf from military property at Apra Harbor to private property at Sella Bay, which would require the acquisition of a very substantial amount of land for safety reasons. Although originally opposed to the Navy plan, Governor Camacho in 1971 approved it and the accompanying land exchange agreement because of "the seeming inevitability of the project in light of past military land acquisitions and the desperate economic needs of the island at the time." The Guamanian community was sharply divided on the issue: the Chamber of Commerce supported the project while environmental groups and Chamorro activists opposed it. After his election to the legislature in 1970, Bordallo organized the opposition to the proposed land agreement. His legal challenge was ultimately successful with the federal appeals court in San Francisco,

---

21. Memorandum, October 15, 1973, Carpenter to Chairman, Under Secretaries Committee; Letter, October 26, 1973, Morton to Camacho.

22. Department of the Interior News Release (November 2, 1973); Memorandum, November 6, 1973, Martin to Director of Territorial Affairs, enclosing talking points for the proposed meeting with Lt. Governor Moylan on November 8, 1973.

which ruled in March 1973 that the land exchange agreement needed the legislature's approval as well as the governor's. This decision fostered more controversy throughout 1973, as the various interest groups waited to see whether either the Navy or the Guam Legislature would change its position on the issue.[23]

Moylan was an experienced Guam politician, having been elected to the Guam Legislature in 1964 and joining Camacho in founding the Republican Party in 1966. On November 8, 1973, he met with Stanley Carpenter, who would be chairing the interagency working group preparing the Guam study, and James V. Martin, Jr., a newly hired outside consultant added to Interior's staff to help with the study. Moylan identified some of the principal concerns that Governor Camacho wanted to have reviewed during the course of the study. He reported that the governor was "grateful that Secretary Morton had seen the need to conduct a review at this time and to consult the Government of Guam in the process" and that "the compelling need for reviewing the Guam-Federal relationship had been lent greater urgency by the status discussions of the United States with Micronesia and the Northern Marianas." He advised that the governor was especially interested in the areas where Guam was seeking greater autonomy: minimum wage laws, immigration laws, shipping laws, communications, land and planning, and banking laws. Moylan recommended that Carpenter and Martin visit Guam later in November to speak with the governor, members of the legislature, and the press. Martin subsequently advised the other members of the interagency working group about the proposed visit and emphasized that limiting the U.S. visitors to Interior personnel "would

---

23. Michael R. Clement, Jr., *The Sella Bay Ammunition Wharf Controversy 1969-1975: Economic Development, Indigenous Rights and Colonialism in Guam* (Unpublished thesis, University of Guam, 2002) [hereafter *Sella Bay Ammunition Wharf Controversy*], 31-38, 56-63.

serve to de-emphasize the military side of the review which Senator Bordallo has already blown way out of proportion."[24]

Subsequent conversations with Moylan, both in Guam in late November and in Washington in December 1973, confirmed that Governor Camacho was unable (or unwilling) to participate in any U.S. review of Guam's status and concerns in light of his conflicts with the legislature and his intention to seek a second term in November 1974. During a private conversation in Guam with the Interior representatives, Moylan opined that Governor Camacho really favored independence and the senator chairing the legislature's status commission favored "free association," but that Guamanians were unlikely to support either alternative. According to Moylan, Governor Camacho had his own status group working on the issues but had made it clear that he would take no action until the legislature's commission issued its report, no earlier than June 1974 and probably much later. During his meeting with Interior in Washington a few weeks later, Moylan stressed that no dialogue on status issues would be possible unless the legislature agreed to participate. He advised that the legislature, despite the assurances that they had received from Martin and Carpenter,

> was nevertheless convinced that status questions were involved in the various matters on which the review would focus—immigration, shipping, minimum wage laws, etc. (In this, said Moylan, the Governor and he had to agree.) The Legislature was now accusing the Governor and Lieutenant Governor of conferring with the Federal Government on status-related issues.

---

24. *Destiny's Landfall*, 239-40; Memorandum of Conversation, November 9, 1973, prepared by Martin; Memorandum, November 13, 1973, Martin to Members of the Guam Working Group. Before departing for Guam, Martin gave the staff of the Office of Territorial Affairs instruction for the preparation of papers on the major issues to be addressed in the study with a deadline of December 7, 1973. On the subject of political status, he asked that the alternatives of status quo with further self-government, incorporated territory, commonwealth, and statehood be considered. However, he stated that the staff "need not evaluate these options at this juncture other than to note under specific political, economic and sociological issues whether a particular political status is essential to a particular option for the resolution of the issue concerned." Memorandum, November 20, 1973, Martin to Staff, Territorial Affairs.

Moylan said that he and the governor would determine if the legislature would participate in the review and, if so, proposed that a joint delegation would come to Washington in February 1974.[25]

The unanticipated publicity about the proposed joint review of Guam's status (by the Republican Administration in Washington and the Republican Administration in Guam) prompted strong reactions from Congress—first by Delegate Won Pat and shortly thereafter by Congressman Burton, both Democrats. In his letter to Secretary Morton, Won Pat suggested that the joint effort by the executive branch and Governor Camacho "closely parallels" his proposal for a presidentially appointed status committee and would be "of significant value as interim steps until such time as" his resolution authorizing a constitutional convention in Guam was acted upon. He also emphasized that any review of Guam's status should have broad representation from Guam, making reference both to the legislature's status commission and his own role as Guam's representative in Congress, which has "exclusive constitutional authority over the territories."[26]

Burton seconded Won Pat's concerns in a strongly worded letter to Secretary Morton a few days later. He too had seen the press comments on the proposed review and was aware of Won Pat's views on the subject. Although he stated that the concept of the review of Guam's status was "praiseworthy," he went on to say that he agreed "with my colleague Tony Won Pat that its limited composition would inevitably deprive it of the broadly-based support which it needs in order to be viable and creditable." More to the point, he advised Secretary Morton that Burton's committee "will be critical of any efforts to alter Guam's relationship with the Federal government without the meaningful participation of the people of Guam." He recommended that steps be taken "to broaden the membership of the joint review committee

---

25. Memorandum of Conversation, (undated but probably November 9 or 10, 1973), entitled "Comments by Lt. Governor Moylan on Guam Situation;" Memorandum of Conversation, December 14, 1973, prepared by Martin.

26. Letter, November 2, 1973, Won Pat to Morton, 1-2.

to include both a bi-partisan representation from the Guam Legislature and the Office of Guam's Delegate to the Congress."[27]

Secretary Morton responded to both letters, expressing agreement with their main point that any change in Guam's political status should be based on a review that had broad and meaningful participation by the people of Guam. But he emphasized as well that the proposed review was only an "initial exploration" within the executive branch and that it would embrace a wide range of issues other than political status. He assured both Burton and Won Pat that the latter's expertise would be sought before any final recommendations might be made regarding changes to Guam's status and that Carpenter had discussed the situation with Won Pat after his trip to Guam in late November. Morton asked Burton if, under the circumstances, the Interior Department could defer its submission to Congress of proposed amendments to the Guam and Virgin Islands organic acts that Burton had requested two months earlier. Burton responded in the negative the very next day. Expressing satisfaction generally with Morton's assurances about the proposed study, he stated that the study did not justify "Carpenter's unilateral abrogation of his commitment to me" and my subcommittee "for departmental recommendations now on stripping the Organic Acts of Guam and the Virgin Islands of cumbersome and superfluous federal oversight provisions, unrelated to protection of the basic interests of the United States."[28]

The Nixon Administration's interagency group met on December 17, 1973, to complete its work on Phase I of the study and to resolve, if possible, some differences that had developed among the agencies. Phase I basically constituted a statement of the problem; it included an introduction, a review of U.S. interests and objectives in Guam, and a discussion of Guam's role in attaining U.S. objectives. All the agencies agreed that Guam played "a pivotal strategic role for the United States" and that it was "in our national

---

27. Letter, November 14, 1973, Burton to Morton, 1-2.

28. Letter, December 4, 1973, Morton to Won Pat; Letter, December 4, 1973, Morton to Burton, 1; Letter, December 5, 1973, Burton to Morton, 1.

interest to preserve Guam's strategic potential and its American identity." Also, the agencies agreed that the Guamanians were justified in "seeking to alleviate the inequities arising from the application of certain Federal laws to Guam" and "desiring to express their self-determination." However, State and Interior took issue with Defense on two points: they believed that "the military are partly at fault for the misunderstandings and tensions between themselves and the Guamanians and for the Guamanian sense of frustration and alienation" and that investments by Japan and China in Guam "do not hold the seeds of grave threat to the United States." The interagency group still had to address the two remaining portions of the study—options and recommendations—in order to meet its deadline of February 1974 for submitting the completed study to the Under Secretaries Committee.[29]

Responding to a series of requests from the interagency working group, the Under Secretaries Committee extended the deadline to June 1974. Early in January, the group advised the Under Secretaries Committee that "the Guamanian leaders are not prepared to consult formally with us at this time" because of "[p]olitical tensions between the Legislature and the Executive." Later in the month, however, Governor Camacho expressed his willingness to participate in the joint review and advised Secretary Morton that his representatives would be headed by Lt. Governor Moylan. Carpenter responded positively on behalf of Secretary Morton, suggested late March as the date for the first session, and solicited Camacho's views as to the subjects that might be considered. No such initial meeting ever took place.[30]

The upcoming election in November 1974 served to heighten the "political tensions" arising from the Sella Bay dispute and other differences between the governor and the legislature. An initially promising effort to develop a joint executive-legislative mechanism for resolving the Sella Bay controversy was put on hold in September 1974 as the election approached.

---

29. Memorandum, December 12, 1973, Martin to Carpenter.

30. Memorandum, January 9, 1974, Carpenter to Chairman, Under Secretaries Committee; Letter, January 24, 1974, Camacho to Morton; Letter, February 19, 1974, Carpenter to Camacho.

Camacho and Moylan intended to seek another term in office and were well aware that their success in 1970 had been due in part to a divided Democratic Party. In 1974 they were concerned about a potential primary challenge within their own party and the prospect of facing a united Democratic Party in the general election. Any participation in the federal government's review of Guam's political status carried with it considerable risk of being used to their disadvantage by their political rivals in both parties.[31]

As the interagency group completed its work on the study, the continued progress in the Northern Marianas negotiations generated more agitation in Guam. Whatever assurances he may have received from Burton, Won Pat took advantage of his privileges as a non-voting delegate to air Guam's complaints on the floor of the House of Representatives. In a speech on January 31, 1974, he charged that many Guamanians were unhappy with the administration's indifference to their aspirations and the fact that the Northern Marianas was well on its way to achieving a degree of political autonomy that Guam lacked. A few weeks later, the Washington lawyers representing the Northern Marianas negotiators met with Won Pat's staff and emphasized that any desirable provisions that the Northern Marianas obtained in its status agreement might well be equally desirable and achievable for Guam.[32]

The Marianas Political Status Commission continued its practice of communicating with Guam officials about the Northern Marianas negotiations. At a seminar in Guam a few days after Won Pat's speech in the House of Representatives, Edward Pangelinan declared that he and other commission members were available "at all times for dialogue on political status" with representatives of Guam and the Trust Territory. At the same meeting, Senator Lujan, chairman of Guam's status commission, asserted that Guam was nothing more than a "colony" of the United States and severely

---

31. *Sella Bay Ammunition Wharf Controversy*, 69-70.

32. Speech of Congressman Won Pat (January 31, 1974); Wilmer, Cutler & Pickering, Memorandum for the File, February 14, 1975, re meeting with Eustaquio and Stillwell of Won Pat's staff.

criticized Puerto Rico's status, as well as the proposed commonwealth status for the Northern Marianas. Lujan, a lawyer who authored Guam's 1974 Court Reorganization Act, was known as "a staunch advocate of indigenous rights" and had joined Senator Bordallo's successful court challenge to Governor Camacho on the Sella Bay issue.[33]

On March 30, 1974, Pangelinan and other Northern Marianas representatives met with Lujan's commission, well aware of his widely known criticism of the U.S. military presence on Guam. Pangelinan subsequently told a U.S. representative on Saipan that the Guamanian representatives had expressed concern about military-civilian relationships on Guam and had given his commission "some timely warnings." Although the fact of the meeting with such a controversial Guamanian group concerned some American officials, others recognized that the Northern Marianas decision to meet with Lujan's commission was "simply good negotiation tactics" and that Pangelinan was fully "capable of evaluating correctly the warnings of Lujan and the Guamanian commission."[34]

With the Northern Marianas negotiations moving to conclusion, Guamanian concerns focused on the financial aspects of the new relationship and the economic and political realities of dealing with a new political entity to the north. When the completed financial arrangements for the proposed Northern Marianas commonwealth were announced in June 1974, a Guam editorial lamented that "Guam Shouldn't Have to Beg for Funds." The writer pointed out that the United States was offering the Northern Marianas the equivalent of $1,300 per capita, which, if applied to Guam, would produce a figure in excess of $130 million for Guam. As the Marianas status negotiations approached their conclusion, Joe Murphy summarized his views of the situation:

> Many of us living on Guam view the proceedings with mixed emotions. We naturally welcome the addition of the Northern Marianas to the American community, and feel that we have, perhaps,

---

33. *Destiny's Landfall*, 248; *Pacific Daily News* (February 2, 1974).

34. *Pacific Daily News* (April 2, 1974); Telegram, April 2, 1974, Trent to Washington; Telegram, April 8, 1974, Westlake to Washington.

contributed something to the desire of the islanders to become a permanent part of America. We have developed a small guilt complex, however, about the negotiations. We feel that somehow, through the lack of leadership on Guam, that Guam has missed the boat. We feel that the Mariana Islands really should be re-integrated, politically, although self-governing. We certainly can't blame the people of the Northern Marianas for that. They tried, and it was Guam that dropped the ball.[35]

Also in June 1974, the interagency working group was attempting to finish its assignment. The inability to consult with Guamanian leaders before issuance of the group's report prompted some disagreement among the agencies. The Defense Department, in particular, was reluctant to approve a study that contained recommendations that had not "been approved in consultation with key Guamanians to insure that the policies will not meet with opposition when implemented." Other agencies, however, believed that the problem could be addressed satisfactorily by dividing the study's recommendations into those appropriate for immediate action and those requiring further study and consultation. The latter approach was adopted in the report submitted to the Under Secretaries Committee. In a modest effort to compensate for this lack of consultation, Interior Secretary Morton announced in early June 1974 that the administration was prepared to consult with Guamanian representatives about their relationship with the federal government.[36]

Before the study was submitted to the Under Secretaries Committee, each participating agency had numerous opportunities to make certain that the study's analysis and recommendations were acceptable. The Defense Department wanted to be sure that the study acknowledged that the joint

---

35. *Pacific Daily News* (June 15 and 23, 1974).

36. Memorandum, February 4, 1974, Carpenter to Chairman, Under Secretaries Committee; Memorandum, February 12, 1974, Martin to Carpenter; Memorandum, June 14, 1974, Carpenter to Doremus, Interior Deputy Assistant Secretary; Department of the Interior News Release (June 6, 1974).

chiefs of staff had not previously addressed "the feasibility and costs of eventual transfer of naval activities from NAS Agana to Andersen AFB, as well as other feasible options on Guam." More fundamentally, Defense believed that "the basic thrust of the study is somewhat obscured" in the final draft under review—namely, that "due to the strategic importance of Guam, it is in the national interest to urgently seek solutions to Guam's problems in the socioeconomic and political status areas." Rather than attempt to rewrite portions of the report at this late date, however, Defense officials proposed that the memorandum to the president that would accompany the study "be the vehicle to correct this deficiency." The deputy secretary of defense, who served on the Under Secretaries Committee, approved the draft study as recommended by the responsible assistant secretary of defense, whose staff served on the interagency working group that prepared the draft. The assistant secretary reported that the revised memorandum for the president "emphasizes that Guam is strategically essential to the United States and fundamental socio-economic problems on Guam must be corrected for the long term to ensure its continued association in a federal relationship, a fact that is clouded in the study and its detailed summary."[37]

On July 2, 1974, the Under Secretaries Committee circulated the revised study and proposed memorandum for the president to numerous federal agencies outside the membership of the working group that had prepared it. The committee requested comments by July 19, 1974 (later extended to July 24), addressing such issues as whether the agency had the legal authority, funding, and personnel to implement those recommendations within the agency's jurisdiction. One thoughtful letter was submitted by Ambassador Williams, whose concern about Guam's legitimate complaints had prompted the study. Williams agreed with the study's two principal recommendations—to offer Guam a change in its political status along "commonwealth lines" and to support the Guam governor's request for a five-year program for capital investment projects. However, he disagreed on

---

37. Memorandum, March 1, 1974, Joint Chiefs of Staff to Assistant Secretary of Defense (ISA); Memorandum, March 28, 1974, Assistant Secretary of Defense (ISA) to Deputy Secretary of Defense.

several other points. First, he suggested that the study unnecessarily raised doubts about the nature and permanence of Guam's relationship with the United States. Second, he thought (along with State and Defense) that Guam should not be given membership in any international organizations, among other reasons because it would complicate his ongoing negotiations with the Northern Marianas. Third, he regretted that the study did not give more attention to "the need for a coordinated policy and an integrated Washington response to the day-to-day relationship between Guam and the Federal Government."[38]

Putting these caveats aside, Williams concluded by stating that "[a]ll efforts should be directed toward making Guam feel it is an integral part of the United States. This objective could be furthered by offering Guam an opportunity to draft its own constitution and to become, if it so desires, a commonwealth under the full sovereignty of the United States." He also had a firm view on the need to move promptly. Williams advised the Under Secretaries Committee that he

> would like to see a new Guam Constitution and a new Guam commonwealth precede the full implementation of the Northern Marianas agreement and the coming into force of a Northern Marianas Constitution. This requires fast action. The Marianas talks could result in an agreement before the end of this calendar year and a Marianas constitutional convention could be called as early as next summer.

Accordingly, he suggested that "the Under Secretaries Committee urge the President to establish in consultation with the U.S. Congress a Joint Status Commission on Guam as soon as possible."[39]

---

38. Memorandum, July 2, 1974, Staff Director Grove to Federal Agencies; Memorandum, July 19, 1974, Radewagen to Under Secretary of the Interior; Memorandum, July 25, 1974, Williams to Chairman, Under Secretaries Committee.

39. Memorandum, July 25, 1974, Williams to the Chairman, Under Secretaries Committee.

Final consideration of the study and the proposed memorandum to the president by the agencies most directly involved proceeded without any significant controversy. The Interior Department's Office of Territorial Affairs thought that some of Ambassador Williams' comments reflected a misreading of the study, especially his concern that the study raised questions about the permanence of Guam's relationship with the United States. The Territorial Affairs Office recommended approval of the study, and the Interior Department sent along its concurrence. The deputy secretary of defense was advised by his staff that the materials now reflected the Defense Department's earlier recommendation that the study expand its analysis of three issues: future political status, financial assistance, and Guam's international role. Having been assured that the views and interests of the department had been fully accommodated, the deputy secretary communicated the department's approval to the Under Secretaries Committee.[40]

The study was formally submitted to the president on August 9, 1974. In the memorandum for the president, the Under Secretaries Committee advised that "due to internal Guamanian political considerations, it was not possible at this time for the Governor to engage in talks related even tangentially to political status. This study has been conducted with limited consultation with the Guamanians, however. And further consultation is planned." The memorandum summarized the study's basic conclusion to the effect "that Guam's strategic importance to the United States is such that its continued association in a federal relationship is essential." To satisfy Guamanians with such a continued relationship, the memorandum recommended that the federal government "in the near future is required to provide an improved political status for Guamanians and to address their economic and social aspirations—including further diversification of the economy." The memorandum stated that two specific recommendations in the study required presidential action—one authorizing an improved political status

---

40. Memorandum, August 2, 1974, Carpenter to the Secretary of the Interior; Memorandum, July 23, 1974, Assistant Secretary of Defense (ISA) to the Deputy Secretary of Defense; Memorandum, August 7, 1974, Deputy Secretary of Defense to Chairman, Under Secretaries Committee.

for Guam and the second supporting increased financial support for capital improvement projects. The Under Secretaries Committee advised the president that "a decision on the status question is desirable in August, if possible, because the status negotiations we are conducting with the Northern Marianas have already resulted in the promise of commonwealth for them, and the Guamanians are anxious about their own future."[41]

---

41. Memorandum, August 9, 1974, Under Secretaries Committee to the President (Appendix 2). The committee also advised the president of the differences that existed between the agencies on other aspects of the study, including the request for financial assistance and what kind of international role, if any, should be extended to Guam. The memorandum to the president was circulated to members of the Under Secretaries Committee by memorandum dated August 14, 1974, from Staff Director Grove.

Chapter Three

Summary of the Study

The Guam study sent to the president in August 1974 consisted of a twenty-nine-page executive summary, the 196-page report, and thirteen annexes. The transmittal memorandum to the president, the executive summary (intended to be read by the president), and the report's list of its recommendations are included at the end of this book as appendices. The report's purpose was succinctly set forth in its first paragraph:

> This is a study of U.S. national objectives, policies and programs to identify prospective courses of action by which U.S. interests in Guam may be most effectively fostered. The core of the problem will be finding means to assist Guam in planning and achieving the goals and aspirations of the local community while at the same time enabling the U.S. to maintain its relationships in the area and an appropriate military posture in Guam.

The Under Secretaries Committee presented its report with a sense of urgency prompted "by the need to determine speedily the best approach before local pressures erupt into demands for changes that are not reconcilable with U.S. interests."[42]

3.1. Background

The report began with a brief review of Guam's history and status as an unincorporated territory of the United States since 1898. It summarized the

---

42. Report, 1. Appendix 3 contains the Executive Summary of the Guam study, which includes its recommendations. A full copy of the Guam study is available at the Micronesian Area Research Center library, University of Guam.

transition from military governance to civilian control (and U.S. citizenship) under the provisions of the Organic Act of 1950 and the more recent federal statutes providing for an elected governor and a non-voting delegate in the U.S. Congress. The report acknowledged that "Guamanians have demonstrated that they are loyal American citizens during the Japanese occupation of the island, through service by many in the U.S. armed forces and through their generally strong sense of patriotism." The report went on to state, however, that the Guamanians were increasingly dissatisfied with their political status and their limited ability to cope with a wide range of issues resulting from recent economic development and the extensive use of their island by U.S. armed forces.[43]

The report's analysis started with the proposition that the Guamanians wanted more self-government. It suggested that their status as an unincorporated territory "has always been vaguely perceived as rather temporary, with the tacit assumption that a progressively greater degree of integration with the United States Mainland lay somewhere in the future." Efforts by the Guamanians to improve their status through a constitutional convention held in 1970 were not acted upon by the U.S. Congress. The report suggested that aspirations in Guam for complete integration through statehood have "faded in recent years," due in part to the status negotiations between the United States and the Trust Territory of the Pacific Islands, especially those involving the Northern Marina Islands. These developments have "sharpened Guamanian desire for greater political autonomy" and fostered a feeling among Guamanians that they are "second class citizens." Although the report estimated that "only a very few" Guamanians would advocate total independence, "there is a growing consensus that the role and status of Guam should be examined more closely, and that options providing for greater rather than less independence from the Mainland may be in the best interest of Guamanians." In this connection, the report pointed out

---

43. Report, 1-3; Executive Summary, v.

that the Guam Legislature recently responded to this sentiment by creating a political status commission in 1973.[44]

Problems other than Guam's dissatisfaction with its status also prompted the 1974 study. The report identified three major issues that needed to be addressed. First, the Guamanians were "afraid that they may lose control of their own island to outsiders," whose presence in increasing numbers had resulted from the major construction projects—both military and civilian—begun in the post-war period and extending to the present growth in the tourist industry. Second, the population growth had precipitated needs for improved water, power, sewerage, and education facilities that Guam was unable to meet without significantly increased subsidies from the U.S. government. Third, the U.S. government (principally the Navy and Air Force) owned nearly one-third of the island and the pressures of the growing civilian population had led to increased tensions between the U.S. military and the civilian community.[45]

3.2. U.S. Interests and Objectives in the Pacific

Reminding readers that the United States had been engaged in three wars in the Pacific region over the past thirty years, the report broadly described U.S. interests in the area as falling into three categories: security, economic, and political. National security interests involved protection of the United States and its possessions, assistance in the defense of its Asian allies, maintenance of regional stability, and preservation of essential lines of communication. Economic interests involved maintaining accessibility in the Pacific region for trade and investment, and promoting a local economy that would be less dependent on U.S. financial aid. United States political interests involved the retention of diplomatic access to the region and obtaining support for U.S. Asian and worldwide policies. On this last point, the report emphasized that the future of the region would be largely determined by relations among the major powers—identified as Japan, China, the USSR,

---

44. Report, 4; Executive Summary, v-vi.

45. Executive Summary, vi.

and the United States. The report recognized that "while the bipolar confrontation of the past has been muted, potential instability is inherent in the development of a new equilibrium" and that "U.S. interests vis-à-vis the lesser powers of Asia are largely determined by their relationships with the major powers." Measured against any of these criteria, the report concluded that "the strategic importance of the Pacific and Indian Ocean is increasing" and emphasized that nearly two-thirds of the world's population live in the area and that trade, travel, and industry were growing rapidly.[46]

The report summarized U.S. national security objectives, policies, and commitments in the Pacific region. The objectives "include deterrence of aggression, creation of an Asia-Pacific power balance in which no single country or combination of countries can dominate the region, creation of a stable environment for trade and development, and reassurance to our allies of our continuing interest and ability to play a stabilizing role." The report identified the principal sources for current U.S. policies in the region, in particular the Nixon Doctrine announced in Guam in November 1969, regarding the use of American troops abroad, and the existing treaties and commitments to various countries in the area with respect to U.S. obligations in the event those countries were threatened by overt aggression. The overall role of U.S. forces in support of these policies was to deter nuclear and conventional attacks or threats to the U.S. itself, its allies, and other nations important to the security of the U.S. and of the region, and if necessary to defeat such attacks. In elaboration of the role of U.S. forces, the report emphasized that "U.S. military bases and forces in the Western Pacific serve as a convincing demonstration of U.S. intent to remain a Pacific power, and to maintain sufficient forward deployed military power to fill U.S. commitments to its allies and protect U.S. interests in that area."[47]

The report discussed the extent and importance of the U.S. military capabilities located on Guam. It identified the strategic forces (bombers and missile submarines) currently based on Guam, as well as the general

---

46. Report, 5-6; Executive Summary, vi.

47. Report, 9; Executive Summary, vii.

operational missions, logistics facilities, staging and transshipment capabilities, and communications facilities located on the island. Guam's military bases and facilities augmented and supported the capabilities of U.S. forces throughout the region, enhancing both the deterrence of aggression and the credibility of U.S. commitments. "Guam's strategic importance is derived from its location and its status as a U.S. territory." Bases located on a U.S. territory "are immune to the pressures which can be exerted by foreign governments on bases in their own countries," but the report observed that the political and economic pressures on the U.S. bases in Guam were "probably more serious that those elsewhere in the U.S." Reflecting the same concerns driving the ongoing separate negotiations with the Northern Mariana Islands, the report observed that Guam's "future role would grow if U.S. basing options in Japan and/or the Philippines were significantly constrained."[48]

3.3. U.S. Political and Economic Interests in Guam

The report identified two basic reasons why it was important to the United States that "the Guamanian people be fundamentally satisfied with their political status." First, their long association with the United States, their consistent loyalty, and their strong support for the U.S. military "constituted compelling evidence that the Guamanians deserve sympathetic consideration of their political desires." Such favorable consideration "would be visible fulfillment of our repeated commitments to the principle of self-determination." Second, improvement in Guam's relationship with the United States was desirable to preserve the favorable environment on the island for the effective maintenance and functioning of U.S. military bases. In short, "if the Guamanians perceive themselves as a people whose interests have been denied, U.S. military forces could hardly expect to enjoy the same spirit of friendly cooperation which they have had in the past."[49]

---

48. Report, 9-11.

49. Report, 11-12.

The report identified another political interest of the United States in addressing the future political status of Guam which related to the current status negotiations with the Northern Marianas and the other districts of the Trust Territory. Looking to the likelihood of three separate entities related to the United States in the Western Pacific—Guam, the Northern Marianas, and Micronesia—the report emphasized the desirability of taking steps to "hold open options which would permit eventual merger of these units, particularly of Guam and the Northern Marianas." A union of Guam with the Northern Marianas would advance both U.S. military interests and administrative efficiency. Accordingly, the United States should "seek a status for Guam which eventually would also be acceptable for the Northern Marianas, with the expectation that both administrations might be incorporated into one governing unit."[50]

International considerations also supported the report's conclusion regarding the desirability of a prompt and favorable consideration of Guam's current political status. Notwithstanding recent steps to improve Guam's self-government, the United States was still required to report annually to the United Nations about its non-self-governing territories, including Guam. The report pointed out that political leaders in Guam had taken advantage of the United Nations to complain about U.S. military activities on Guam and the lack of meaningful self-government. Such Guamanian advocacy and the present nature of Guam's government under the organic act "would tend to deter the UN from recognizing that Guam governs itself until such time as a positive act by the electorate, such as approving a constitution, or electing a governor on the issue of preserving the status quo, can be taken as clearly representing an act of self-determination."[51]

Separate from considerations of Guam's political status, the report identified an important United States interest in promoting steady and broad-based economic development on Guam with a more equitable distribution

---

50. Report, 12-13.

51. Report, 13.

of income. Such an objective was justified not only because the United States "has an obligation to promote the highest standard of life possible for its citizens, but also because a favorable socio-economic climate enables the U.S. to carry out its strategic and political objectives more effectively." The report emphasized the economic advantages to the United States that flowed from Guam's geographic location—including U.S. control over sea and air shipping through Guam, the island's development as a commercial center for U.S. economic enterprises, and its potential as a tourist destination for Asians. But the report observed that "the unprecedented boom of the past few years has introduced some distortion." In particular, uncontrolled development had resulted in serious strains on Guam's infrastructure and a sizeable gap in income distribution between the rich and the poor. According to the report, the Guamanians recognized the need to address these problems but "are sensitive to imposition of solutions by federal agencies, considered to be 'outsiders,' and initiatives for the creation of economic policies to benefit Guam will have to flow from suggestions made by the Guamanians themselves."[52]

3.4   Guam's Importance in Attaining U.S. Objectives

This section of the report addressed the major issues in the relationship between Guam and the federal government. It divided the discussion into three areas of interest: national security, political, and socioeconomic. In each area the report identified the major objectives of both the United States and Guam and discussed the current and potential areas of conflict between the two entities.

3.4.1   National Security Issues

Objectives and Evaluation: The report concluded that the current Guam-based U.S. forces played a vital international role that was both military and political. After reiterating the various military objectives served by these forces, the report indicated that the existing levels of military activity

---

52. Report, 15-16.

on Guam (about 12,000 to 14,000 personnel) would probably be maintained for the foreseeable future. It pointed out that the strategic importance of Guam was not likely to decrease and there was no likelihood of a substantial reduction in its strategic military mission. Guam's military bases advanced U.S. political objectives as well; the maintenance of these forces "serves to remind Asian powers—allies and potential adversaries alike—that the U.S. is and intends to remain a resident Pacific Power and is a geographic neighbor to nations along the East Asian littoral." This capability and visible resolve to meet commitments "is particularly important in Asia where, historically, regional military cooperation has depended on U.S. initiatives and financial support." As a cautionary note, the report added that it is "especially significant" that the military and political objectives of the U.S. forces in Guam "can be fulfilled without substantial political frictions with the residents of Guam."[53]

Looking ahead to possible contingencies, the report evaluated Guam as a possible location for additional forces and facilities in the event that some combination of foreign and domestic political pressures forced the relocation of military activities based in Japan or the Philippines. Based on its current assessment of relations with these two countries, the report concluded that such a relocation of U.S. forces was not likely in the foreseeable future. Nevertheless, the report analyzed such a contingency and suggested that a maximum redeployment of U.S. forces to Guam and the Trust Territory of the Pacific Islands would require "almost all of the lands presently held by the military on Guam as well as substantial areas in the TTPI." Considering the political implications of any such full or partial relocation of U.S. forces from Japan or the Philippines, the report recognized that moving such forces to Guam may be preferable to moving them to Hawaii but still suffered "in terms of political utility to true forward bases in Japan and the Philippines." Although the political consequences of such relocation were unclear, the report concluded "it would be prudent, therefore, to maintain the option of transferring to Guam appropriate activities now based forward."[54]

---

53. Report, 16-17.

54. Report, 19, 21.

40

With respect to Guamanian attitudes and objectives, the report concluded that generally Guam's population accepted "the continuation of Guam's historic role as a military bastion." However, the report acknowledged Guam's desire to develop its economy and community "with more Guamanian identity and less dependence upon the military bases." It identified some of the major areas of development where the Guamanians were seeking to establish a greater role for themselves, ranging from electric power generation and distribution to operation of the civil airport terminal. Although manufacturing and tourist development had increased significantly in the last five years, the report concluded that these activities "cannot yet provide the basis for long term economic growth and stability. Guam's economy for the foreseeable future will remain heavily dependent on military presence and federal spending no matter how much Guamanians would wish it were otherwise."[55]

Current and Potential Areas of Conflict: The report briefly assessed the general status of civilian-military relations in Guam. It found a generally favorable attitude towards the military among the civilian community, but noted several frictions in the relationship which, if left unaddressed, "have the potential for serious damage." The report suggested several causes for the lack of rapport and understanding between the military and civilian communities—the lack of an aggressive and effective military public relations program; the protected status of the military with regard to prices, supplies, and housing; a local press perceived as antagonistic to the military; a growing impression among the Guamanians that the military lacked understanding of local problems; and "prejudices on both sides stemming from race and language, differing standards of living, and different work habits."[56]

One overriding problem related to the competition for the use of the limited amount of land available to both the U.S. military and the civilian community. The U.S. Defense Department owned one-third of the

---

55. Report, 22.

56. Report, 23.

island; the Guam government owned one-third; and the remainder was in private hands. Of the privately held land, the report estimated that about one-fourth of the commercially most desirable land was owned by foreign interests. It acknowledged growing pressure on the U.S.-held land resulting from population growth, economic development, infrastructure needs, and increasing foreign investment. The report indicated that some of the federally held land was for military contingency purposes which could not be openly discussed with the Guamanians. The report warned: "Guamanian desires for ownership or use for public purposes of more land held by the military could, if not properly dealt with, develop into political pressures on the U.S. military presence."[57]

The report discussed six land-related issues or disputes between the U.S. military and Guam: (1) Sella Bay Land Exchange Agreement; (2) Naval Air Station Agana; (3) the port; (4) Northwest Field; (5) the beaches; and (6) Won Pat's proposal for transfer of unused U.S. lands to Guam's government. The proposed Sella Bay Land Exchange Agreement, which had been negotiated between the Navy and the governor of Guam but then rejected by the Guam Legislature, received the most attention. As described in the report, the agreement would have addressed satisfactorily several land needs on both sides. It would have enabled the Navy to build a new ammunition pier on land owned by the Guam government and private parties at Sella Bay to replace the inadequate and unsafe one located in Guam's only port. Guam in return would have acquired needed lands from the Navy to build schools, to construct a power plant on Cabras Island, to expand the Guam International Air Terminal (which shared the runways of the Naval Air Station at Agana), to develop facilities of the port, and to establish recreation areas. Certain federal funds could not be made available for some of these projects until the land exchange agreement was consummated.[58]

The report attributed the rejection of the Land Exchange Agreement to the political rivalry between the governor and the legislature facing an

---

57. Report, 24.

58. Report, 25-26, Executive Summary, ix.

election year in 1974. At the request of certain legislators, the courts had effectively invalidated the land exchange pending its approval by the legislature. The report pointed out that two or three of the objecting legislators owned land at Sella Bay whose value would be diminished if the Land Exchange Agreement was implemented. These same legislators exhibited "[r]adically separatist attitudes" evidenced by talk of independence and total exclusion of the U.S. military from Guam. According to the report, "the majority of Legislators were probably content simply to frustrate the Governor (of the opposing political party) and make it appear in the election campaigning later this year that the Governor is more interested in looking after the military than taking care of the people of Guam." According to the report, rejection of this agreement affected several other land-related issues. The exchange of land involved the construction of three public parks about which there was no real dispute. It prevented the full implementation of a joint use agreement regarding the runway and related facilities at the Naval Air Station Agana and the receipt of needed federal funds by Guam for improvements of the facilities in anticipation of increased civilian aviation traffic. The report stated that alternative arrangements in place of this land exchange agreement had to be worked out; and that "some arrangement is imperative to satisfy both Navy and GovGuam requirements." Although focused on current land issues, the report referred also to its earlier discussion of possible contingencies and observed that any "significant expansion and/or increased utilization of Guam bases could be a source of friction with Guamanians," thereby reemphasizing the need to remove "unnecessary frictions" between the military and civilian communities.[59]

3.4.2 Political Issues

Objectives and Evaluation: The report began its discussion of Guam's political status—past, present, and future—with a brief statement of United States policy on the issue: "The basic political objective of the United States is to preserve tranquility on Guam and to ensure the conditions for continued Guamanian identification with the interests of the rest of the United

---

59. Report, 26-27, 33; Executive Summary, ix.

States." After summarizing the key provisions of the Organic Act of 1950, the report turned to its assessment of current Guamanian political motivation and long range political objectives.[60]

The report attributed Guam's growing dissatisfaction with its present political status in large measure to worldwide political developments over the past few decades. The transformation of former colonies into independent states claiming their place at the United Nations, especially those Pacific islands with which Guam naturally identified, and the agitation in Puerto Rico for "more self-assertiveness and greater independence" were followed closely by Guam's political leaders and commentators. Most significant, however, were the status negotiations between the United States and the Trust Territory of the Pacific Islands, especially the Northern Mariana Islands. According to the report,

> Looking particularly at the Northern Marianas, with which Guamanians feel some kinship, they see their fellow Mariana Islanders driving a hard bargain with the United States, using political status as a lever against the land needs of the federal government. Rightly or wrongly, Guamanians feel, in retrospect, that their unquestioning acceptance of territorial status has operated to their disadvantage.

As a result of these growing sentiments, Guam's status was under review by a political status commission appointed by the legislature and an advisory council appointed by the governor. The report observed that Guam's desire for greater autonomy "could be accommodated within a wide range of different forms—commonwealth status, full self-government, 'free association'—any one of which Guamanians might eventually advocate. In the present status of political awareness, Guamanians are far from agreement on any particular solution."[61]

---

60. Report, 34; Executive Summary, x.

61. Report, 35-36, 42.

In assessing Guam's long range political objectives, the report focused on (1) the degree of integration into the U.S. political family; and (2) the relationship with Micronesia (especially the Northern Marianas). The report observed that political proposals to enhance Guam's self-government in the late 1960s and early 1970s were generally predicated on long term Guamanian aspirations for statehood. However, the report noted that this commitment to statehood appeared to be lessening in the past few years, citing the results of the informal survey of Guamanians conducted by Delegate Won Pat. Notwithstanding the obvious statistical deficiencies in the poll, the report thought that its "results may give some notion of current thinking." The key results showed 40 percent of the respondents favoring commonwealth status, 28 percent favoring statehood, 15 percent favoring the current status, and only 2 percent favoring independence. There was also some indication that both the status commission appointed by the legislature and the governor's advisory council would be recommending commonwealth when their reports came out later in 1974.[62]

Without expressly so stating, the report suggested that the growing support for commonwealth status (largely undefined) over statehood was both fortuitous and well advised. It concluded that the U.S. Congress "would be unlikely to confer statehood on Guam because of its distance from the North American continent, its small population, and federal economic dependence." It also pointed out that, upon further study of the necessary consequences of statehood, the Guamanians might not wish to give up their favorable tax status and other economic advantages which they enjoyed as an unincorporated territory. According to the report, the growing support for commonwealth was based principally on the Northern Marianas negotiating objectives, with one of the greatest attractions of commonwealth being the right of the Guamanians to draft their own constitution. Other aspects of this newly developed goal for commonwealth, or closer integration into the United States, related to the desire to vote in U.S. presidential elections and to have full representation in the U.S. Congress—both of which raised

---

62. Report, 37; Executive Summary, x.

fundamental policy and constitutional issues that the report indicated were not likely to be addressed favorably by the Congress.[63]

After a brief discussion of a possible, but most unlikely, merger between Guam and all of Micronesia, the report turned to the more discussed prospect of union between Guam and the Northern Marianas. The report indicated that Won Pat's informal poll showed 86.2 percent of the respondents favoring reunification—a significant change in sentiment since the 1969 referendum at which Guamanian voters rejected such a proposal. But the report went on to note that political leaders in the Northern Marianas, although characterizing such reunification as a "natural solution" and "inevitable," were now expressing reservations about reunification because of Guam's larger population and more developed economy.[64]

Areas of Conflict: Before identifying the principal conflicts in the political area between Guam and the federal government, the report reiterated the overriding U.S. political status objective in Guam—to ensure "the permanence of a Federal relationship with Guam," an objective which might be met by modified territorial status, commonwealth, or statehood. But it emphasized a subsidiary objective as well—to accomplish a merger of two or all three of the governments in Micronesia. To achieve this objective, the report suggested that Guam might be given a status which, from an economic standpoint, "is a little more favorable than whatever the others [the Northern Marianas and the other TTPI districts] get in their negotiations with us." According to the report,

> If Micronesia and the Northern Marianas see Guam with no benefits over and above what they themselves already have, merger will hold no attraction, especially since, in the traditional hierarchy of U.S. territorial status, the Northern Marianas will be starting out at or near the top position. Economic advantages would provide the sugar coating on the merger pill—but in any case, the pill should be freely taken to avoid animosity.

---

63. Report, 38-40.

64. Report, 41-42.

With these overall objectives in mind, the report discussed some of the key issues or disputes currently complicating the federal government's relationship with Guam.[65]

The report acknowledged that Guam's current status "fails in many ways to address the special problems of this small group of citizens on a remote little island" nearer to Tokyo, Manila, and Taipei than any American state. Furthermore, potential sources of conflict characterize the entire range of the relationship with the federal government—from the adverse effects on Guamanians of various federal laws, the limitations on self-government imposed by the organic act, and the limited ability of Guam's U.S. citizens to participate fully in the American electoral process. According to the report, the conflicts "are of two kinds, reflecting the ambivalence with which Guamanians view their present status. On the one hand, they want closer ties with the United States, and greater representation in its councils. On the other hand, they feel oppressed by U.S. laws applied indifferently to their special circumstances, and they seek greater autonomy." These relational problems were summarized as Guam's desire for more effective representation of its interests in the shaping of federal policies, more autonomy in the application of federal laws, release from most of the restrictions contained in the organic act, some meaningful participation in international agencies, and its concern that the Northern Mariana Islands will achieve "a more prestigious or advantageous status."[66]

3.4.3 Socioeconomic Issues

Guam's more specific complaints with its status were discussed in this section of the report. It addressed the impact of selected federal laws and programs; policy with respect to foreign investment; the federal/territorial financial relationship; the role of the military in the economy; and policy on participation in international agencies.

---

65. Report, 43.

66. Report, 43-46.

The Impact of Selected Federal Laws and Programs: The report pointed out that the overall objective in applying U.S. laws and programs to Guam "has been to improve the well-being of the inhabitants"—on the general assumption "that what is good in America is good in Guam." The report identified a related objective of maintaining U.S. presence and providing stability. But it recognized that "neither objective is always served, especially on those occasions when conditions are so different in Guam from those on the mainland for which they were tailored as to make a program counter productive." The report found examples in federal minimum wage laws, immigration laws, shipping laws, and banking laws.[67]

The interrelated problems of applying federal minimum wage and immigration laws to Guam related to the island's desire to exercise more control over its economy and the flow of foreigners into the island. In Guam, federal laws resulted in higher wage levels for unskilled labor and lower levels for skilled occupations than was customary on the mainland; the "disparity of pay rates with Asian countries, combined with the absence of indigenous skilled labor, has created an attraction for Asian labor during the recent boom on Guam." According to the report, Guam's growing dependence on alien laborers had led to two major problems with respect to the federal immigration laws: many Guam employers were unable to get access to the alien laborers that they needed; and Guam's government could exercise no control over the immigration to the island of aliens and their families where they put pressure on existing infrastructure and social service programs and, under U.S. law, may ultimately be eligible for U.S. citizenship. This latter possibility had prompted concern among Guamanians that they would lose political control over their island. The report pointed out that the Northern Marianas negotiators were currently seeking control over immigration in their status talks and warned: "Should the United States grant autonomous control over immigration to the Northern Marianas, equal autonomy cannot be denied Guam without serious repercussions."[68]

---

67. Report, 51.

68. Report, 47-49, 52.

The report characterized the shipping and banking laws as presenting important, but somewhat less complex, issues. The Jones Act, which was the shipping law in question, required shipping between U.S. ports, including Guam, to be on U.S.-flagged ships. According to the Guamanians, this had led to higher transportation costs, which in turn had led to higher prices for goods on Guam. The report questioned whether Guam's analysis on this point was accurate or that an exemption from the Jones Act would be as beneficial as they had hoped. But the report recognized that the application of the Jones Act, which did not apply to the Virgin Islands and American Samoa, was a constant source of Guamanian complaint. With respect to the banking laws, the Guamanians were seeking exceptions from federal law that would permit its banks to create anonymous accounts as in Switzerland—an outcome that the report suggested would not be "desirable or sufficient in itself to make Guam a major financial center."[69]

Foreign Investment: The federal agencies had divided views on the potential impact of increased foreign investment in Guam. The majority thought that U.S. national security interests and concerns might justify some limitation on continued foreign investment. The majority view emphasized the risk of Guamanian dissatisfaction and instability if the local residents felt that they had lost control over their land to foreign interests. In addition, "to the extent that a U.S. objective is to maximize U.S. presence and to keep control over the economy within the American family, serious questions would arise if both prime land and major economic activities should rest chiefly in the hands of foreigners, which could occur if present trends continue." The State Department disagreed: it emphasized the strong international support for the free flow of capital and the lack of support for the majority's national security concerns with respect to Guam. It recognized that U.S. restrictions on foreign capital in Guam might have the effect of slowing the rise in land values, but such restraints "might also retard economic development and employment growth in Guam" and generate resentment in the community, whose leaders "should be free to decide what

---

69. Report, 49-50.

measures they want to take to promote their own capacities." The report concluded that these questions of land ownership and foreign investment "are likely to be among the most difficult to resolve." But, after a further discussion of the risks and benefits attached to such foreign investment, the report decided that "[t]he benefit outweighs the risk."[70]

Federal/Territorial Financial Relationship: The report acknowledged the general obligation of the United States to concern itself with the well-being of Guamanians as U.S. citizens and its legal obligation under the Organic Act of 1950 to rebate to Guam all federal income taxes collected on Guam. It focused on direct federal support (not including Defense Department military funding of its activities), which amounted to about $29.7 million including the rebate of federal taxes ($11.7 million), federal categorical grants ($10.6 million), federal rehabilitation fund ($6.3 million), and economic development fund ($1 million). These federal funds provided about 23 percent of Guam's combined budget in 1973, compared with 29 percent in 1971, and as much as 40 percent back in 1953. The report pointed out some of the significant changes in Guam's financial situation over the past two decades: the growth in the income tax collected by Guam (as contrasted with that collected by the U.S.) and the growth of Guam's business privilege tax and real property tax, both attributable to the recent rapid growth of the local economy. Because Guam benefited from the rebate of federal taxes, it was not eligible for the general revenue sharing available to the states.[71]

The report summarized Guamanian objectives in this area as twofold. The first was "to obtain federal financial assistance in funding maintenance and expansion of the social and economic infrastructure both to provide for current social needs and to facilitate future economic growth." The second was to secure more federal categorical and state formula grants to support health, education, and other Guamanian needs. Guam had focused on obtaining federal assistance in three areas—schools, water supply, and sewerage—and was seeking a federal grant in the amount of $56.1 million over a

---

70. Report, 53-55, 58.

71. Report, 59-60, 62; Executive Summary, xii.

five-year period from 1975 through 1979. The report concluded that "there are no major areas of conflict between the Federal Government and Guam with respect to financial relationship."[72]

Role of the Military in the Economy: The report described the impact of the U.S. military presence on Guam by reference to population and expenditure figures. It pointed out that military personnel and their dependents numbered about 30,000, some 29 percent of the total island population of 105,000. Annual Defense Department expenditures in Guam were nearly twice the amount of Guam's budget. A very large number of military-dependent wives worked in a variety of skilled positions—school teachers, secretaries, lawyers, and architects. The report suggested that "in the long term" Guam may be able to develop a more diversified economy in which the military role and influence may be significantly smaller, emphasizing the number of Guamanian youth in school, the growth in the civilian economy, and the increase in per capita income in recent years. Nevertheless, the report concluded that "the military will play a dominant role in Guam's economy for the foreseeable future."[73]

The report addressed several areas of conflict between the federal government and Guam with respect to the role of the military. The first and most significant related to the extent of military and other federal land holdings on the island—amounting to about 34 percent of the total land area. The second arose from the higher standard of living in the military community and the fact that the rapidly increasing cost of living (and inflation) was having a much greater impact on the Guamanians. The report concluded: "While it cannot be effectively argued that Guamanians are suffering severe economic hardship, nevertheless, the contrast between the large proportion of lower income Guamanians and the more affluent resident military population carries with it the potential for conflict." Another problem stemmed from the frequent shipping strikes which impacted the civilian community most severely because the unions did not stop military shipments during a

---

72. Report, 62-64.

73. Report, 64-67.

strike. Any fluctuation in the military population, especially a significant reduction in the military population, could also be a source of conflict given the economy's continued dependence on the military presence on the island.[74]

Policy on Participation in International Agencies: The last subject discussed in this portion of the report related to Guam's continued interest in participating more extensively in international organizations. It did participate in the South Pacific Conference and in regional World Health Organization activities. But the Guamanians were seeking membership in U.N. regional organizations, which provided direct financial and technical assistance, and the Asian Development Bank. The report acknowledged that Guam's desires in this area conflicted with the general United States policy that Guam, as part of the United States, was not eligible to participate and that "the limited resources of international development organizations should be utilized for the benefit of less developed countries and that countries able to provide for their own needs should do so and should not request assistance even for their less developed territories." Acknowledging that Guam had not been persuaded by these U.S. policies, the report concluded that "a better definition of Guam's eligibility for membership in and assistance from international organizations" was needed.[75]

3.5   Policy Options and Recommendations

The remainder of the report included a detailed discussion of the options available to address the disputes or areas of concern identified in its early sections. It advanced recommendations regarding military changes, socioeconomic policy, and Guam's international role. It summarized the discussion in each of these areas, identified those recommendations for immediate action and those requiring further study or consultation, and specified the U.S. government office or department that was responsible for implementing each particular recommendation made in the report.[76]

---

74. Report, 67-68.

75. Report, 70.

76. The recommendations are set forth in the Executive Summary (Appendix 3).

The discussion of options and recommendations relating to Guam's political status was predicated on the report's earlier review of U.S. objectives on the subject, the many sources of Guam's present dissatisfaction, the apparent trends in Guamanian sentiment, and the desirability of a merger with the Northern Marianas. Although conceding that Guamanian opinion on the issue "cannot be precisely measured," the report concluded that "politically articulate Guamanians probably cannot be satisfied short of obtaining a political status adjustment which involves drafting their own constitution and moving in either of two directions (1) toward greater autonomy from the United States, or (2) toward greater integration with the United States in an manner that permits a larger voice in U.S. policies affecting Guam." The first course might lead to independence and the second to statehood, but the report observed that neither of these extremes "has any major backing in Guam." Even though statehood was not presently being sought, the report recognized that "it is a possible ultimate goal."[77]

Before discussing any specific status option that might be pursued, the report reviewed Guam's most important interests and desires, other than drafting its own constitution, relating to such matters as better relations with the U.S. military, a workable land exchange method, substantial federal financial assistance, more ready access to federal officials, and relief from some onerous federal laws. The report then reiterated the essential U.S. interests and objectives with respect to Guam, ranging from maintaining a strong military posture, a workable land exchange program, preservation of political tranquility, preservation of economic stability, and preventing foreign domination. It stated further that other important interests and desires are: "(1) retention of all currently held land likely to be needed, (2) preservation of a close political relationship with Guam, (3) preservation of the option of future Guam-Northern Marianas unification, and (4) promotion of prosperity with equitable income distribution." The report acknowledged that a change in status alone—without addressing some of their respective major concerns—would not satisfy either the United States or Guam. But

---

77. Report, 171-72; Executive Summary, xxiii.

it found enough overlapping in their respective interests and objections that "the situation is not therefore a straightforward adversary situation at all. However, compatibility of future political status with the major interests of Guam and the United States is essential."[78]

By way of defining those status options that accommodated the major interests of both Guam and the United States, the report declared that such an altered status in order to meet Guam's requirements would "involve Guamanian drafting of the basic organ or constitution" and "be no less favorable than the arrangement for the Northern Marianas." In order to meet U.S. requirements, it must "be consistent with the U.S. Constitution, preserve U.S. control over defense and foreign affairs, create no obstacles to unification of Guam and the Northern Marianas, [and] preserve a close political relationship with the U.S." Having already rejected independence and statehood as viable options, the report added "that outright continuation of the status quo also is not a viable option because it lacks the essential element of a self-drafted basic organ or constitution." The report concluded that three options deserved detailed consideration: (1) modified unincorporated territorial status with greater self-government through amendment of the organic act or congressional authorization and acceptance of a Guamanian-drafted constitution, (2) incorporated territorial status with further self-government achieved through either of the same two alternatives, and (3) commonwealth status.[79]

3.5.1   Modified Unincorporated Territorial Status

Although this option would serve U.S. objectives, the report concluded that it probably would not address the current concerns of the more

---

78. Report, 173.

79. Report, 173-74. The report emphasized that all three options have several basic features in common: U.S. sovereignty, full U.S. control over foreign affairs and defense; consistency with the U.S. Constitution, U.S citizenship for Guamanians, a republican form of government for Guam, federal financial assistance, the future options of unification with the Northern Marianas and statehood would be kept open, and congressional approval would be necessary. Report, 175.

articulate Guamanians. Whether the improvements in status were accomplished by a revision of the organic act (as proposed by a Guamanian constitutional convention in 1970) or by a Guamanian-drafted constitution approved by the U.S. Congress, such a revised status would be seen as inferior to the "commonwealth" status being negotiated with the Northern Marianas. In order to keep open the option of future unification between Guam and the Northern Marianas, the report concluded that "it will be necessary to make unification attractive to the Northern Marianas, and to meet this objective Guam should have a status no less favorable than that of the Northern Marianas."[80]

3.5.2   Incorporated Territorial Status

Under this option Guam would have all the elements of self-government that Hawaii and Alaska had before they became states and the additional feature of an elected governor. Incorporated territorial status involved full application of the U.S. Constitution and carried with it the anticipation of ultimate statehood. The report concluded that this status would meet virtually all U.S. interests and objectives and, if accompanied by some kind of referendum, would satisfy international public opinion. However, the report opined that Congress was unlikely "to incorporate Guam within the Union now in view of its distance, its small population, and its economic circumstances." In addition, statehood would be financially disadvantageous to Guam, relief from onerous federal laws would be more difficult, and this option "would in all probability lack appeal to Guamanians." Therefore the report concluded that this option "appears not to be a course we should propose but which, under circumstances hard to visualize, we might accept."[81]

3.5.3   Commonwealth Status

The report decided that this third option was the one most likely to meet the major objectives of both the United States and the Guamanians.

---

80. Report, 179.

81. Report, 180-81.

The report acknowledged some of the uncertainty flowing from the Spanish language term for commonwealth (free associated state), the flexibility inherent in the term "commonwealth" currently being explored in the Northern Marianas negotiations, and the likelihood that free association of the kind being discussed with the other five districts of the Trust Territory would not be very attractive to the Guamanians. Although the specifics of an appropriate commonwealth status for Guam could not be spelled out at this time, the report emphasized the need to address Guamanian concerns about the Northern Marianas negotiations and to preserve the option of future unification by doing the following: "(1) that at the earliest possible date we assure the Guamanians that we are prepared whenever they are ready to work with them to establish for Guam a status no less beneficial than that which the Northern Marianas will get, and (2) that we give the Guamanians the opportunity to express their own desires." It cautioned against any "premature" offer, which "would rob the Guamanians of the politically needful conviction that they at last are becoming masters of their own fate."[82]

The commonwealth status discussed in the report would be modeled after what was being negotiated with the Northern Marianas. It would involve a locally drafted and adopted constitution consistent with the U.S. Constitution. It would be subject to the plenary legislative authority of the U.S. Congress, "even though the Congress may decide to limit the scope of its exercise of that authority, particularly concerning the internal affairs of Guam." The relationship, like that being negotiated with the Northern Marianas, contemplated "tighter U.S. control" than provided under the enabling legislation affecting Puerto Rico. The report concluded that Guam "will not be satisfied with anything less than the Northern Marianas get. Should it ask for more, we can probably resist successfully."[83]

According to the report, "there are no forceful arguments against this option." It detailed the specific respects in which commonwealth status for Guam served "all essential interests of the Guamanians and would satisfy

---

82. Report, 182-83.

83. Report, 184.

their other important desires as successfully as would modified territorial status, better than incorporated territory status." Exemption from the coast-wise shipping laws might be more easily achieved under this status than under incorporated territory status. It was also a more attractive status to Guamanians because of its name. It would be compatible with all U.S. essential interests and better serve other important U.S. interests than would modified territorial status because it would facilitate future unification of Guam and the Northern Marianas. International and public opinion pressures "would be well taken care of by commonwealth status, probably better served by this option than by modified territorial status." In a separate note on reintegration of Guam with the Northern Marianas, the report reiterated Guamanian concerns about the ongoing Northern Marianas negotiations, but observed that union now between the islands was not feasible "because public opinion in neither place is yet prepared." But it was in the interest of the United States "to treat the Guamanians as well as the Northern Marianas until such time as union becomes a realistic possibility."[84]

3.5.4   Recommendations

The study then set forth recommendations relating to Guam's future political status. As to immediate actions, it found that the U.S. should:

1. Be prepared to accept a commonwealth or modified territorial status for Guam as selected by Guam itself. This status and its specific arrangements should be as good as what is worked out for the Northern Marianas. (Executive Office of the President)

2. Permit the Guamanians to draft their own constitution subject to the acceptance of the United States. (Executive Office of the President)

3. Be prepared to establish with Guam a Joint Status Commission or some other forum that is mutually agreeable in which to discuss Guam's future as soon as the Political Status Commission appointed

---

84. Report, 184-87.

by the 12th Guam Legislature has submitted its report to the Legislature and the Governor has had an opportunity to present his views. (Executive Office of the President)

As to further study or consultation, it found that:

4. In order to avoid misunderstanding and efforts at cross-purposes, key Congressmen should be informed that the [above three] recommendations embody the preferred policy of the Executive Branch. (White House)

5. In order to forestall Guamanian jealousy of the Northern Marianas and to avoid unnecessary frustration or confusion which might affect U.S. negotiations in Saipan, the Governor and key Legislators in Guam should, after the foregoing Congressional consultations, be informed promptly though informally that the United States wants Guam to have a status and arrangements no less favorable than those which will obtain in the Northern Marianas and that the Federal Government will be ready to entertain Guamanian views regarding future arrangements as soon as Guam is prepared to present them. (Interior, Office of Micronesian Status Negotiations)[85]

Although the report suggested that it was too early to suggest a negotiating scenario with respect to Guam's future status, it declared that "it is necessary even at this early stage both to anticipate what steps must be taken and in what order, and to get a general understanding of the time element likely to be involved." The report then proposed a ten-step implementation process—beginning with the president's approval of the study's recommendations in July 1974, informing congressional leaders and seeking enabling legislation in August 1974, advising Guamanian leaders in September 1974, conducting first round of talks with Guamanian leaders in January 1975, conducting a second round in May–June 1975, preparation of draft Guamanian constitution in August 1975 and, after approval of constitution by Congress, the new status would become effective in January 1976. The

---

85. Report, 188, 196.

report acknowledged that this is "the fastest practicable time table" and that "[a]ctual developments are likely to take longer." But it saw "urgency in the first three steps," approval by the president, informing congressional leaders, and informing Guamanian leaders of the new U.S. position regarding Guam's political status.[86]

Some parts of the now-completed study and certain of its appendices contained specific information about the Defense Department's contingency plans that the department probably designated as classified with a "secret" designation, meaning that this information could be circulated only to persons with an appropriate security clearance. Although much of the study constituted publicly available information about the political and economic situation on Guam, analyses of political status alternatives, and other routine information, the entire study was stamped "Secret." This probably violated the regulations in effect at the time governing the use of the "Secret" classification, and had far-reaching effects. It meant that copies of the study could not be kept in routine government files, but had to be locked up in classified storage facilities. And it meant that the study was closely held within the small group of government officials who prepared it and were responsible for its implementation.

---

86. Report, 189.

Chapter Four

Approval by the President

The Under Secretaries Committee anticipated a presidential decision on the study's principal recommendation regarding Guam's political study in August 1974 soon after the recommendations were delivered to the president through National Security Adviser Henry Kissinger. Kissinger's staff had participated in the deliberations both of the interagency working group as the report was developed and of the Under Secretaries Committee as the report was refined and its cover memo to the president was drafted. Kissinger was advised that the departments principally concerned with Guam's affairs were in agreement on virtually all the recommendations set forth in the report. Unexpected political developments, however, complicated these plans for speedy presidential approval.

On August 9, 1974, the day after President Nixon resigned, the Under Secretaries Committee forwarded its recommendations. It was Gerald R. Ford's first day as president of the United States. National Security Adviser Kissinger arranged a meeting of the National Security Council for the next day, August 10, 1974, and used the occasion to educate the new president regarding the council's structure and functions. He urged President Ford to affirm his strong interest in the "NSC system as a vital aid to your decision making in national matters."[87]

While the Guam study waited for White House action, the Northern Marianas status negotiations were moving rapidly toward conclusion. The study had been stimulated in large measure by the Guamanian reaction to

---

87. Memorandum, August 9, 1974, Kissinger to the President regarding the NSC meeting set for August 10, 1974.

the second round of these negotiations in May–June 1973, at which the parties had agreed to the broad outlines of a "commonwealth" relationship between the United States and the Northern Marianas involving a locally drafted constitution, an essential element of self-government not available to Guam. Over the next eighteen months, the unfolding specifics of the new relationship were extensively publicized in Guam. As a result of negotiations in December 1973 and May 1974, the parties had reached tentative agreement on such matters as exceptions to the U.S. Constitution, limitations on federal authority, guaranteed local self-government, increased federal funding, limitations on certain federal laws (such as shipping), and temporary local control over immigration and minimum wage requirements. During the summer months of 1974, the lawyers for the United States and the Northern Marianas were working out the differences between two competing draft status agreements and identifying those issues that needed to be resolved by their principals at the next—and perhaps final—negotiating session tentatively set for December 1974. Many of the issues addressed in the Northern Marianas negotiations were those of greatest interest also to the Guamanian leaders, as reflected in the conversations between Interior personnel and Lt. Governor Moylan in late 1973.[88]

The draft agreement that emerged from these discussions was not warmly received by lower level Interior officials who had participated in the study of Guam's political status. After President Nixon appointed Ambassador Williams in March 1971 to be his personal representative in dealing with the Micronesian (and later the Northern Marianas) negotiations, Interior no longer was the key federal agency in managing these status negotiations. As was the case with the Defense and State Departments, Interior had to work under the direction of Ambassador Williams and the newly created Office of Micronesian Status Negotiations. But Interior continued to exercise authority in the unincorporated territories such as Guam, the Virgin Islands, and American Samoa. When Interior's Stanley Carpenter, who chaired the interagency group that drafted the Guam study, saw the proposed Northern Marianas status agreement, he complained:

---

88. *An Honorable Accord*, 114-19, 160-62, 169-87.

In our opinion the agreement generally creates a new group of U.S. citizens who will be favored above all other U.S. citizens while…it will require of them virtually none of the usual duties and obligations of U.S. citizens. The governmental entity proposed will be practically autonomous, although principally funded by the United States for the foreseeable future. We find many of the [Northern Marianas] positions unacceptable and we have problems with a number of the U.S. positions.

Carpenter's harsh criticism of the draft status agreement had no impact on the successful completion of the Northern Marianas negotiations. But it did not bode well for the Interior staff's future treatment of the Guam study which, if approved by the president, would assure Guam a political status equivalent in all important respects to the one obtained by the Northern Marianas.[89]

After waiting for three months, the Defense and Interior Departments urged Deputy Secretary of State Robert S. Ingersoll, who was chairman of the Under Secretaries Committee, to stimulate the needed presidential review of the Guam study. The deputy secretary of defense advised Ingersoll that the Northern Marianas negotiations might be completed in mid-December. On a recent trip to Guam, he noted "a continuing high interest in their future political status and a desire for greater recognition of their concerns in Washington," and a recent resolution by the Guam Legislature inviting a United Nations committee to visit Guam to examine "firsthand the federal presence on Guam and in order to establish a dialogue with Guam concerning the issue of political status." These factors prompted him "to urge strongly that the White House staff be pressed to obtain an early decision, at least on the question of Guam's political status," so that we "can then take the initiative to settle this domestic issue, turn away international meddling in U.S. Government affairs, and better look after its national interests in

---

89. *An Honorable Accord*, 25, 186-87.

the Pacific." Interior's under secretary supported the Defense "call for early White House action" on the study.[90]

On December 23, 1974, John A. Froebe Jr. of the National Security Council staff forwarded his analysis of the study and recommendations to Kissinger (now secretary of state). Froebe was very familiar with the work of the Under Secretaries Committee, having participated as the NSC representative in the interagency group's deliberations. Because Kissinger was obviously not so well informed on this minor issue, Froebe prepared an eight-page memorandum regarding the study and attached two documents—a draft seven-page memorandum from Kissinger to the president and a draft three-page directive from Kissinger on behalf of the president to the chairman of the Under Secretaries Committee. Without any reference to the delay since August, Froebe advised Kissinger that "there is some urgency in our beginning talks with the Guamanians" on what he saw as the key issues requiring presidential attention: Guam's desire for an improved political status, its interest in some participation in international agencies, and the level of future U.S. financial support for Guam. He suggested that discussions with Guam might begin as early as January 1975 "so that we can then proceed to sign the agreement with the Marianas on a commonwealth arrangement without implying that Guam is being left in an inferior political status."[91]

Kissinger's memorandum to the president essentially adopted Froebe's analysis and recommendations. By way of background on the political status question, Kissinger emphasized that Guam's discontent with its status "has grown slowly over the past decade," but that its reaction to the U.S. offer of commonwealth to the Northern Marianas, "which they believe is less advanced than they, is that Guam is being shortchanged." Kissinger advised the president that "our essential needs in our political relationship

90. Memorandum, November 9, 1974, Clements to Chairman, Under Secretaries Committee; Memorandum, November 18, 1974, Carpenter to Under Secretary of Interior; Memorandum, December 2, 1974, Under Secretary of the Interior to Chairman, Under Secretaries Committee.

91. Memorandum, December 23, 1974, Froebe to Secretary Kissinger, 1.

with Guam are control over Guam's defenses and foreign affairs and continued military basing rights. To achieve this, we need a political framework
that will continue Guam's close relationship with the Federal Government,
but that will keep the island's growing political demands within manageable bounds." He set forth the three policy options discussed in the study
regarding Guam's future status. He reported that all the agencies involved in
the study recommend that the United States "should work out with Guam
some form of commonwealth status that would be at least equal to that
which we have negotiated with the Northern Marianas, and which would
allow for a Guamanian-drafted constitution that would be acceptable to
Congress."[92]

Kissinger endorsed this recommendation for action by the president.
He concluded that commonwealth status

> meets basic U.S. needs and offers probably the most effective
> means for satisfying current basic Guamanian political aspirations
> . . . . It would create a political framework that would accom-
> modate basic Guamanian interests as well as our own, and would
> therefore probably be more stable over the longer run. In addition,
> commonwealth status would conduce toward Guam's eventual in-
> tegration with the Northern Marianas, which is in our interest.

His proposed directive for the president to approve reflected this recommendation.[93]

Uncertainty when the president would review Kissinger's memorandum
on the Guam study prompted some debate within the executive branch
whether the signing of the Northern Marianas status agreement should be
delayed until the president acted. After the December negotiations with the
Northern Marianas, both parties had agreed to a short recess before recon-
vening for the signing ceremony in early February 1975. Williams needed
this time to secure presidential approval for certain tentative commitments

---

92. Draft Memorandum, (date unknown), Kissinger to the President, 2-4.

93. *Id.*, 4.

that he had made to the Northern Marianas negotiators. The NSC staff was recommending a delay of a few weeks to provide additional time for the president to make his decision. Faced with the unresolved issue of Guam's future political status, which he had consistently urged be addressed before any status agreement with the Northern Marianas, Williams now recommended that the proposed conclusion of the Northern Marianas negotiations go forward on schedule "in advance of specific action on Guam's future status." Williams was proposing an accelerated schedule of events that would permit a plebiscite in the Northern Marianas on the status agreement by late June. In a meeting on January 21, 1975, with Deputy Secretary of State Ingersoll, the chairman of the Under Secretaries Committee, Williams acknowledged his change of position on the issue, but maintained that there should be no delay in resuming the Northern Marianas negotiations in early February even if a presidential decision on the Guam study might be forthcoming within the next few weeks. Ingersoll agreed with this course of action.[94]

On February 1, 1975, Kissinger advised Ingersoll that President Ford had reviewed the Guam study and decided the three key issues placed before him. Before setting forth the presidential direction on these issues, Kissinger's memorandum instructed the Under Secretaries Committee to implement the policies set forth in order "to give effect" to these objectives:

> To retain U.S. sovereignty over Guam, and, in particular, to maintain U.S. control over Guam's foreign affairs and defense and to preserve U.S. military basing rights to Guam.

> To enable Guam to move toward complete self-government in internal affairs under a self-drafted constitution consistent with the U.S. Constitution, in order to enhance prospects for Guam's continued close relationship with the Federal Government and for long-term stability of the island.

> To help promote the material well-being of Guamanians, in order to maintain stability on Guam.

---

94. *An Honorable Accord*, 211-14.

To enhance the prospects for the ultimate integration of Guam with the Northern Marianas, if this accords with the desires of the majority of Guamanians.

Specifically with respect to political status, Kissinger directed the committee to "seek agreement with Guamanian representatives on a commonwealth arrangement no less favorable than that which we are negotiating with the Northern Marianas. If, however, Guamanian representatives prefer a modified unincorporated territorial status, we will be willing to accept such an arrangement."[95]

The directive specified that, under the general supervision of the Under Secretaries Committee, "the Assistant Secretary of Interior for Program Developments and Budget should develop and implement a negotiating approach that will give effect to the above instructions, and should organize a U.S. negotiating team that will include representation from the Departments of State and Defense as well as the Department of Interior." By assigning responsibility for implementation at Interior to an assistant secretary, Kissinger made clear that the task should be handled at a policy level within the department, rather than by the Office of Territorial Affairs, and by a presidential appointee sensitive to the importance of implementing President Ford's directive. Regarding the role of the U.S. Congress, the directive provided that "the Congress should be kept informed of significant developments in the negotiations with Guamanian representatives."[96]

---

95. Memorandum, February 1, 1975, Kissinger to Chairman, Under Secretaries Committee, 1-2 (Appendix 1). The memorandum also instructed the committee with regard to the issues relating to Guam's international status and federal financial assistance. Reflecting the disagreement among the agencies on the international issue, the decision made by the president in reliance on Kissinger's recommendation was to clarify the specific nature of Guam's interest in entering into international trade agreements, try to satisfy Guam's reasonable and practical needs through means that would not lead to a separate international status for the island, and maintain the basic U.S. policy to discourage membership for U.S. territories in international organizations. *Id.*, 2. With respect to financial assistance, the committee was authorized to offer up to $75 million in U.S. funds for Guam's capital improvement program, "with a maximum of one-half this amount to be in the form of a federal grant' and the remainder to be through federal loans. *Id.*

96. *Id.*, 3.

Chapter Five

Thwarting the Presidential Directive

The Department of the Interior was responsible for implementing President Ford's directive approving the Guam study. It bears full responsibility for failing to undertake an affirmative course of action designed to achieve the national security objectives underlying the president's order that Guam be offered a commonwealth relationship comparable to that negotiated with the Northern Mariana Islands. Whereas the study attached the highest priority to prompt notification of Guamanian officials of the newly established federal policy, Interior decided that Guam's elected leaders should not be informed of the U.S. readiness to negotiate such a new political relationship with Guam. Rather than initiating an effort to begin meaningful negotiations with informed Guam representatives, Interior embarked on a dilatory and indefensible deliberative process, internally and with the other federal agencies, about how to deal with the presidential directive. Interior staff imposed a series of obstacles and conditions that had to be met by Guam's political leaders before the United States would discuss political status with them. Although State and Defense representatives would occasionally question Interior's leadership on the Guam project, they had many higher priority problems and deferred to Interior's increasingly obvious program to subvert the presidential directive and ignore the findings of the Guam study. Confusion in the White House as to whether Guam was a domestic or national security question served only to highlight the lack of White House leadership necessary to ensure that President Ford's directive was faithfully implemented.

5.1 Failure to Inform Guamanian Officials

The Interior Department was required to address the issue of advising Guam's leaders about the new federal policy within a few weeks after the presidential directive. The newly elected governor of Guam, Ricardo J. Bordallo, was planning to visit Washington in mid-February 1975 to attend the annual session of the National Governors Association and to meet with various federal officials. Bordallo had been first elected to the Guam Legislature in 1956 and was described as "a loquacious, energetic populist." His defeat by Camacho for governor in 1970 has been attributed in part to the three-way competition in the Democratic primary "which left the Democratic party badly divided." Bordallo had another struggle to win the nomination in 1974, but in the village "pocket meetings" his "emphasis on Chamorro rights, expressed fluently and emotionally in English and in Chamorro, attracted the biggest crowds." Reliance on his "grassroots political infrastructure proved decisive"; his ticket "swamped" the other Democratic tickets. The general election was another story; he and his running mate, Rudolph G. Sablan, "squeaked by Camacho-Moylan with 51.3 percent of the vote," aided considerably by a write-in campaign for a second Republican ticket.[97]

Early in February, Governor Bordallo met with Ambassador F. Haydn Williams, who was in Guam before completing the status negotiations with the Northern Marianas in Saipan that resulted in the signing of the Northern Marianas Covenant on February 15, 1975. At the time of his meeting with the governor, Williams had not yet learned of President Ford's approval of the study and his directive to the Under Secretaries Committee. He did, however, repeat the assurances offered to Bordallo's predecessor that the United States had a "continuing US interest in exploring with Guamanians [a] possible change in Guam's future status," was prepared "to work with Members of US Congress regarding [the] future status of Guam," and that the United States "in no way [was] attempting to give [the] Northern Marianas [a] preferred status at expense of Guam." Williams reported that

---

97. *Destiny's Landfall*, 234-35, 250-51; *Sella Bay Ammunition Wharf Controversy*, 71-72.

Governor Bordallo appreciated this advice but then "launched into [a] long explanation [of] his personal view that unification with Guam should have been original goal of Marianas negotiations and that anything setting up separate commonwealth in Northern Marianas would make unification that much more difficult in his opinion."[98]

Anticipating meetings by Governor Bordallo with Secretary Morton and several other federal officials during his visit, Interior officials considered how to respond to any overtures by him about political status. This was one of many issues raised by Emmett M. Rice, who was serving as acting director of territorial affairs since Carpenter's return to the Department of State in late 1974. Rice was a career federal official in the small staff office that handled federal relationships with the territories. The large, sprawling Interior Department had high priority missions with respect to water, timber, grazing lands, mineral leases, and similar politically charged matters. The business of the territorial affairs office rarely gained the attention of the cabinet officer. In addition, Interior during this period suffered from a revolving door as its leaders frequently changed. Rogers C.B. Morton, an experienced congressman from Maryland, took over as secretary after President Nixon fired Walter J. Hickel, his first secretary of the Interior. Morton left in April 1975, leaving the office vacant until his successor Stanley K. Hathaway was confirmed on June 11, 1975. Hathaway served only for a few months. After another period without a confirmed replacement in office, Thomas S. Kleppe took office on October 17, 1975. Under these conditions, low-level officials like Rice could have an impact disproportionate to the position they held.

Rice traveled to Guam to meet with Governor Bordallo on the afternoon of Saturday, February 15, 1975, the day before Bordallo left for Washington. In a memorandum to an assistant to Secretary Morton, Rice identified some of the important issues that had to be addressed regarding Interior's responsibilities to implement and develop a negotiating approach pursuant

---

98. Cable, February 3, 1975, Williams to Secretary of State, 1-2. Williams was informed of President Ford's directive a few days later. Cable, February 7, 1975, from Secretary of State to Williams.

to the presidential directive, such as staffing and funding of the effort, the role of the U.S. Congress, and development of a negotiating strategy. As to dealing with any inquiries by Governor Bordallo, he recommended

> that any response be limited to assurance already given ex-Governor Carlos Camacho that we look forward to opening a dialogue on Guam-Federal relations. Ambassador Williams has already indicated to Governor Bordallo in general terms that this invitation is still open. If pressed on timing, we should respond that that is largely up to Guam and we will be interested in knowing the plans of the Governor in that regard.[99]

The Department of Defense was also concerned about Governor Bordallo's visit. His schedule included a meeting with Deputy Secretary of Defense William P. Clements Jr. on February 25, 1975. Bordallo had requested the meeting to discuss various issues raised by the department's use of land on Guam and its plans to build additional housing units there for military personnel and their families. The deputy secretary was informed that Governor Bordallo had been recently advised "that Guam's ultimate status will be no less favorable than that promised the Northern Mariana Islands," but that "the Governor still may raise issues related to political status." The briefing memorandum went on to say that "he is considered somewhat unpredictable in this regard and has not had the time in office to develop fully most future status objectives." At the meeting, Governor Bordallo, accompanied by Joseph F. Ada, the Republican Speaker of the Guam Legislature, responded to inquiries about the recent signing of the Covenant with the Northern Marianas by emphasizing again the desirability of reintegration of Guam and the Northern Marianas, the rejection of such a proposal by Guamanian voters in 1969, and "the possibility that integration would become even less desirable after the people of the Northern Marianas experienced

---

99. Memorandum, February 14, 1975, from Rice to Herge, 2; Official Schedule Book 1975, Papers of Ricardo J. Bordallo, Micronesian Area Research Center. The schedule shows a meeting with Rice at 3 P.M. on the afternoon of February 15, 1975. Rice had traveled with Ambassador Williams to Saipan for the signing ceremony of the Northern Marianas Covenant on the morning of February 15, 1975.

greater self-government." None of the participants apparently discussed Guam's political status aspirations or United States policy regarding improvements in Guam's relationship with the federal government.[100]

Governor Bordallo also scheduled a meeting at the White House for February 27, 1975. Within the White House staff, it was decided that Norman E. Ross Jr. of the White House Domestic Council staff would see the governor, although the Guam study had been the responsibility of the National Security Council staff. Ross had received a copy of the Froebe memorandum regarding the Guam study and was fully informed regarding the action taken by the president. However, the Domestic Council had no active participation in the work of the Under Secretaries Committee and Ross was aware that Interior had been assigned the lead role in implementing the presidential directive. For those reasons, Ross may have concluded that he should not be the principal spokesman in delivering a message on the new federal policy.

In a letter to Ross after the meeting, Governor Bordallo expressed the hope "that we will be able to work closely in the future concerning Guam and its relations with the federal government." His letter indicated that nothing was said about the newly established U.S. policy regarding Guam's status at the meeting. Instead, Bordallo asked that Ross forward to him "any information you may obtain concerning Guam, and, in particular, the progress of the recently-appointed Presidential Task Force." It is unclear, of course, exactly what was said about any presidential task force at this meeting; Ross may have made a general reference to the past interagency work developing the Guam study or may have anticipated the creation of a new task force to implement the presidential directive. But whatever was said the end result was evident: Governor Bordallo left the meeting wholly uninformed about current U.S. policy regarding Guam's status and misinformed

---

100. Memorandum, February 20, 1975, Carter to Jones; Memorandum, February 20, 1975, Assistant Secretary of Defense (ISA) to the Deputy Secretary of Defense, 1; Memorandum of Conversation, March 25, 1975, prepared by Assistant Secretary of Defense (ISA), 1.

about a non-existent task force whose deliberations might at some point in the future be of interest to him.[101]

Three months later, Governor Bordallo requested a meeting with President Ford to discuss "questions within the Territory regarding its future role within the United States in light of recent events in Indochina." The Domestic Council staff recommended that the president meet with the governor for ten minutes, advising that Bordallo wanted to express "a desire on the part of the Guamanians for closer identification with the U.S." and "will raise sensitive issues relating to the Commonwealth status of the Marianas and the desire of Guam to be included in future status considerations." The president's schedulers turned down the request. Governor Bordallo met instead with the recently appointed Secretary of the Interior Stanley K. Hathaway on June 19, 1975, who, like most of his predecessors, was not familiar with his department's responsibilities for distant insular areas. An interagency group, including Fred M. Zeder, a Texas businessman recently appointed as Interior's new director of territorial affairs, considered how Secretary Hathaway should respond to any inquiries from Governor Bordallo about political status. Based on this discussion, Secretary Hathaway was advised if the subject came up to make the following points:

> Inquire of the Governor as to how Guam is proceeding with respect to the question of a new status for the territory. The Secretary should express the hope that the Executive and Legislative branches [of Guam] will be able to arrive at a joint position. He should indicate that the Executive Branch [of the U.S.] will be receptive to a formal request for Guam-Federal talks and that the Executive is preparing to open a dialogue on this matter.

---

101. Letter, March 1, 1975, Bordallo to Ross. After his meeting with Ross, the governor's schedule was apparently amended to include the subject of "Presidential Task Force" on his agenda for meetings on February 28, 1975, with Secretary Morton, Senator Inouye, and Representative Matsunaga. No memorandum regarding his meeting with Secretary Morton was produced by the Department of the Interior. The governor's subsequent letter to Secretary Morton about the meeting made no reference to political status but concentrated instead on Guam's pending request for $56 million in the 1976 fiscal year budget. Letter, March 13, 1975, Bordallo to Morton.

As the meeting turned out, Governor Bordallo mentioned future political status only in passing and Secretary Hathaway did not make any of the carefully scripted points prepared for his use.[102]

To be sure, Guamanian officials during 1975 were given general assurances about future improvements in their political status—usually in the process of securing Guamanian support in Congress for approval of the Northern Marianas Covenant. In May 1975, a report from Guam suggested growing opposition among Guamanian businesses to certain provisions of the Covenant, especially its restriction on land ownership and exemption from the federal minimum wage law. Williams dispatched Richard Wyttenbach, a Navy officer then working for Williams in the Office of Micronesian Status Negotiations, to deal with the problem. Wyttenbach had recently returned from an assignment as the Navy's political advisor on Guam, during the course of which he had established valuable personal contacts with a wide range of influential political, business, and social leaders on the island. In Guam, Wyttenbach drafted a resolution supporting the Covenant, which he delivered to Speaker Ada, and visited with Governor Bordallo. He told the governor that he had been authorized by Brent Scowcroft, the assistant to the president for national security affairs, to say: "If you support us in Washington for the Covenant of the Northern Marianas, to get it through the Senate, we guarantee you, Guam, at least as good a deal as the Marianas are getting. That is the phrase I used."[103]

Later in 1975, when the Covenant encountered unexpected opposition in the Senate, Ambassador Williams turned to Guam for assistance. The Guam Legislature passed a resolution on November 12, 1975, which asserted

---

102. Memorandum, June 16, 1975, Falk to Rustand; Memorandum for the Record, June 19, 1975, prepared by Elster and Whelan of Defense (ISA), 2; Briefing Notes for Secretary Hathaway, June 19, 1975, 1; Memorandum for the Files, July 7, 1975, prepared by Knowles of State (EA/ANP), 1; Governor Bordallo's subsequent letter did not refer to any discussion of political status at the meeting. Letter, June 27, 1975, Bordallo to Falk.

103. *Oral Histories*, Interview of Richard Wyttenbach-Santos; *Pacific Daily News* (March 6, 1975); Report on *Foremost International* (newsletter), May 15, 1975, prepared by Schmitz.

that "the people of Guam are pleased that their cousins in the Northern Mariana Islands, to whom they are bound by blood, history, culture and language, have successfully negotiated a covenant under which they are willing to live as citizens of the United States" and urged that the U.S. Congress approve the new relationship. Won Pat put into the Congressional Record a letter to Senator John Sparkman in which he emphasized the national security and defense interests involved and the need to honor the humanitarian and political obligations imposed by the Trusteeship Agreement. Near the end of congressional consideration of the Covenant, Governor Bordallo weighed in with letters to several U.S. senators seeking their support for the Covenant. The Covenant was approved by the Senate on February 24, 1976, and signed by President Ford on March 24, 1976. [104]

5.2 Interior's Failure to Implement the Presidential Directive

The Under Secretaries Committee first considered implementation of President Ford's directive on March 11, 1975. Chairman Ingersoll emphasized that Guam's future political status was essentially a domestic matter and that the Interior Department should take the lead in developing a new political relationship with Guam. Assistant Secretary Hughes assumed this responsibility for Interior, but asked for some additional time within which to address Interior's personnel and organizational problems. He advised the Under Secretaries Committee that Interior would be prepared within two to four weeks to proceed to develop "a game plan" for consideration by the committee. The committee recommended an early approach to the U.S. Congress regarding a new political status for Guam. Interior was instructed to prepare "an options paper concerning our negotiating approach" as soon as "Interior has completed its internal organization and staffing arrangements." It took more than twelve months before Interior presented the

---

104. *Commonwealth of the Northern Mariana Islands: Hearing on H. J. Res. 549*, 94th Cong., 1st Sess. (November 5, 1975), Appendix, 170–71; *Congressional Record*, 94th Cong., 2nd Sess., 1976, 122, pt. 1:49; *Pacific Daily News* (February 10, 1976). No suggestion of Guamanian opposition to the Covenant, or Guamanian insistence on equal treatment, is found in the congressional record of deliberations regarding the Covenant

requested "options paper" to the committee—an unjustifiable delay that led inevitably to new complications and made implementation of the presidential directive even more difficult.[105]

Interior's approach to its assignment was initially designed by Rice as acting director of territorial affairs, but was wholly embraced by Zeder after his appointment as director. As revealed by the briefing of Secretary Hathaway before his meeting with Governor Bordallo, Interior's Office of Territorial Affairs planned to impose the burden on Guam's political leaders to form a negotiating committee representing both its executive and legislative branches and to approach the federal government with an agenda regarding improvements in its status. This would be done without telling any Guam official about the existence or substance of the president's directive. In addition, Interior's approach included these other important ingredients: (1) members of Congress would be invited to participate in any discussions with Guam about its status; (2) no invitation would be extended to Guamanian leaders for status discussions until congressional participation was determined; (3) discussions with Guam would not be considered as "negotiations;" and (4) many substantive issues would have to be addressed by the U.S. government "before full scale talks can begin."[106]

On Rice's advice, Hughes recommended to the Under Secretaries Committee in August 1975 that appropriate members of Congress be invited to join as full participants in any status discussions with Guam's representatives. Rice acknowledged that members of Congress, in particular Representative Burton and Senator Henry M. Jackson, had been satisfied during the Micronesian and Northern Marianas negotiations to leave the negotiating to the executive branch so long as they were regularly kept advised regarding the substance and direction of the negotiations. Rice contended, however, that direct congressional involvement was preferable with respect to Guam because "Congress is the final authority for any alterations in the Guam

---

105. Memorandum, March 25, 1975, Staff Director Gathright to USC members re meeting of March 11, 1975, 2-3 (Appendix 4).

106. Memorandum, February 24, 1975, Rice to Hughes, 4.

Organic Act and for any Federal grants or loans which may result from the Guam discussions." In addition, he pointed out that including members of Congress on the federal team "will encourage the Guamanians to represent themselves similarly thereby preventing a one-branch or one-party domination of the discussions." Because the Guamanians might be influenced by the composition of the U.S. team, Rice recommended that no invitation be extended to Guam to participate in status discussions until the question of congressional participation was resolved. Rice's recommendations along these lines were presented to Hughes in April 1975, but not acted upon until late August when Hughes incorporated these recommendations essentially verbatim in a letter to the Under Secretaries Committee. No member of Congress was consulted about such proposed direct participation before the recommendation was forwarded to the Under Secretaries Committee.[107]

Interior elected not to share with the other agencies at this time its views about the format and substance of any discussions with Guam's representatives. Notwithstanding the clear language of the Guam study recommendations and the presidential directive, Interior argued that any discussions with Guam should not be characterized as "negotiations." Rice argued that basic U.S. interests in Guam, such as U.S. sovereignty, control over foreign affairs, and defense, "are not considered negotiable by the U.S. and probably not by Guam." With respect to other areas where a change in Guam's status might be contemplated—internal self-government and local constitution—"there is no reason to believe that U.S. and Guamanian objectives are very different." Lastly, he pointed out that "financial assistance is a poor tool for negotiations . . . because Congress is the provider of such assistance" and "its attitude is not likely to be easily influenced by a negotiation even if Congressional representatives are included on the negotiating team."[108]

---

107. Memorandum, February 24, 1975, Rice to Hughes, 2-3; Memorandum, April 23, 1975, Rice to Hughes, 1-3 (Appendix 5); Letter, August 27, 1975, Hughes to Ingersoll, 1-3 (Appendix 7).

108. Memorandum, February 24, 1975, Rice to Hughes, 4.

Interior's view of the subjects that might be considered in any status negotiations with Guam reflected its disposition to dismiss the conclusions and recommendations of the Guam study, notwithstanding the fact that they were based on some twelve months of interagency collaboration chaired by Interior personnel. Rice proposed that the federal government would have to "make up its mind on various substantive issues" before talks could begin because the "issues of most importance to Guam are not addressed in the February 1 memorandum to the Under Secretaries Committee." He identified "immigration, federal land, military expenditures, environmental concerns and any number of federal programs" as falling in this category. Such an approach obviously ignored the facts that only three major issues were submitted by the Under Secretaries Committee to President Ford for decision and that the detailed findings and recommendations of the Guam study on the very subjects identified by Rice constituted the established positions of the federal government. Interior's early and consistent attitude towards any status negotiations with Guam might be explained, if not excused, by its history of reactive and unimaginative administration of U.S. territories and its disapproval of the Covenant negotiated with the Northern Marianas. But its position wholly ignored the major conclusion of the Guam study approved by the president that moving promptly to improve Guam's political status was necessary to address Guam's legitimate complaints about its status and to protect and advance American national security and defense interests in the Western Pacific.[109]

5.3 Delay Inevitably Produced Complications

Governor Bordallo and Speaker Ada, although of different political parties, were well aware of the tension that had developed between their predecessors on the issue of Guam's political status. The status commission, created by Guam's legislature in 1973 and chaired by Senator Lujan, reported in late 1974 that a good "interim status would be similar to the commonwealth status granted Puerto Rico and that which is being discussed with the Marianas." Rather than consider seriously such a short-term strategy, the new political leadership in Guam decided to start afresh with a new political

---

109. *Id.*, 4.

status commission. Unlike the earlier commission, this Special Commission on the Political Status of Guam had the support of both the governor and the legislature. Senator Frank F. Blas was elected chair of the new commission; its members were drawn from both parties; and the commission was declared to be the sole body to represent Guam in any status negotiations with the federal government.[110]

Chairman Blas wrote President Ford shortly after the commission was organized to advise him regarding its membership, functions, and desire to promptly establish a liaison with the White House. He emphasized that the commission's members "include representatives of the general public and representatives of the Executive and Legislative branches of the Guam government." He quoted the legislative finding in creating the commission that "a resolution of some of Guam's basic economic, social and political questions should be sought within the framework of political status negotiations with the federal government with all due speed." His letter referred to the meeting between Governor Bordallo and Norman Ross of the White House staff at which "a Presidential Task Force was mentioned by Mr. Ross as one method of studying all aspects of Guam's political status." Referring to the recently concluded Northern Marianas negotiations, he urged the president to appoint a representative "for the purpose of establishing initial dialogue" with the commission "in order that proper coordination can be maintained throughout our efforts to resolve the important question of the future relationship of Guam to the United States of America." Reflecting a dysfunctional White House staff and Interior's antipathy to meaningful discussions with Guam, this letter, and a follow-up letter from the commission's staff director, went unanswered for more than thirteen months.[111]

---

110. *Destiny's Landfall*, 250, 253-54; *Pacific Daily News* (May 10, June 14, and July 19, 1975).

111. Letter, August 22, 1975, Blas to the President, 1-2 (Appendix 6); Letter, September 16, 1975, Bacchi to Falk. In his letter to James H. Falk of the White House Domestic Council, Bacchi asked who at the Domestic Council was responsible for Guam in light of Ross' departure and inquired about the status of the chairman's earlier letter. On behalf of the commission, he asked for the opportunity to discuss its function and its request for a presidential representative during an upcoming visit to Washington. No documents were produced regarding any such meeting during a Bacchi visit.

However timely and appropriate, Guam's creation of a new status commission offended Antonio Won Pat, who was not officially consulted about the commission or included among its members. Reportedly "antagonized" by this slight, Won Pat in June 1975 introduced a joint resolution calling for creation of a status commission by the U.S. Congress, composed of the chairman of the Subcommittee on Territories of the House of Representatives and other members appointed by U.S. and Guamanian executive and legislative officials to study and recommend changes in the Guam organic act and Guam's political status. Following up on an earlier resolution, Won Pat in September 1975 introduced legislation authorizing the convening of a constitutional convention to prepare a constitution for Guam, providing for a republican form of government and a bill of rights. The proposal also called for approval of such a constitution by Guam's voters in a referendum and subsequent review by the president of the United States. Once approved, the legislation provided that the constitution "shall supersede such provisions of the Organic Act of Guam as may be inconsistent with such constitution."[112]

Notwithstanding Won Pat's disapproval and the lack of any response from the federal government, the Special Commission continued to study the issues and develop a strategy for pursuing its objectives. Its members included former lieutenant governor Kurt Moylan, Vice-chairman Pedro Sanchez, and Senators Tommy Tanaka, Ed Duenas, Carl Gutierrez, Frank Santos, and Benigno Palomo. At the commission's direction, Blas wrote to Won Pat emphasizing the need for an overall political agreement between the United States and Guam before Guam drafted its own constitution. When the commission learned that Governor Bordallo's subcabinet had taken a different position and endorsed Won Pat's constitutional convention proposal, commission member Santos was reported as saying, "oh, my God, don't they know that we exist?" He suggested that the Bordallo subcabinet

---

112. H.J.Res. 489, 94th Cong. 1st Sess. (June 5, 1975); H.R. 9492, 94th Cong. 1st Sess. (September 9, 1975); *Destiny's Landfall*, 254.

be invited to observe a regular commission meeting "so we don't duplicate our efforts and waste time."[113]

These developments did not go unnoticed within the federal agencies charged with implementing President Ford's directive regarding Guam's political status. Rice advised Assistant Secretary Hughes in June that Won Pat "had publicized his introduction of [the status commission] resolution heavily on Guam during his recent visit" and that action on Rice's then-pending proposed draft letters to the congressional leadership "outlining the Administration's approach to Guam-Federal discussions is called for." The conflicting status approaches by Guam's representatives provided Interior's personnel with an additional reason for delaying any federal initiative until Guam's political leaders had agreed on their priorities and preferred mechanism for dealing with the federal government. The proposal for a congressionally approved constitutional convention in Guam before any review of Guam's political status as directed by President Ford was particularly troublesome, especially to those who had participated in the Northern Marianas negotiations and wanted to avoid the risk of a Guamanian convention that might be tempted to address federal relations issues.[114]

5.4   Other Departments Defer to Interior

Shortly after sending their August letter to Deputy Secretary of State Ingersoll, who still served as the Chairman of the Under Secretaries Committee, Interior officials visited with him to discuss the matter. Assistant Secretary Hughes, accompanied by Zeder, assured Ingersoll that "they had not forgotten the assignment he had given them to prepare a study on the implementation of the President's instructions on Guam's political status." They explained the delay in part because the Interior Department lacked a secretary and under secretary, but represented that they now were prepared

---

113. *Pacific Daily News* (September 10, 1975); Letter, September 17, 1975, Blas to Won Pat.

114. Memorandum, June 11, 1975, Rice to Hughes; Memorandum, September 26, 1975, Crowe to Abramowitz, 1.

to make the approach to Congress that they had previously recommended. Based on his recent trips to Guam, Zeder reported "a general attitude of impatience on Guam with the Federal Government" but thought that "the climate was good now for following up on the President's instructions" and that the Guamanians "were now ready to get into political status discussions." Hughes, whose regular duties as assistant secretary for programs and budget spanned a broad range of tasks, asked Ingersoll if Zeder could take Hughes' role "to chair the negotiations with Guam." Ingersoll responded that he thought that Zeder could play such a leading role without seeking any revision in the presidential instructions. They agreed that an interagency meeting should be held within the next seven to ten days "to consider the question of touching base with Congress as well as other steps that should be taken." Ingersoll hoped that "everything necessary could be done in time for Mr. Zeder to discuss political status with Governor Bordallo when he visits Guam on October 5."[115]

Interior convened a meeting of the interagency working group in late September to consider its proposed negotiating approach and organizational structure. It circulated in advance its draft memorandum to the Chairman of the Under Secretaries Committee, which outlined the negotiating approach that had long been germinating within Interior. It emphasized that any discussions with Guam not be characterized as "negotiations" because the basic U.S. interests in Guam were not considered negotiable, creating a constitution was an internal Guam matter, financial assistance to Guam came from Congress "and therefore would not be a proper subject in negotiations," and "negotiations tend to make adversaries of the negotiating parties." As to the question of congressional involvement, Interior's draft letter reflected a changed approach based on its informal (and long overdue) consultations on Capitol Hill. Interior reported that the United States-Puerto Rico Ad Hoc Committee was "severely handicapped" by the inability of its Congressional members to attend scheduled meetings. In addition, "informal

---

115. Memorandum to the Files, September 26, 1975, prepared by Knowles, 1-2. Ingersoll confirmed his readiness to let Zeder take the lead in that department in a letter to Interior's acting secretary. Letter, September 25, 1975, Ingersoll to Frizzell.

soundings with staff members on the House Committee on Interior and Insular Affairs indicate that the key Congressmen [ie. Burton] are not interested in direct participation in discussions with Guam as long as they are kept fully informed as the discussions proceed." Therefore, the attached draft letter to the president of the Senate and the speaker of the House proposed that these congressional leaders designate members of their respective bodies who would be involved by means of regular consultation.[116]

On the organizational side, Interior's draft memorandum proposed that Zeder be designated by the president to undertake and conduct all discussions with Guam regarding its political status, economic well-being, financial assistance, and international status. He would be staffed by an interagency committee to be chaired by Rice, now the deputy director of Interior's Office of Territorial Affairs. The draft letter reiterated the view that any formal invitation to the Guamanians or response to their initiative to begin status discussions "should be delayed until after the question of U.S. Congressional involvement is settled." The letter suggested that Zeder would be meeting informally with key members of Congress (including Burton) "as soon as possible to sound them out on proposed Executive Branch and Congressional involvement in any Guam-Federal relations discussions." Once the question of congressional involvement was resolved, Interior proposed that Zeder open "an informal dialogue" with Guamanian officials during his visit to Guam, now scheduled for late October. However, the draft letter emphasized "that these discussions would not involve any substantive issues on political status or commit the Federal Government to a specific course of action" but that it was hoped "that some indications of Guam's intent could be determined." Conspicuously absent from Interior's draft was any reference to the presidential directive instructing that Guam be offered a political status comparable to that of the Northern Marianas.[117]

---

116. Memorandum, September 29, 1975, Rice to State and Defense officials. Draft Memorandum for the Chairman, Under Secretaries Committee, September 29, 1975, prepared by Interior, 1-2.

117. *Id.*, 3-4.

The members of the interagency group generally approved Interior's approach at their meeting on September 29, 1975. Some concern was expressed at the lack of action implementing the presidential directive of February 1,1975. Admiral William J. Crowe Jr., who had participated in both the Micronesian and Northern Marianas status negotiations, complained in advance of the meeting to Deputy Assistant Secretary of Defense Morton I. Abramowitz about this lack of action and pointed out that, in the meantime, "the Guamanians are moving in all directions" to establish a status commission, to have a presidential representative named with whom they can negotiate, and to get authorization for a constitution to replace the organic act. At the meeting, Admiral Crowe expressed his preference (differing from Interior) for an overall agreement which "would then become the framework for the Guam Constitution." The group generally endorsed "a very low-key approach" by Zeder to key members of Congress regarding their involvement in any discussions with Guam, but "should avoid communicating with any other Members on this subject until after the Marianas Covenant is approved." This cautionary comment reflected a growing concern that the opposition to the Covenant which had developed in the U.S. Senate might use any apparent readiness to alter Guam's status to strengthen their position in opposing the Covenant. The interagency group acknowledged that a written response to the Guamanian status commission was in the hands of the White House Domestic Council, but believed that it should be delayed until Zeder's meeting with congressional leaders and timed so as not to jeopardize Senate action on the Covenant. State representatives at the meeting advised that both the answer to the commission's letter and designating Zeder as the president's representative "would require clearance from the USC Chairman to assure compliance with the relevant Presidential directive."[118]

---

118. Memorandum, September 26, 1975, Crowe to Abramowitz, 1; Memorandum, September 29, 1975, Rice to State, Defense, NSC, and OMB officials, 1-2.

5.4   Congressman Burton Intervenes

These leisurely deliberations within the executive branch regarding possible status negotiations with Guam soon conflicted with the preferences of Congressman Burton. Following through on his representations to the Guam Legislature in January 1974, Burton in September 1975 was aggressively pushing the legislation authorizing a Guam constitutional convention through the House of Representatives. He could not understand why some Guamanians were opposed to the proposal, which he described as another key step toward "getting rid of the trappings of colonialism" and moving "down the road of self-government." His critical comments were directly aimed at Guam's Special Commission and its earlier letter to Won Pat. When Burton's criticism was publicized in Guam, the commission felt compelled to meet and reconsider its position on the bill. Burton reportedly had asserted "emphatically that in matters of U.S. territories and possession, his word is final." He had emphasized that he was planning to become the House of Representatives majority leader when Speaker Carl Albert stepped down and that Won Pat "might replace him as territories subcommittee chairman." Burton's comments had their intended effect; nearly all the commission members present at the meeting "spoke in terms of newfound respect and awe for Burton's self-stated powers." They hastened to make amends with Burton and Won Pat by reversing their earlier position opposing the constitutional convention bill and settling for a modest request that the proposed legislation acknowledge the existence of their commission and the desirability of negotiations between Guam and the federal government.[119]

---

119. *Sunday News* (September 21, 1975); *Pacific Daily News* (September 23 and 24, 1975). Meanwhile Won Pat had requested the Director of the Congressional Research Service to address several legal questions raised by the Special Commission's letter to him. For example, he asked whether there was any legal basis or precedent for an unincorporated territory to negotiate its political status with the United States. Letter, September, 26, 1975, Eustaquio to Jayson.

Without consideration of any Guamanian views, Interior urged that the legislation should not be enacted:

> We believe that enactment of these bills would be premature at this time because the Administration has not had sufficient time to consider the broad issues surrounding such changes and to develop its position on them. Specifically, whether they will adequately protect the Virgin Islands/Federal and the Guam/Federal relationships, and we need to examine this more thoroughly. Accordingly, we recommend that the Committee defer its consideration of these bills until the Administration has developed its position on them.

Given the administration's signing of the Covenant for the Northern Mariana Islands in February 1975, after more than two years of negotiations, and the president's approval of the Guam study after extensive deliberations by the Under Secretaries Committee, Interior's claim that the administration "has not had sufficient time to consider the broad issues" regarding the proposed legislation was simply incredible.[120]

Within the Department of Defense, Admiral Crowe opposed the legislation on the very practical grounds that it appeared to bypass all current efforts to seek revisions in Guam's political status through amendments of the organic act. According to Crowe, "this approach is fraught with difficulties. It could confront this Administration with local political choices which clearly are inconsistent with federal-territorial relations." He observed that two steps were necessary before developing a new constitution for Guam: "(1) an indication from the Legislative and Executive branches on Guam that they are ready to proceed with political status discussions and (2) a federal-territorial dialogue which addresses practical alternatives to the more restrictive provisions of the Organic Act."[121]

---

120. Letter, September 17, 1975, Hughes to James A. Haley, Chairman, Committee on Interior and Insular Affairs, 2.

121. Memorandum, September 24, 1975, Crowe to DOD assistant general counsel. He also pointed out that consideration of the bills should be delayed until Congress acted on the Covenant.

Interior's plea for delay on the Guam legislation did not deter Burton, who acknowledged that "we probably move a little too fast for the Interior Department. . . . We've been writing the policy from up here—not them—but it's been bipartisan all the way." He pointed out that "the legislative process is not neat—you have to take what action you can as it comes up" and claimed that "it would be 'foolhardy' to wait around for ideal solutions when real improvements can be made." Interior was more successful in the Senate, where it succeeded in eliminating the flexibility provided in the House version, which would have permitted the president to disapprove portions of the constitution, and assured automatic repeal of conflicting organic act provisions. Interior also persuaded the Senate to adopt limitations on the subject matter that the convention could consider—in effect requiring the convention to proceed within the existing federal-territorial relationship—while knowing that substantial changes in that relationship were being sought by Guamanian officials, many of which would be acceptable to the federal government under the president's directive.[122]

In Zeder's absence, Rice visited with Burton and his assistant, Adrian Winkel, on October 7, 1975. At the outset of the meeting Burton stated "emphatically that no action or discussion on Guam's political status would take place until after Marianas Covenant Bill was passed by Congress." That bill was under consideration by the Senate at the time, and ultimately passed about four months later in February 1976. As Rice outlined the approach of Guam's status commission and the interagency deliberations regarding possible negotiations, Burton strongly disagreed. He made the following points: there should be no negotiations; he wanted to push the constitutional convention bill through Congress; he maintained that Guam should first adopt a constitution and then Burton "would make some changes in the Organic Act and broaden scope of Federal programs and services applicable

122. Public Law 94-584; 90 Stat. 2899 (October 21, 1976); Penelope Bordallo Hofschneider, *A Campaign for Political Rights on the Island of Guam 1899-1950* (Saipan, MP: CNMI Division of Historic Preservation, 2001) [hereafter *A Campaign for Political Rights*], 177; Arnold H. Leibowitz, *Defining Status: A Comprehensive Analysis of United States Territorial Relations* (Dordrecht: Martinus Nijnoff, 1989) [hereafter *Defining Status*], 377; *Sunday News* (September 21, 1975).

to Guam." His position, in short, was directly contrary to President Ford's directive and the express desire of Guamanian officials to have a thorough review of their political status. When Rice raised the issue of a presidentially appointed representative to discuss status and other issues with Guam, Burton dismissed the idea and maintained that the director of territorial affairs at Interior (Zeder) "had the authority now to work with Guam and that is the way it should continue."[123]

With little apparent resistance or thought, the interagency working group accepted Burton's position regarding discussions with Guam. They were influenced to some extent by the disintegrating economic situation on Guam, which was viewed as close to bankruptcy, and the perceived inclination of some Guamanian officials to "use the political status issue to focus federal attention on their economic plight." So the group concluded that "our central problem in dealing with the Guamanians is how to avoid a Constitutional Convention in an atmosphere of government bankruptcy, business failure, and unemployment." Nevertheless, the group "agreed that the Burton approach to political status is the best way to protect federal interests, i.e., speed passage of legislation now before Congress to authorize a Constitutional Convention on Guam." After some desultory discussion about addressing Guam's economic problems, the meeting concluded with the further direction that Interior should draft an appropriate reply to the letter received two months earlier from Chairman Blas of the Guam status commission.[124]

---

123. Memorandum for the Record, October 7, 1975, prepared by Scott, 1-2 (Appendix 8). Burton advised the Interior officials that he saw little chance of exempting Guam from the Jones Act (which the Covenant provided for the Northern Marianas), was sympathetic to Guam's desire for more control over immigration, and supported Won Pat on the need to inventory military land holdings on Guam to determine which lands are in excess.

124. Memorandum for the Record, October 9, 1975, prepared by Elster (DOD), 1-2. Zeder's trip to Guam was directly related to Guam's economic situation. Governor Bordallo had written the Secretary of the Interior "requesting either forgiveness of the remaining debt on the Rehabilitation Loan or deferred payments on the loan for five years." Interior's response indicated that Zeder would be in Guam on October 16-20 and would be prepared to sit down with the responsible executive branch officials, including the governor, as well as the legislature's budget committee. Memorandum, October 6, 1975, Rice to Zeder, 1.

Rice sent Zeder a brief report by cable about the meeting with Burton and the subsequent conclusions of the interagency working group. He reported that the group was working on the negotiating approach paper for submission to the Under Secretaries Committee, but suggested that Zeder should meet with that committee before the paper's submission. He also reported that an interim response to Blas was being prepared under White House direction to the effect that Blas's request for appointment of a federal representative was under active consideration but, until a presidential decision was made, the director of territorial affairs "would continue to be [the] responsible official and point of contact for Government of Guam initiatives with [the] federal government." He advised Zeder that Won Pat might be in Guam during Zeder's visit, perhaps "trying to mend some fences in preparation for upcoming political campaign," in which Won Pat would be facing the vice-chairman of the Guam's Special Commission as a candidate for Won Pat's Congressional Delegate seat. He reminded Zeder that the Special Commission "took strong exception to Won Pat's Con Con bill, saying that Won Pat had agreed not to submit bill until [the] Commission had completed its work."[125]

Shortly before Zeder returned from his trip, Assistant Secretary Hughes in early November 1975 wrote the chairman of the Under Secretaries Committee following up on some of Rice's suggestions. He reported very briefly about the meeting of the interagency group on September 29, 1975, Zeder's initial contacts with members of Congress regarding their involvement in any discussions with Guam, and Rice's meeting with Burton. He advised that the working group was still drafting a negotiating approach for presentation to the committee in November. But before making any further recommendations to the chairman about a negotiating approach and congressional involvement, Hughes suggested that the Under Secretaries Committee "will want to assess the results of the meetings with Congressman

---

125. Cable, October 10, 1975, Rice to Zeder, 33-34. Rice subsequently prepared two draft replies to Blas and sent them to the NSC staff at the White House for review and decision. Memorandum, October 21, 1975, Rice to Taylor (NSC).

Burton and Senator Jackson's staff and Mr. Zeder's meetings with Guamanian officials."[126]

5.6 The Under Secretaries Committee Finally Makes a Decision

Early in January 1976, Rice circulated to the working group a revised version of the draft memorandum to the Under Secretaries Committee. With no effort to explain the inaction over the past several months, Rice's draft reported that "two separate but related events have occurred which may affect the timing of any official approach to the Guamanians." First, action by the Senate on the pending constitutional convention bill was not expected until after the Northern Marianas Covenant was voted upon and Won Pat (assuming favorable action by the Senate) projected that convention delegates would be elected in September 1976. Second, Guam's Special Commission on the Political Status of Guam was proceeding on a course in conflict with Won Pat's and planning to conduct a plebiscite of Guamanian sentiment in September, following which the commission would "enter into negotiations with the Federal Government leading to an 'Agreement' and then hold a Constitutional Convention." Overriding both considerations, according to the draft memorandum, was Congressman Burton's insistence that there be no contact with Guamanian representatives regarding a change in its political status until after a vote on the Covenant.[127]

Before outlining three options for consideration by the Under Secretaries Committee, the draft memorandum reiterated Interior's position that any discussions with Guam should not be characterized as negotiations. It also reviewed Guam's severe financial condition resulting from the current

---

126. Letter, November 3, 1975, Hughes to Ingersoll, 2.

127. Memorandum, January 7, 1976, Rice to Inter Agency Group on Guam-Federal Relations; Draft Memorandum to Chairman, Under Secretaries Committee, 2. The memorandum reported incorrectly that an interim response to the chairman of the Guam Special Commission was sent by the White House informing him that his request was under consideration but, until a presidential decision was made, the director of the Office of Territorial Affairs would continue to be the official representative of the executive branch with respect to Guam. *Id.*

recession and high inflation, emphasizing Interior's continued efforts to address the issue in consultation with Guam's officials, and recommending that President Ford's directive regarding financial assistance to Guam should be deleted so as remove this issue from further consideration by the Under Secretaries Committee. The draft memorandum then assessed three approaches to political status discussions with Guam: (1) status quo; (2) executive branch initiative with a presidentially appointed representative; and (3) appointment of a joint U.S./Guam commission. Interior's draft memorandum recommended the status quo alternative: (1) it was the only alternative acceptable to Congressman Burton; (2) it placed the burden for initiating status discussions on the Guamanians; and (3) it obligated the federal government only to address specific legislative issues affecting Guam on an individual basis as they were raised.

Between the alternative approaches recommended by Guam's status commission and Won Pat, Interior now endorsed Won Pat's preference for a prompt constitutional convention. Interior emphasized that Burton was wholeheartedly supporting this approach and that a recent poll conducted by the University of Guam indicated that Won Pat enjoyed a much higher level of popular support than either Guam's governor or legislature. Interior again stressed the "internal" nature of Guam's constitution, but emphasized that both the Guamanians and Interior had "to insure the integrity of the constitution as a locally drafted document reflecting the wishes of the convention while insuring that the provisions of the constitution will be acceptable to the President and to the Congress." According to the draft memorandum, this alternative enables the administration to stay "clear of internal in-fighting over timing of Constitutional Convention," does not put the "Administration in position of appearing to get out ahead of Congress . . . in its efforts to have the Guamanians hold a constitutional convention," and is the "most acceptable way of treating Guam question according to Congressman Phillip Burton."[128]

---

128. Draft Memorandum, 7-8; Option One, 2-3.

Under Interior's recommended approach, "the federal government should not take the initiative in suggesting a beginning of such [political status] discussion until requested by the Governor." Interior suggested that the absence of any further inquiries from Guam's commission or the governor over the past several months may be due to the fact that "the Guamanians have not agreed amongst themselves on an approach to these discussions." It acknowledged that the federal agencies know generally the areas of interest to Guamanian officials, including those addressed in the Guam study, and stated that the working group "will develop position papers on the other aspects of Guam's political status over the next few months once these have been identified with more clarity." Interior offered in further support of its "status quo" approach the results of the recent poll showing that "status quo is preferred over commonwealth, statehood, union with Hawaii or the Northern Marianas, or independence by a margin of 3 to 1." According to the draft memorandum, "if this poll does represent the current mood on Guam, it strengthens the reasons for the Federal Government not to take the initiative at this time in proposing specific areas of discussion on political status."[129]

Disturbed by the delay in implementing President Ford's directive of nearly a year ago, State Department officials rejected Interior's proposed "status quo" alternative. Under the leadership of Richard L. Williams, State's representative on the interagency working group, State decided that a more active approach to negotiations with Guam should be considered. After consultation with representatives from other State Department bureaus interested in the problem, Williams delivered State's comments to the interagency group at its meeting on January 19, 1976. He pointed out that under each of the three options set forth by Interior "active or formal negotiations, except perhaps for piecemeal legislative revisions, would be deferred until the Marianas legislation has been acted upon and until the Governor of Guam has officially asked the President for talks."

---

129. Draft Memorandum, 8-9.

State urged that "a more active approach" be considered for several reasons. First, "presidential guidance directs us to seek agreement with the Guamanians on political status, not to wait for them to request discussions." Second, prompt action now "may forestall potential future Guamanian dis-satisfaction over Federal inaction," which "could make the negotiating task easier and have beneficial effect on Congressional, press, and UN opinion." Third, a Guamanian constitutional convention before meaningful status negotiations would run the risk that the convention "might reach results unforeseen and undesirable from a Federal Government standpoint," citing the Micronesian convention of six months earlier as an example. Accord-ing to State, a proposed constitution for Guam "which went beyond Fed-eral preferences in asserting elements of sovereignty or international status" could cause "friction in the Federal-Guam negotiations and unnecessary difficulty or embarrassment with Congress, the press, the UN and even the White House, which might ask us why we had not more actively pursued its February 1975 directive calling on us to seek agreement with the Guamani-ans within certain parameters."[130]

State submitted an Option Four to the interagency group at this meet-ing. As soon as Congress passed the Marianas Covenant bill, but no lat-er than April 1976, State proposed that "the Federal negotiating team or its representative should convey to principal Guamanian political figures a statement that the Federal Government wishes to enter into discussions with Guam's representatives intended to lead to revisions in Guam's politi-cal status consonant with the wishes of the people of Guam as well as of the rest of the United States." Before conveying such a statement, how-ever, State's option recognized that consultation with selected members of Congress was required, and left it to the working group to decide whether members in addition to those of the Interior Committees, such as those on the Armed Services, Foreign Relations, or other committees, should be consulted. State's proposal acknowledged also that the working group would be required to "consider possible modifications to the approach in re-sponse to any Congressional objections or advice." The proposed statement

---

130. State Department Comments on the Draft Negotiating Approach, undated but at-tached to Memorandum, January 19, 1976, Williams to Mickey, 1-2.

to Guamanian officials was fundamentally different from any approach that Interior had contemplated. It would recognize that the relationship of Guam "to the rest of the US needs clarification and redefinition," indicate "that the Federal Government is ready for discussions at any time," advise the Guamanians "that the Federal Government has Commonwealth status in mind but would be willing to see modified unincorporated territorial status continue if the Guamanians prefer the present arrangement," recognize Guam's right to draft its own constitution, "offer assurance that political status negotiations can be scheduled so as to take any Constitution-drafting process sensibly into account," and "call for preliminary discussions between a Federal team and a Guamanian team this summer."[131]

Although three members were not present, the interagency group at its meeting of January 19, 1976, agreed to add Option Four to its memorandum to the Under Secretaries Committee. The group also accepted State's view that no formal revision to the February 1975 presidential directive should be sought as recommended by Interior. The representative from the Office of Management and Budget, within the Executive Office of the President, "said that his office shared State's concern at the long delay in implementing the February 1975 NSC guidance." The representative of the Joint Chiefs of Staff agreed to "endorse Option Four as the preferred option so long as the current round of Congressional action on the Marianas was first completed." Given this unanimity of views, Rice said that he too would support Option Four, would agree that no revision of the 1975 directive was required with respect to its financial provisions, "but said that he would need to reserve on the proposal about Mr. Zeder's position until he could speak with Mr. Zeder."[132]

---

131. Option Four, 1-2, attached to Memorandum, January 19, 1976, Williams to Mickey.

132. Memorandum, January 19, 1976, Williams to Mickey, 2. The representatives of the National Security Council, the Office of Micronesian Status Negotiations, and the Department of Defense (ISA) were not in attendance. Some consideration was given to eliminating Option Three, in light of the difficulties that such an approach had encountered in the Puerto Rico context, but the working group concluded instead to leave it in so as to avoid criticism "but beef up the reasons against this being an acceptable option." Memorandum for the Record, January 20, 1976, prepared by Herndon (DOD/Joint Chiefs of Staff), 3.

It took another two months before the working group could finalize a memorandum for the Under Secretaries Committee. Interior continued to press—and State continued to oppose—a formal effort to amend the year-old presidential directive. Anticipating that the working group would reach agreement on some version of Option Four, Williams at State advised his colleagues that "we will soon need to delineate State's interests in the Guam negotiations." Much of Interior's advocacy focused on Zeder's continued insistence on a designation by President Ford that Zeder was the president's personal representative in any status discussions with Guam. Shortly after his arrival at Interior as director of the Office of Territorial Affairs, Zeder had mounted a determined bureaucratic campaign to replace Ambassador Williams as the president's personal representative in the Micronesian status negotiations. Having failed in that effort, Zeder was even more strongly motivated to seek such a presidential seal of approval as the official in charge of discussions with Guam.[133]

A meeting by Rice with members of the Guam commission during February 1976 provided some additional impetus for submitting the memorandum to the Under Secretaries Committee. During his visit to Guam, Rice also met with Governor Bordallo, Speaker Ada, and several members of the Guam Legislature. He advised Zeder that all of the Guam representatives "were delighted to meet with me as they are tired of 'fencing in the dark'" and "look forward to opening official discussions at an early date." Rice advised that the members with whom he met were "not interested in titles like Commonwealth but only in Federal laws as they affect Guam." They were intending to recommend legislation by June to authorize a plebiscite by December 1976 which would solicit the views of the voters on the specified options presented to them. According to Rice's report, the commission wanted to have formal discussions with U.S. representatives and seek to "reach a definite agreement prior to the plebiscite" on those options which would be acceptable to U.S. representatives. The commission was seeking

---

133. Memorandum, February 6, 1976, Williams to State officials, 1; Memorandum, February 10, 1976, Williams to Scott (Interior); Guam memo, February 10, 1976, prepared by Williams, 2-3.

"official recognition of their group by the United States," which they told Rice "will help to meld the Legislative and Executive Branches together for the common good." They expressed a fear that "an anti-military faction" would develop "if recognition is delayed" and "advised that Governor Bordallo's three appointees took the position of the Twelfth Guam Legislature, which is somewhat anti-United States and anti-U.S. military."[134]

On March 25, 1976, Under Secretary of Interior Kent Frizzell, formerly the department's general counsel, sent the Under Secretaries Committee the letter that had been under discussion by the working group for at least six months. The letter acknowledged that it was responding to the committee's direction at its March 11, 1975, meeting that Interior should "develop and implement a negotiating approach" to effect the presidential decisions on the Guam study. By way of background, Interior's letter advised that "the pressures for change" in the Guam-Federal relationship "are not so much aimed at a modified or revised political arrangement as they are at restrictive Federal statutes and regulations that in Guam's view inhibit economic development and financial self-sufficiency." After providing some examples of this dissatisfaction, the letter identified the amount of land used for military purposes as another significant issue that would have to be addressed in any discussions. Interior concluded this portion of its report to the Under Secretaries Committee by emphasizing that "another factor that has commanded more immediate attention amongst the people of Guam than changing Guam's basic relationship with the Federal Government is the Territory's financial plight."[135]

Interior advised the Under Secretaries Committee of its intention to commence discussions (not "negotiations") with Guamanian representatives

---

134. Memorandum, March 1, 1976, Rice to Zeder, 1-3. Those present at his meeting with the commission were Chairman Blas, Vice-chairman Sanchez, members Tanaka and Moylan, and staffer Bacchi. He also enclosed copies of a recent letter dated February 12, 1976, from Blas to Zeder, Blas' earlier (and still unanswered) letter to the president, and information regarding the commission's background and activities.

135. Memorandum, March 25, 1976, Frizzell to Chairman, Under Secretaries Committee, 2-3 (Appendix 9).

"as soon as possible after receiving Congressional acquiescence of the approach recommended in this memorandum." It advised, however, that "progress in the discussions with the Guamanians may hinge on resolution of Guam's domestic political problems" and proceeded to elaborate on the different approaches being pursued by the Special Commission and Won Pat. Interior reported that Won Pat's bill calling for a constitutional convention was not "necessarily in conflict with the Commission's objectives, but that it is premature to draft a constitution until it is known what status is desired by the people." Discussions between Won Pat and the Special Commission reportedly "did not result in a compromise solution" and Won Pat, with Burton's full support, "envision[ed] an election of delegates to the convention in September 1976." Interior added that 1976 is an election year for both Won Pat and the legislature and that, although Won Pat is likely to be reelected, "he looks upon the Commission as a challenge to his stature as the advocate for improving Guam's relationship with the Federal Government. If he could delay any substantive work of the Commission until after the 1976 elections, he feels the Commission may cease to exist."[136]

Interior also told the Under Secretaries Committee that there were several aspects of the presidential directive "which if read literally are inaccurate, undesirable or required some clarification due to changed circumstances." The under secretary "would like to consider it as within Mr. Zeder's discretion to interpret these passages in the spirit of the directive without NSC modification of the directives." Recognizing that the USC chairman might believe that a formal request was necessary, Interior identified some of the specifics in the directive that required clarification or amendment. Referring to perhaps the most important aspect of the presidential directive—namely, that the U.S. "should seek a commonwealth arrangement no less favorable that that which we are negotiating with the Northern Marianas"—Interior advised that the term "commonwealth" "is an imprecise term which strictly speaking might require further definition," and that if the "no less favorable" qualification was deemed to cover the financial provisions of the Covenant

---

136. *Id.*, 4-5.

"the financial assistance due Guam would be difficult to define comparably and would be potentially exorbitant in amount." Interior found similar problems with defining the phrase "modified unincorporated territorial status" and any suggestion that a final agreement with Guam should provide "for U.S. military basing rights on Guam," because it ignored "the fact that the U.S. already has military base rights which it simply wishes to continue as they now exist and which the Federal side may not wish to include explicitly in the negotiations." Lastly, Interior recommended that the directive be amended by substituting the words "Director, Office of Territorial Affairs, Department of the Interior" for the words "Assistant Secretary of the Interior for Program Development and Budget" so that Zeder could represent himself as a presidential appointee.[137]

With respect to the substance of the approach to the Guamanians, Interior basically recommended a watered-down version of Option Four as discussed within the working group, which would lead to letters from the president to appropriate Guamanian officials suggesting a meeting of two delegations as early as May 1976. But Interior stressed that "perhaps the most important aspect of the Administration's initiative to enter into discussions with Guam is to make a prior determination that the [Democratic-controlled] Congress has no serious reservations or objections to our recommended approach." Interior recommended that Zeder be instructed to meet with selected members of Congress to solicit their views on the subject, beginning with the "minority [Republican] leaders of Congress and the ranking minority members of the Senate and House Committees on Interior and Insular Affairs" and after that "the [Democratic] chairmen of these committees and the chairman of the House Subcommittee on Territorial

---

137. *Id.*, 5-7. On this last point, Interior's memorandum reported that this change can be effected by a letter of notification from the Under Secretaries Committee to the National Security Council and that, "inasmuch as no NSC approval is required, it is recommended that the USC send such a letter forward." Id., 7. Later in the memorandum, Interior recommended that Zeder be expressly appointed by the president as his personal representative on the grounds that the Guam commission had expressly requested such an appointment and that it "would have the advantage of elevating the importance, in the eyes of the Guamanians, the Federal Government attaches to these discussions." *Id.*, 8.

and Insular Affairs." The memorandum outlined the presentation to be made to Congress, including the schedule for discussions with Guam, their overall objectives, and the intention to consult fully with Congress along the way. If "one or more Members seriously object to the proposal as outlined by Mr. Zeder . . . and persist in their objections after attempts by Mr. Zeder to dissuade them, Mr. Zeder will make recommendations to you as to how next to proceed."[138]

After considering the comments of the concerned agencies, the Under Secretaries Committee acted on May 17, 1976. The new chairman of the committee, Deputy Secretary of State Charles W. Robinson, advised Interior's under secretary that the approach set forth in his memorandum was approved "subject to several modifications and comments." First, the interpretations proposed by Interior regarding the presidential directive relating to political status "are approved on the understanding that the United States is willing to discuss a commonwealth status or a modified unincorporated territorial status for Guam if Guamanian representatives so desire." Second, the director of Interior's Office of Territorial Affairs "should head the federal delegation" without the need for any other action on the grounds that the authority is sufficiently based on the presidential directive and the letter of September 25, 1975, from the chairman of the Under Secretaries Committee and "will ensure effective coordination of the views of the interested US agencies." The proposed approach to the U.S. Congress and the proposed initial communication with Guam's representatives were also approved with instructions that draft letters to the president of the Senate and the speaker

---

138. *Id.*, 9-11. In fact, the proposal advanced by Interior in this memorandum fell far short of the proposal advocated by State in the working group. Not only does it purport to take several issues off the table of any discussions, but the planned public announcement of such discussions would make no reference to the federal government's willingness to consider commonwealth status or some comparable alternative desired by the Guamanian people.

of the House of Representatives, as well as to Guamanian officials, be prepared and sent back to the Under Secretaries Committee for approval.[139]

5.7   The White House Attempts to Get Involved

White House staffers for both the Domestic Council and the National Security Council were well aware of Guam's interest in improving its political status. Governor Bordallo's visits to Washington in February and June 1975 made this abundantly clear. In addition, White House staffers had to respond to letters from the newly appointed Guam status commission in August and September 1975. Both letters requested that the president appoint a special representative to open discussions with the commission. Another letter from Governor Bordallo in January 1976 to the president prompted White House officials to confront their record of inaction on the earlier letters. Referring to the Bicentennial Year celebration of the Declaration of Independence, Governor Bordallo emphasized that the people of Guam still lacked certain fundamental democratic rights available to all other American citizens. He stated that he was "compelled to bring to your attention the existence of many federal statutes and constraints that affect Guam's ability to advance politically and economically" and that "increased economic self-sufficiency demands increased local autonomy." He requested the president's "personal attention in resolving some of the imperfections of Guam's relationship with the federal government" and, in particular, the

---

139. Letter, May 17, 1976, Robinson to Frizzell (Appendix 10). The Under Secretaries Committee decision was promptly circulated to members of the committee. The Interior memorandum of March 25, 1976, had been circulated by USC's staff director to members of the committee by memorandum of March 30, 1976, asking for comments by April 13, 1976. Memorandum, March 30, 1976, Gathright to Members of the USC. The Defense Department comments on Interior's proposed approach confirmed that department's views on what issues affecting it were clearly not on the negotiating table: it agreed with Interior's concerns about the scope of the presidential directive and stated that Defense "does not envisage the negotiation of U.S. base rights on Guam, the conversion of land held in fee simple to land held under a long term lease, or the renegotiation of various agreements pertain [sic] to the joint use of facilities on Guam." Memorandum, undated, Defense (ISA) to Staff Director, Under Secretaries Committee.

appointment of "a Personal Representative to begin talks with Government of Guam officials."[140]

The need to respond to Governor Bordallo's letter, as well as the earlier ones from the commission, prompted a debate within the White House staff whether Guam's political status was a domestic problem or a national security issue. In order to respond appropriately to the governor's letter, one Domestic Council staffer asked his boss whether Guam fell within his duties for intergovernmental relations and, significantly, inquired: "Are we committed to a course of upgrading the political status of Guam?" The head of the Domestic Council staff, James Cannon, raised the subject with the head of the National Security Council staff, Brent Scowcroft, mentioning the letter from the governor, and stated that changing the status of either Guam or Puerto Rico "would have far-reaching domestic and international implications."[141]

Although Cannon and Scowcroft met on February 19, 1976, to discuss the matter, the jurisdictional issue relating to Guam remained unresolved for many months. A fact sheet prepared after the meeting for Scowcroft referred to the presidential directive of a year earlier as "setting out broad objectives in negotiating a new status for Guam" and reported that Interior had "delayed doing anything until recently, partly because of bureaucratic reasons and partly because it felt that we should not engage in serious

---

140. Letter, January 13, 1976, Bordallo to President Ford, 1. Upon receipt of this letter, Won Pat promptly wrote to Burton expressing his "intuitive reaction" that "whatever agreement or compact is agreed upon, the Subcommittee on Territories should reserve the right to amend the agreement rather than for the committee to accept or reject the proposal in toto." Letter, January 21, 1976, Won Pat to Burton. Won Pat continued to pursue a separate course on status issues in 1976, often in conflict with the objectives of Guam's governor, legislature, or Special Commission. His stated determination to pursue his legislative proposal for a congressionally created status commission prompted inquiries from the Special Commission about his intention. Letter, April 2, 1976, Blas to Won Pat. When he learned of the legislature's intention to hold a referendum on political status, Won Pat queried the Congressional Research Service whether the legislature had the authority to take this step. Letter, June 30, 1976, Won Pat to Glass.

141. Memorandum, January 29, 1976, McConahey to Cannon; Memorandum, January 29, 1976, Cannon to Scowcroft.

talks with the Guamanians until after the passage of the Northern Marianas Commonwealth Covenant." Scowcroft sent this memorandum to Cannon for his information, but neither official seemed prepared to address the jurisdictional question.

One result of this indecision was that representatives from both the domestic and national security areas participated in a meeting with Guam Senator Concepcion Cruz Barrett in early March 1976, shortly after the Covenant finally cleared the Congress. Senator Barrett outlined some of Guam's principal concerns regarding its status, including the need for more control over immigration, the need for a Guam Supreme Court, and an exemption to the Jones Act. She stressed that the Guam organic act "was obsolete and needed revising," but thought that Guamanians did not want "statehood or commonwealth status but preferred an enhanced territorial status that would, among other things, give them control over immigration." One of the White House staffers at the meeting assured the senator that "with the final Congressional approval of the Northern Marianas Covenant, the U. S. Government would be ready to focus on the Guam question."[142]

Following through on this representation, a member of the Domestic Council staff reported to Cannon in mid-April (after the Covenant was signed by President Ford) that agreement had been reached on the allocation of responsibilities with respect to the Guam issue. He advised that "Interior will take the lead on routine discussions with issues relating to the Guamanian Commission, NSC will continue to provide a substantive review and input from a security standpoint, and we will perform the major contact point on an intergovernmental basis." He reported that two Guam senators (and members of the Special Commission) had recently met with him to request "prompt negotiations on their status and relationship with the Federal Government" and that the NSC advised these senators that it was "prepared to begin such discussions later this spring." Accordingly,

---

142. Memorandum, February 20, 1976, Barnes to Scowcroft, 1; Memorandum, February 23, 1976, Scowcroft to Cannon; Memorandum of Conversation, March 10, 1976, prepared by Taylor, 1-2.

he recommended that Cannon sign the attached draft responses to both Governor Bordallo and Chairman Blas of the commission "indicating our understanding of their concerns and our willingness to begin serious discussions with them later this spring."[143]

By this time, however, the Under Secretaries Committee was considering the negotiating approach recommended by Interior's under secretary. The timing and nature of the responses to the Blas and Bordallo letters depended to some extent on the decision of the committee and its implementation by the Department of the Interior. Interior's effort to implement the committee's decision of May 17, 1976, encountered opposition from Burton that delayed any response to these letters for several months. The jurisdictional question in the White House regarding Guam remained unresolved: the National Security Council staff thought that the Domestic Council should be responsible and the Domestic Council staff believed that the National Security Council should be responsible. In the absence of any meaningful presidential interest with respect to Guam, the White House staff obviously felt no pressure to resolve this ongoing debate—a judgment that essentially left them with little choice but to defer to Interior's future recommendations on the matter.

---

143. Memorandum, April 19, 1976, McConahey to Cannon. One member of the NSC staff, Jay Taylor, was a member of the interagency working group chaired by Rice and was the principal person involved in trying to coordinate White House action with the deliberations of the working group and the Under Secretaries Committee.

Chapter Six

The Guam Study Fades into History

Interior was charged with the duty of ascertaining congressional reactions to the proposed approach to the Guamanians approved by the Under Secretaries Committee. Not surprisingly in light of his earlier comments, Congressman Burton in his meeting with Zeder on June 24, 1976, strongly objected to the appointment of a federal negotiator to deal with Guam's political status. Zeder reported that Burton would oppose any formal administration initiative to begin discussions with Guam's status commission. Although Burton expressed concerns relating to the Puerto Rico Compact, Zeder reported that "his primary reason for opposing was Guam politics." Burton was concerned that Won Pat was going to be opposed in his party's primary election in September by Pedro Sanchez, the vice-chairman of Guam's Special Commission. According to Zeder's report, "Burton, a strong supporter of Congressman Won Pat, believes that Sanchez would use the forum of Federal relations discussions with the Special Commission to campaign against Won Pat."[144]

Zeder met with the Special Commission at their request a month after his meeting with Burton. The commission gave Zeder a set of papers setting forth its negotiating objectives on a number of issues relating to the application of federal laws in Guam. The members were very concerned about the failure of the White House to respond to their several letters requesting

---

144. Memorandum, July 19, 1976, Rice to McConahey, 2; Debriefing Memorandum of Zeder's Meeting with Guam's status commission, August 10, 1976, prepared by Interior, 1. This second memorandum reported that Burton considered the Special Commission "to be too politically oriented," but that the ranking minority member of Burton's Subcommittee, Congressman Clausen, endorsed the proposed approach to Guamanian officials approved by the Under Secretaries Committee. *Id.*, 1.

that the president appoint a special representative to initiate a dialogue with them. Zeder attributed the delay to White House concerns about Puerto Rico, suggesting that they were apprehensive about taking "any definitive action on status negotiations anywhere in [the] world." Assuring the commission members that there were "no two sides" to these discussions, Zeder asked the members to consider him as "their representative in Washington." He then proceeded to discuss briefly several of the federal law issues raised by the commission, such as the Jones Act, customs, air transportation, income tax exemptions, and a duty-free allowance increase. With respect to these and other issues discussed, Zeder offered little hope for satisfying Guam's concerns as he pointed out the existing political, legal, or economic obstacles pertaining to each. He stressed the need for the commission to provide his office with more convincing documentation to support their requests.[145]

Because of Burton's opposition to any initiative until after the Guam Democratic primary election in September, Interior now reverted to its original status quo approach. Interior recommended that interim responses to Blas and Bordallo be approved by the White House, which would state that Zeder would continue to represent the executive branch in matters affecting the Guam-Federal relationship "pending a final decision by the President."[146]

Interior's pressing for interim responses and designation of Zeder as the representative of the federal government was not well received in the White House. One staffer wondered who had commissioned Zeder to describe himself as representing President Ford at Guam's bicentennial celebrations in early July and challenged Zeder's reported public statement in Guam "that he was shortly expecting instructions from Washington appointing him as the Special Negotiator on the future political status of Guam." He

---

145. Debriefing Memorandum (handwritten five pages), (undated), probably prepared by Interior; Debriefing Memorandum of Zeder's Meeting with Guam's status commission, August 10, 1976, prepared by Interior.

146. Memorandum, July 19, 1976, Rice to McConahey.

advised Cannon that "the NSC believes that our negotiator with Guam should be a different individual, possibly a distinguished citizen operating directly under the authority of the White House, since Guam involves the interests of at least three Departments: Defense, Interior, and State." He did agree, however, that interim responses to Blas and Bordallo should be approved and sent. By way of footnote, he suggested to Cannon that "there is also the need to 'de-activate' Mr. Zeder in this matter, appropriately through a communication with Secretary Kleppe."[147]

The results of Guam's primary election in early September were not helpful in advancing discussions within the federal government about Guam's status. Won Pat easily defeated his opponent to be the Democratic Party's candidate for the Congressional Delegate seat. The plebiscite organized by the Special Commission on the Political Status of Guam had placed five alternatives before the voters with the following results: (1) Status Quo (9 percent); (2) Improving Present Status (58.1 percent); (3) Independence (5.6 percent); (4) Statehood (23.8 percent); and (5) Other (3.5 percent). The voters participating in the plebiscite represented 65.4 percent of the registered voters. After the plebiscite results were certified by the election commission in Guam, Interior learned that the chairman of the Special Commission planned "to write the president, informing him of the results and desire to move ahead with discussions leading to an improved relationship with the Federal Government."[148]

With this information in hand, Interior asked the White House again to send the interim responses to Blas and Bordallo. Zeder's office reminded the Domestic Council staff that he had been assured before his last trip to Guam that such responses were on the way, that it had become "very difficult for Guamanian leaders to explain why an answer has not been received," and that Zeder planned another trip to Guam in early October. This request for

---

147. Memorandum, August 13, 1976, Hanzlik to Cannon, 1-2.

148. Memorandum, September 17, 1976, Scott to Director of Territorial Affairs. Chairman Blas did shortly thereafter write such a letter. Letter, September 28, 1976, Blas to the president.

action reached the White House while National Security Adviser Scowcroft was reviewing a recommendation from Cannon "that the White House responsibility for Guam should remain with the NSC." Cannon pointed out: "For the most part, the questions relating to Guam deal with foreign policy and defense posture in the Pacific region, and your staff, more than the Domestic Council, has been involved in the question of opening negotiations with Guam on their status." After receiving this request, Scowcroft's staff reminded him "of the continuing confusion with the Domestic Council regarding an appropriate division of responsibility on matters dealing with Guam" and that the NSC staff had "been trying for many months to have the Domestic Council" reply to the letters from Blas and Bordallo. The staff recommended that Scowcroft agree "that the NSC will continue to exercise White House responsibility on matters relating to Guam's status" so long as "the Domestic Council continue to provide a formal communication channel because we want to treat Guam as a domestic rather than an international matter."[149]

Compelled to make a decision in advance of Zeder's next visit to Guam, Cannon finally agreed to sign the two letters to Blas and Bordallo on October 1, 1976. The letters informed the Guamanians "that the President delegated to the Secretary of the Interior the responsibility for naming a Special Representative" and that the secretary has designated Zeder. The letters concluded with the recognition that "Mr. Zeder has worked closely with you in the past in finding ways to solve Guam's financial and economic problems and it is logical that he expand his scope to include ad referendum discussions and exchange of views on the Guam-Federal Government relationship with you." The internal debate within the White House continued throughout October 1976, eventually resulting in a complicated allocation of shared responsibility that was viewed by some of the staff involved as not in fact changing anything. But attention within the White House regarding Guam—or indeed the many more important subjects on the staff's

---

149. Memorandum, September 7, 1976, Cannon to Scowcroft; Memorandum, September 17, 1976, Mauldin (Interior) to Humphreys (Domestic Council); Memorandum, September 29, 1976, Gleysteen to Scowcroft.

agenda— was fading under the public relations and other demands of the presidential election campaign.[150]

The long-pending legislation providing for constitutional conventions for Guam and the Virgin Islands reached the president's desk in October, requiring his action by October 25, 1976. As finally approved by Congress, the bill authorized the Virgin Islands and Guam to organize territorial governments under constitutions drafted by their own elected constitutional conventions. The bill required that such constitutions:

- recognize, and be consistent with, the sovereignty of the United States over the Virgin Islands and Guam, as well as all other provisions of the U.S. Constitution, treaties, and laws of the United States applicable to them;

- provide for a republican form of government, consisting of executive, legislative, and judicial branches;

- contain a bill of rights; and

- provide for the establishment of a system of local courts.

After completing its work, each convention would submit a proposed constitution to its governor, who would transmit the proposed constitution to the president. The president within sixty days would then forward the constitution, with his comments, to the Congress. Under the bill, Congress would then have sixty days to approve, amend, or modify each constitution by joint resolution; if Congress failed to act within the prescribed sixty days, the constitution would be deemed approved. Once approved or modified by Congress, the proposed constitutions would then be submitted to the qualified voters of Guam and the Virgin Islands.[151]

---

150. Memorandum, October 1, 1976, Humphreys to Cannon; Letter, October 1, 1976, Cannon to Bordallo; Letter, October 1, 1976, Cannon to Blas; Memorandum, October 11, 1976, Scowcroft to Cannon; Memorandum, October 19, 1976, Cannon to Scowcroft.

151. Public Law 94-584, 90 Stat. 2899 (Oct. 21, 1976).

Three deficiencies in the legislation were singled out for the president's consideration. One referred to an ambiguity in the bill's provision relating to the establishment of a local court system. Another referred to the bill's failure to specify which parts of the organic legislation of Guam and the Virgin Islands "will cease to be operative when the constitutions become effective." The president was informed, however, that the Senate committee report acknowledged the problem and stated that it was anticipated that the president would transmit "a list of those provisions as part of his comments on the constitution[s]." The most significant deficiency was the bill's requirement that Congress review, and be allowed to amend, the proposed constitutions before they were voted on by the people of Guam and the Virgin Islands. This procedure departed from the precedent of the Northern Marianas Covenant, which provided that the proposed constitution of the Commonwealth of the Northern Mariana Islands would be presented to the federal government for approval only after it had been approved by the Northern Marianas voters. The Office of Management and Budget advised the president that it, as well as the Interior and Justice departments, had opposed this scheduling of congressional review and that, to this extent, the bill "defeats its basic intent of enabling the people of the two territories to organize their governments pursuant to constitutions of their own adoption." Despite these reservations, the federal agencies submitting comments, the Office of Management and Budget, and the White House Domestic Council staff all recommended approval. President Ford signed the proposed legislation on October 21, 1976.[152]

The interagency group on Guam chaired by Rice had not met since it had finalized its proposal for submission to the Under Secretaries Committee on March 25, 1976. By October 1976, it had been five months since the committee had generally approved the recommended approach to status discussions with Guam and four months since Congressman Burton had

---

152. Memorandum for the President from the Acting Director of OMB, October 19, 1976, 3-4; Memorandum, October 20, 1976, Cannon to the President; Letter, October 6, 1976, Interior to OMB; Letter, October 12, 1976, Justice to OMB; Letter, October 13, 1976, State to OMB; and Letter, October 13, 1976, from Defense to OMB.

objected to the opening of such discussions—at least until after Guam's primary election in early September. No effort had been made by Interior to develop an alternative approach that might be pursued in the face of Burton's opposition, although this eventuality had been recognized as a possibility in Interior's memorandum to the Under Secretaries Committee. In the meantime, of course, Zeder had visited Guam on at least two occasions; the long-delayed responses to the earlier Blas and Bordallo letters had been sent by the White House; and Zeder had finally succeeded in having himself officially designated as the representative of the federal government in any status discussions with Guam's commission.

Some preparation for eventual discussions with Guam seemed necessary in light of Chairman Blas's recent letter to the president suggesting that "formal discussions between the Commission and a Presidential representative begin immediately following the November election." Notwithstanding the uncertainties presented by the U.S. presidential election, in which Ford was challenged by the Democratic nominee Jimmy Carter, Rice wrote the members of the interagency group on October 20, 1976, asking that they undertake an appropriate review by November 10 of the issues that had been identified by the Guam commission in its series of position papers entitled "Specific Goals of Status Commission," which had been given to Zeder during his July visit. Rice advised the members that Zeder "has indicated a willingness to discuss these goals with the Special Commission in late November, but has informed the members that more convincing documentation will have to be presented showing how socio-economic conditions on Guam are adversely affected because these goals are not attainable under existing federal laws."[153]

---

153. Memorandum, October 20, 1976, Rice to Inter-Agency Working Group, 1. Five follow-up studies were assigned by Rice to specified federal agencies: (1) exemption of Guam from coastwise laws (Commerce); (2) limitation of number of resident aliens entering Guam (Justice and State); (3) prevent abuses of system for entry and control of non-immigrant aliens (Justice); (4) return unused Federally-owned land to Guam (Defense); and (5) permit Guam to join and participate in international organizations (State). With respect to the last four topics, Rice's assignment referred to designated pages in the 1974 Guam study, which had directed various follow-up studies of the kind now contemplated for the first time by Rice. *Id.*, Enclosure (2).

On November 2, 1976, the voters in the United States went to the polls in the presidential election. Jimmy Carter emerged as the victor. President Ford's defeat marked the effective end of Zeder's leadership of Interior's program for dealing with Guam's still unaddressed status aspirations. Following the November election, Zeder wrote to congratulate Chairman Blas on his reelection to the Guam Legislature, suggesting that this result as well as the earlier plebiscite "can only be interpreted as endorsements of your leadership and of the direction taken by" his commission. He advised Blas, however, that given the political nature of Zeder's position, he expected to be replaced by the incoming president soon after January 20, 1977. Under these circumstances, he concluded that it would not "be appropriate for me to schedule at this time a series of talks that may be delayed or not come to fruition because of conflicts with a new Director's priorities." He observed that "we have made a good beginning" and assured Blas that he "will make a strong recommendation to my successor that he follow the same approach to Guam-Federal relations discussions with the Special Commission as I have." In particular, he emphasized that he would recommend that the director of territorial affairs at Interior "continue as the White House-designated Federal government official for these discussions" and that, contrary to the views of unnamed Guamanian officials, "it would be entirely inappropriate to appoint a United States Ambassador as the Federal representative."[154]

---

154. Letter, November 19, 1976, Zeder to Blas, 1-2. Notwithstanding the election results, a few agencies began the process of responding to Rice's October 20 request. State was inclined to oppose any move to exempt Guam from federal regulation of Guam-foreign shore air routes, but was more favorable with respect to its desire for some special immigration rules. Memorandum, November 9, 1976, Brown to Williams; Memorandum, November 17, 1976, Williams to Rice. Defense looked at several "goals" that fell within its jurisdiction and generally took issue with the underlying assumptions of Guam's status commission. According to Defense, the department had not "retained certain acres of land for which no justification exists," past and current studies confirm that the department has "exercised prudence in the acquisition of real property on Guam," and "there is no valid reason for a one year suspension of the Statute of Limitations in that properties were legitimately acquired in Guam by DOD pursuant to the procedures for acquiring lands for federal public purposes." Memorandum, November 22, 1976, Blastos (Joint Chiefs of Staff) to Rice, 1-2.

Zeder's optimistic assessment of his contribution to the work of the Special Commission was not shared by its members. Although Zeder had the authority to implement a clearly defined presidential directive, his discussions with the commission left a very different impression. According to the Special Commission's vice-chairman,

> Zeder kept in touch with the commission as best he could but offered no substantial contribution to the work of the commission. He had no authority to do so. The absence of a designated representative of President Ford with whom the commission could dialogue on issues and the general apathy in official Washington about Guam's political status drive was frustrating to the commission.

This sentiment and frustration were shared by the other members as well, as reflected by the decision of Senator Blas and other commission members reelected to the Guam Legislature in November 1976 to make no effort to continue the Special Commission when the new legislature convened in January 1977.[155]

Zeder's final report to the Under Secretaries Committee in January 1977 contained a dramatically different approach to Guam-Federal status discussions from the one that he and his subordinates had so carefully nurtured and advocated during the past eighteen months. His memorandum briefly summarized his discussions with Congressman Don H. Clausen, a Republican from California, and Congressman Burton in June 1976; and expressed the view that, even after Won Pat's victory in September, Burton "was too preoccupied this fall with the business of Congress to reconsider the Administration's approach and Congressional involvement in Guam-Federal relations discussions." Zeder stated that this "apparent lack of interest on the part of key Committee chairmen, absent specific objections, has caused me to reconsider the need to arrange formal coordination procedures with the Congress, as recommended in the March 25, 1976, memorandum to you."

---

155. Pedro C. Sanchez, *Guahan/Guam: The History of our Island* (Agana, Guam: Sanchez Publishing House, 1989) [hereafter *Guahan/Guam*], 431.

He reported on his discussions with Guam's status commission and his letter to Blas after the election indicating that it would not be appropriate to engage in substantive discussions with the commission in late November or early December as originally planned.[156]

Zeder advised the Under Secretaries Committee that the recently enacted constitutional convention legislation precluded implementation of the earlier approach recommended by Interior and approved by the committee. According to Zeder, the earlier approach "recommended that improvements in the relationship and amendment of the Organic Act result from Guam's Constitutional Convention treatment of several issues related to the Organic Act, and development by the Secretary of the Interior of a legislative package for submission to Congress which addressed changes to existing legislation affecting Guam's socio-economic development." But now, he concluded, "following this approach will not obtain the desired results" because the legislation "specifies that the constitution shall deal with subject-matter of those provisions of the Organic Act which relate to local self-government" and "must be consistent with those provisions of the Organic Act which do not relate to local self-government." As though it were an entirely new thought, he advised the committee that this meant that "for all practical purposes the Organic Act, which was drafted by the U.S. Congress without benefit of Guamanian participation, will continue to govern the relationship between Guam and the Federal Government, and this is the crux of the relationship." He went on to state the obvious: "Guamanians want to replace the Organic Act with an agreement which defines Guam's status" and cited as an example the Northern Marianas Covenant.[157]

Having provided this basis for his recommendation, Zeder in a stunning 180-degree reversal of position contended that the Northern Marianas precedent should be followed with respect to Guam. He recommended: "Instead of treating revisions to the Organic Act and changes in the application

---

156. Memorandum, January 5, 1977, Zeder to Chairman, Under Secretaries Committee, 2-3.

157. *Id.*, 3-4.

of Federal laws and regulations in a piecemeal fashion, I propose that the Federal Government enter into a formal agreement with the Government of Guam, which would then be submitted to the people of Guam in a plebiscite, then to the U.S. Congress for enactment and to the President for final approval." He suggested that this approach would satisfy the general objectives of the 1974 Guam study and President Ford's directive approving its major provisions. Zeder attached to his final report to the committee a draft "Covenant to Establish the Commonwealth of Guam in Permanent Union with the United States of America." His draft document was based on the Northern Marianas Covenant (in some sections almost verbatim). Zeder recommended that it be circulated to the Under Secretaries Committee and that an interagency working group, chaired by the new director of territorial affairs, "develop an agreed paper to be used as the basis of continued Guam-Federal relations discussions over the next several months before Guam's constitutional convention convenes in July 1977." The chairman of the Under Secretaries Committee acknowledged receipt of Zeder's letter and advised him that the documents "will be referred to those in the next Administration who will be responsible for overseeing the negotiations on the Guam-Federal relationship" and that he was "sure that your recommendations will be helpful to them."[158]

---

158. *Id.*, 4; Letter, January 19, 1977, Robinson to Zeder.

Chapter Seven

Epilogue and Prologue

President Ford's directive in early 1975 to improve Guam's political status provided a unique opportunity for successful status discussions between the federal government and Guam. It could have produced solutions to some, if not all, of Guam's grievances and a commonwealth status comparable to the Northern Marianas. Whether this improvement of Guam's political status would have been supported over the long term by Guam's diverse constituencies is uncertain. What seems clear, however, is that it would have been preferable to the twenty-five years that followed, marked by turmoil, frustration, and lack of success in addressing Guam's status aspirations.

Guam's inability to take advantage of the presidential directive in advance of its 1977 constitutional convention predictably led to dissatisfaction both within the convention and the community at large. The convention's draft constitution, although professionally done and approved by the federal government, was rejected overwhelmingly by the voters in 1979 for a variety of reasons, including their displeasure at being required to adopt a constitution before having their relationship with the federal government improved through status negotiations. In 1980, Guam created its first Commission on Self-Determination, which conducted two polls of public opinion in 1982. After only 37 percent of the electorate participated in the first poll, a second was conducted between two alternatives—statehood or commonwealth. Commonwealth was preferred by 73 percent of the voters.

A proposed commonwealth act was completed in January 1984 under the auspices of a new Commission on Self-Determination. This act was discussed with various members of Congress, who were proposing that Guam submit its proposal to Congress directly rather than deal with a very reluctant executive branch. After many revisions, and growing political differences within the Guamanian community, the proposal was approved by the voters in 1987. Beginning in 1989 there were four years of negotiations about its provisions between Guam's representatives and a federal task force of more than twenty separate agencies. At the end of the Bush Administration in early 1993, however, there remained fundamental disagreements about many of the act's most important provisions. Negotiations continued under the Clinton Administration, with the assistance of three special representatives appointed to deal with the situation, but were equally unsuccessful in resolving the key differences. After introduction of the Guam Commonwealth Act in Congress in 1997, extensive hearings were conducted at which this history of Guam's efforts to improve its status and the critical issues in dispute were fully discussed. No action was taken on the bill.[159]

7.1   What Went Wrong

Although the Guam study and the presidential directive of 1975 may seem like distant history in light of the intervening decades, three conclusions can be usefully drawn from this experience. First, an effective reexamination of Guam's political status requires presidential leadership and supervision so that the Interior Department is not left substantially in charge of the assignment. Second, Guam needs to present a unified voice with respect to status issues and reshape its priorities in a realistic manner that reflects the political, economic, and legal concerns of all its citizens and the federal government. Third, the U.S. Congress has to be persuaded to let the executive branch, under presidential direction, shape and conduct the negotiations with Guam so that no single Congressman can exercise the kind of veto

---

159. An overview of most of this period from 1977 to 1997 can be found in Hearings on H.R. 100 before the House of Representatives, 105th Cong. 1st Sess. (1997). See also *Destiny's Landfall*, 262-64, 271-75, 284-85; *A Campaign for Political Rights*, 177-83, *Defining Status*, 336-38, and Richard H.J. Wyttenbach-Santos, "The Status of Guam's Quest for Commonwealth Status" (1996). During the hearings the federal government opposed the mutual consent provision, the Chamorro-only vote, the transfer of immigration and labor control to Guam, and the creation of a joint commission under Guam's control to make final determinations on the application of federal policy to Guam and to determine military lands to be transferred to the new commonwealth government.

power that Burton used repeatedly in connection with proposals to address Guam's political status.

7.1.1 Presidential Leadership and Supervision

Appointment of a presidential special assistant to conduct status discussions with Guam, reporting to a high-level committee such as the Under Secretaries Committee, would be essential to a favorable outcome. The experience of successive administrations in dealing with both the Northern Marianas and the Micronesian status negotiations in the 1970s and 1980s confirms the need for such a mechanism when there is an overriding national security interest and several different agencies are involved. This was not done in connection with the Guam study, in large measure because Guam was viewed (especially by Interior) as a domestic issue. But the national security interests emphasized in the study definitely justified such high level attention; it would also have served early on to require White House personnel to resolve their jurisdictional dispute so that the presidential assistant had a clear line of reporting to a responsible White House official. An experienced and sophisticated appointee to implement President Ford's directive would have been far better prepared both to manage the interagency consultations inherent in the project and to deal with the responsible members of Congress in a timely and effective manner.[160]

Even if Interior had been favorably disposed towards the Guam study and its implementation, its personnel basically lacked the capacity and the stature to handle such an assignment. The interagency committee did a competent job in preparing the Guam study submitted to the president in August 1974. But as the implementation discussions indicated, the permanent staff at Interior lacked any enthusiasm for an improved status for

---

160. It was especially unfortunate that Ambassador Williams, who was instrumental in originating the study, resigned from his duties in mid-1976 after serving more than five years on a part-time basis and achieving success with the Northern Marianas negotiations and considerable progress in the Micronesian negotiations. Although Guam's political status was not on his agenda, he would certainly have been offended by Interior's delay in implementing President Ford's 1975 directive.

Guam and, most importantly, concluded that it had no choice but to defer to the wishes of the dominant Congressman whose committee controlled the department's budget. The Office of Territorial Affairs (now the Office of Insular Affairs) has always been a small staff office in the Department of the Interior, and the department has many more politically significant functions which have necessarily commanded the attention of its top-level officials. With the possible exception of Secretary Walter J. Hickel, who had been governor of Alaska, during his brief service from 1969 to 1970, no Interior secretary in the last forty years has been prepared to assign a high priority to the department's responsibilities with respect to the U.S. territories under its jurisdiction, especially when challenged by a powerful Congressman with influence over its budget.[161]

Interior was not in fact favorably disposed to carry out the presidential directive that Guam be offered commonwealth status no less favorable than that afforded the Northern Mariana Islands. To some extent, this reflected the department's historic reluctance to accept any comprehensive improvement in a territory's status. During the 1960s, for example, Interior resisted efforts by the Department of State to negotiate a future political status for the Trust Territory of the Pacific Islands that would provide more self-government. Under the influence of the then-powerful Congressman Wayne Aspinall, Interior preferred the incremental process of providing for an elected governor, then a non-voting delegate, and then perhaps the right to draft a local constitution. The Northern Marianas Covenant, however, reflected a more comprehensive approach to political status and was resisted as such by Interior's territorial experts. As Interior viewed the situation, not only had the status negotiations with the Northern Marianas been taken out of its control, but the end result also threatened a substantial reshaping of the political status of Guam and the Virgin Islands.[162]

---

161. *National Security*, 14-15, 47-48, 114-21, 138-50; *An Honorable Accord*, 140-41, 357.

162. *National Security*, 70-73, 78-82, 113-22; *An Honorable Accord*, 186-87.

Interior's approach to the Guam study and the presidential directive consistently failed to acknowledge the basic findings and goals of these documents: the need to respond affirmatively to the reasonable complaints of the Guamanians and to protect the national security and defense interests that depended on the Guamanians' feeling that they were being treated fairly by the federal government. It was only after nearly a year of procrastination by Interior that representatives of State and other agencies protested Interior's "status quo" strategy as being inconsistent with the presidential directive and possibly subjecting them to criticism by the White House staff. No excuse can justify the delay from March 11, 1975, when Interior received its assignment from the Under Secretaries Committee, to March 25, 1976, when Interior finally sent its recommendation to the Under Secretaries Committee. As the professional staff at Interior was well aware, delay would almost certainly result in the appearance of external factors that might be used to justify further delay. This certainly proved to be the case: opposition to the Northern Marianas Covenant in the Senate and Burton's endorsement of the constitutional convention legislation provided additional excuses for Interior's phlegmatic approach to the problem. The fact that the Under Secretaries Committee failed to insist on a more responsive approach by Interior is due in large measure to the absence of an advocate, either a special presidential appointee or a designated member of the White House staff, who had the obligation to ensure the implementation of the presidential directive.

Interior's dealings with Guamanian officials during this period reflected a remarkable lack of candor. Never did Zeder or Rice tell Governor Bordallo, Speaker Ada, Chairman Blas of the status commission, or any other elected Guamanian official that the president had decided to offer Guam a commonwealth status like the Northern Marianas or some comparable status if that is what Guam preferred. At no point did Interior take any affirmative steps to convene a meeting with Guamanian officials, in particular the Special Commission, to address the preliminary questions that would necessarily precede any meaningful negotiations: issues such as scheduling, agenda topics, and the formation of joint working groups to explore the various issues. State suggested such an approach generally in January 1976, but it was significantly weakened by the working group and by the Under Secretaries Committee—all of whom seemed reconciled to letting Congressman Burton control any status discussions with Guam, whether public or private. In fact, a forthright and prompt response by Interior to the Special Commission's letter of August 1975 might have resulted in some meaningful preliminary work that could have led to substantive discussions between the two parties soon after the Covenant was passed by the Senate in February 1976.

Rather than adopting such an affirmative approach, Interior imposed the burden on Guam's officials to formulate a position to which Interior would then respond. This enabled Interior to take advantage of the apparently different strategies being pursued by the Special Commission and Delegate Won Pat, with some considerable doubt as to where Governor Bordallo stood on the critical issues. Of course, in anticipation that at some point discussions might take place, Interior had early on developed an approach—and secured the approval of the other agencies—that was calculated to frustrate and almost certainly antagonize the Guamanians. An approach such as Interior's—refusing to use the word "negotiations," taking several critical issues off the table such as finances and U.S. military needs, and prematurely rejecting other Guamanian positions—was certainly not well calculated to persuade the Guamanian representatives that the federal government was committed to substantial improvements in Guam's political status. Yet that was precisely what the Guam study recommended and what President Ford ordered the agencies to accomplish.

Interior's failure to implement the presidential directive was characterized by an aggressive effort to ensure that Interior was the lead agency and that its director of territorial affairs was designated as the federal government's representative in dealing with Guam. For months Interior recommended interim responses to Bordallo and Blas that would name Zeder as the government's representative pending some further decision by the president. This pursuit of self-aggrandizement provoked some members of the White House staff, but their own disorganization left them no choice but to designate Zeder as their representative in early October 1976. By then it was basically too late to initiate meaningful discussions and Zeder later used President Ford's defeat as an excuse for not meeting with the Special Commission. His suggestion to the commission's chairman that Zeder's successor might have different views on such status discussions tellingly reveals his misconception of Interior's assignment: the policy to be implemented was that specifically set forth in the Guam study and President Ford's directive, not the personal preferences of either Zeder or his successor.

Interior's position regarding the constitutional convention bill supported by Burton (and Won Pat) also contributed significantly to the non-implementation of the presidential directive and the frustrating course of events since 1976. Interior personnel, as well as those from State and Defense, recognized that a constitutional convention before any meaningful status discussion between Guam and the federal government was fraught with difficulty and more likely than not to lead to a convention determined to examine all aspects of Guam's current status. Once Burton appeared committed to this course, Interior (and the Under Secretaries Committee) concluded that they had no choice but to go along with his approach. But Interior then compounded the difficulties inherent in the situation in two important respects. First, it was instrumental in obtaining amendments in the Senate that expressly limited Guam's constitutional convention to those provisions of the organic act that pertained to local self-government; in effect the convention was compelled to draft a constitution within the current political framework defined by the organic act. Second, Interior's dilatory strategy regarding the presidential directive precluded the substantive status discussions sought by the Special Commission in 1976 that might have influenced the legislation while it was still before the Senate or the parameters within which the 1977 convention operated. The impact of these actions was seen in the overwhelming rejection of the draft constitution by the

Guamanians in 1979 as a way of expressing their frustration with Guam's present political status.[163]

When assessed against this record, Zeder's last-minute conversion in January 1977 to a different approach was both cynical and politically motivated. His newly developed recognition that the convention would have to work within the confines of those organic act provisions that did not relate to self-government cannot be fairly reconciled with the fact that he had personally urged such restrictive legislative provisions. His surprise that the Guamanians wanted to replace the organic act with an agreement that redefined its status and addressed some of their other problems with federal laws cannot be taken seriously. That is precisely what the Guamanians had been urging for years and was one of the underlying justifications for the Guam study. His recommendation that his successor adopt an approach directly contrary to the one pursued by Zeder for the past eighteen months was obviously calculated to tempt his Democratic successor to proceed in a manner that had been repeatedly rejected by Congressman Burton.

Having failed to honor and attempt to implement the directive of a Republican president, Zeder wanted to be remembered as an enlightened participant in the process who had tried valiantly to address Guam's political status issues and had equipped his Democratic successor with an approach that would build on Zeder's efforts.

Because the Guam study had been classified "Secret" in its entirety, its few existing copies were kept in secure storage facilities. After the 1976 election, when the Carter transition team arrived at the Interior Department to consider its staffing by the new president and the major policy issues to be

---

163. *Guahan/Guam*, 438-39. Guam's voters were not alone in rejecting a constitution resulting from the 1976 legislation. The voters in the Virgin Islands did likewise in 1979 and 1981, with 62 percent of the voters indicating in a 1982 referendum that they preferred to deal with political status issues before dealing with constitutional issues. University of Guam and University of the Virgin Islands, *A Time of Change: Relations between the United States and American Samoa, Guam, the Northern Marianas, Puerto Rico and the United States Virgin Islands* (*Conference Proceedings*, February 8-11, 1993) (1994) [hereafter *Conference Proceedings*], 230.

faced by the new administration, the Guam study was nowhere in sight. No one could provide a copy of a classified document to someone without the necessary security clearance, and the members of the transition team probably had no such clearances. The staff in the Office of Territorial Affairs at Interior opposed the recommendations of the Guam study and the resulting presidential directive, and had no reason to cause its possible resurrection by disclosing its classified status or resting place in secure storage.[164]

7.1.2 Guam's Responsibilities

In any discussions with the federal government to improve Guam's political status, it is essential that Guam speak with a single voice. The few years embracing the preparation of the Guam Study and its non-implementation (1973–1976) highlight the problem when this does not occur.

The federal government's initial efforts to engage Guamanian officials in the preparation of the Guam study were rejected by Governor Camacho because the Guam Legislature, controlled by Democrats, had appointed a status commission to report in the fall of 1974. The new Democratic administration that assumed office in January 1975, headed by Governor Bordallo, paid no attention to that commission's recommendations and created a new status commission. But this action reportedly antagonized Delegate Won Pat who, although of the same party as Governor Bordallo, wanted to play a leading role in any political status discussions. So he adopted an approach that conflicted with the objectives of the newly appointed Special Commission and efforts to reach some compromise were apparently unsuccessful. To add to the confusion, there was considerable uncertainty within the federal government where Governor Bordallo stood on the critical status issues; he added to the uncertainty by his repeated expressions of support for reintegration of Guam and the Northern Mariana Islands and his regret

---

164. After Professor Ballendorf submitted his FOIA request to the Department of the Interior in late 2000, an official in charge of locating such documents reported to his lawyer in 2001 that there was a safe in the Office of Territorial Affairs where such a classified document might be located, but the safe had not been opened in years and no one in the department knew the combination.

about the outcome of the recent Northern Marianas negotiations. These different points of view enabled Interior, and the other federal agencies to a lesser extent, to justify their inaction regarding the presidential directive because, in their opinion, Guam "had not gotten its act together." One can only speculate whether a more candid approach by Interior and the Under Secretaries Committee in 1975 might have provided the needed impetus for Guam's leaders to put their differences and political ambitions temporarily to one side so that they could negotiate with the federal government as a unified team.[165]

Although one can admire his decades of service to Guam, Won Pat's strategy during 1975–76 without doubt contributed to Guam's failure to take advantage of the Guam study and President Ford's directive. He knew about the executive branch study but made no effort to ascertain its progress, its recommendations, or its fate. His proposal to have the U.S. Congress create a commission composed of representatives from both the executive and legislative branches of the United States and Guam predictably gained no support in Congress, among other reasons because the experience with such a joint commission dealing with Puerto Rico had been a disappointment.

But it was Won Pat's endorsement of the constitutional convention legislation, over the objection of Guam's status commission, which proved more troublesome. Won Pat certainly appreciated the risks involved in such an approach. Interior personnel speculated that he adopted this different course because he hoped that the status commission would expire at the end of 1976 and leave him as the paramount leader in addressing Guam's status concerns. On the other hand, he may have believed that he had no choice but to take the course in Congress that Burton would support. He had constantly been assured by Congressman Burton that he would take care

---

165. One of the consistent strengths of the Northern Marianas effort in seeking and conducting separate status negotiations with the United States during the 1960s and early 1970s was that its leaders of both political parties generally shared the same political objectives—in particular, U.S. citizenship and affiliation with the United States. Guam's political leaders did present a united front in supporting the Commonwealth Act before Congress during the 1997 hearings.

of Guam as soon as the Northern Marianas Covenant had been approved. Under the circumstances, Won Pat's support for the constitutional convention approach might be understandable. Certainly Won Pat's deference to Burton over the years had resulted in substantial financial and other benefits for Guam. But in this case, the consequences of following Burton's lead, and endorsing a constitutional convention before important status issues were addressed, were not benign: the end result marked a serious blow to Guam's ability to secure the benefits of the Guam study and the presidential directive.

Any revived movement to address Guam's status concerns should include a greater effort to reach a consensus regarding its priorities. For example, at several points during the 1975–76 period Guam's representatives in meetings with White House staff or Interior personnel would emphasize their concerns about specific federal statutes and downplay their interest in improving their status. It is certainly true that individual problems arising from federal laws dealing with coastwise shipping and immigration, or U.S. military land needs and use, might be addressed separately and apart from any overall review of Guam's status and lack of a locally drafted constitution. However, unless popular sentiment has changed significantly over the past few decades, it seems more advantageous for Guam's leaders to consider an effort to put all the issues on the negotiating table at one time, in the expectation that an overall agreement that meets Guam's principal needs would be seen by the voters as a substantial improvement in Guam's status. This was certainly the approach taken with respect to the drafting and advocacy of a commonwealth act in the 1980s and the 1990s. If such an agreement could be negotiated, then another constitutional convention could almost certainly produce a draft constitution that would enjoy a better outcome than the one rejected in 1979. But the assessment of priorities, and the weighing of alternative strategies, necessarily involve political and other judgments relating to the federal government's readiness to participate in such discussions and to the disposition in the U.S. Congress to consider their results favorably.

7.1.3 Dealing With the United States Congress

At key stages during Interior's handling of the presidential directive, Congressman Burton intervened in a decisive manner. When consulted by Rice in October 1975, Burton was strongly opposed to the opening of any status discussions with Guam until the Northern Marianas Covenant was approved by the Senate. He objected as well to the appointment of any special presidential assistant to represent the federal government in such discussions. Later, in June 1976, several months after the Covenant had been approved by the Senate, Burton still opposed the opening of any status discussions with Guam, this time reiterating some of his earlier objections and adding his additional concern that Won Pat's opponent in the upcoming Democratic primary elections might use the start of any negotiations to Won Pat's disadvantage. After the primary elections, Interior personnel were of the impression that Burton was simply too busy to concern himself with Guam's political status. Although trying to explore Burton's reasons comes close to a fruitless exercise, it may help illuminate some of the perennial issues that Guam must face as it seeks any significant reshaping of its relationship with the federal government.

The unexpected difficulties encountered in the Senate with the Northern Marianas Covenant may have persuaded Burton that a different approach had to be followed with respect to Guam. According to Roger Stillwell, who as an aide to Won Pat observed Burton for many years at close range, Burton viewed the Marianas negotiations as "a wonderful testing ground to see how far we could bend the Constitution, as it were, what could be done to create a whole new political relationship between off-shore areas and the United States. It was very much an experimental process, and he worked hard at it." But Stillwell emphasized that Burton also was a political realist and concluded that the take-it-or-leave-it approach with respect to the Marianas Covenant could not be followed for Guam. According to Stillwell, Burton was "adamant" that he would take care of Guam's problems on a "piecemeal" basis and Won Pat (and other Guamanian leaders) really had no alternative but to accept his judgment on the matter. Although plausible to a point, it is hard to reconcile this view with Burton's unchallenged power in the only house of the U.S. Congress that he cared about and his demonstrated creative use of such power to achieve his political ends.[166]

Other factors were certainly influencing Burton's opposition to any substantial federal initiative with respect to Guam. He might well have seen the constitutional convention legislation as all that he could reasonably do at the time, especially if such an effort would enhance Won Pat's political standing in Guam. The fact remains that Burton did not take care of Guam's major problems on a "piecemeal" or any other basis before his death in 1983. There is some indication that Burton had always been motivated to use his power to persuade Guam and the Northern Mariana Islands to reunite in a single political entity. He was heard to say on one occasion that, if the Northern Marianas wanted a non-voting delegate in Congress, they should reintegrate with Guam, and on another occasion that, if Guam wanted the special advantages provided the Northern Marianas in the Covenant, Guam should seek reintegration with the Northern Marianas. At this point, in 1976, Burton was at the peak of his power in the House of Representatives, preparing for an effort to become Democratic majority leader of that body. There is no question that he was faced with multiple challenges and the need to address more significant legislative and personal goals than those relating to another small island out in the Pacific.[167]

Burton's changing reasons for opposing any executive branch initiative were reported to the Under Secretaries Committee by the Interior personnel who met with him. As emphasized above, Burton exercised great influence over Interior, whose personnel would be predisposed to accept his informal, but forcefully expressed, views as his final words on the subject. Interior personnel had neither the authority nor the stature to take issue with Congressman Burton and here, in fact, his reported views tended to support Interior's own biases with respect to any status discussions with Guam. Burton was

---

166. *Oral Histories*, Interview of Roger Stillwell. For examples of Burton's use of power in matters under consideration by the U.S. Senate, see *A Rage for Justice*, 373-79.

167. For Burton's campaign to become majority leader and his defeat by a single vote, see *A Rage for Justice*, 245-79, 296-327.

not influenced by the political affiliation of those who came before him on status issues. He was very supportive of the Republican initiatives with respect to Micronesia and the Northern Mariana Islands, where he dealt fairly with Ambassador Williams and the Micronesian and Northern Marianas negotiators. On the other hand, when the Carter Administration continued the Micronesian negotiations with a Democratic replacement for Williams, Burton exhibited great difficulties in dealing with the administration's efforts to the point that the successful outcome of the negotiations was placed in serious doubt. The continuation of the Micronesian status negotiations through a change in administrations nonetheless suggests that a bona fide effort to begin status discussions with Guam in 1976 under presidential leadership could have been productively continued under the Carter Administration. With the momentum generated during the last year of the Ford Administration and the careful (and constant) handling of Congressman Burton by the Carter Administration, he might ultimately have been persuaded that U.S. national security interests and the obligation to treat Guam fairly justified a comprehensive improvement in its relationship with the federal government.[168]

The problems that Guam faces in Congress, however, go far beyond any single Congressman's sense of power or predilections with respect to the insular areas. As former Guam Delegate Robert A. Underwood has pointed out:

> In general, territories are seen as a drag on the national treasury. Collectively, they are thought of as very minor jurisdictions to which the national government distributes large sums of money, most of which is undeserved because of their tax status. The economies are not viable without a heavy infusion of federal cash. The governments that exist in these islands are mismanaged and frequently corrupt. Federal officials, auditors and the federal

---

168. Memorandum, April 26, 1979, Rosenblatt to Nimetz; Memorandum of Conversation, June 15, 1979, prepared by Rosenblatt; Letter, November 1, 1979, Burton to Rosenblatt; Memorandum, November 5, 1979, Rosenblatt to Joseph.

bureaucracy (not to mention real corruption and mismanagement) insure a steady stream of information along these lines.

Recent efforts by the District of Columbia to achieve voting representation in the U. S. Congress comparable to the states distinguished the "taxpaying Americans" in the District of Columbia from "the [non-taxpaying] Americans who live in the territories."[169]

7.2   Looking to the Future

Since the 1997 congressional hearings on the Commonwealth Act, political status issues in Guam have been generally subordinated to pressing economic concerns resulting from the Japanese recession and the post-September 11 repercussions that severely impacted Guam, the Northern Mariana Islands, and other popular tourist destinations in the Pacific. Within the last few years attention has focused on a plebiscite under the auspices of the legislatively created Commission on Decolonization originally scheduled for July 2000. Only "native inhabitants" as defined by the legislation would be authorized to vote in the plebiscite and express their preference among the three stated choices for Guam's future political status: statehood, independence, and free association. The plebiscite has been deferred continually since 2000 because of limited funding, inadequate voter education, and the relatively few eligible voters who have registered to participate. Although the issue is a very sensitive one for Guam's political leaders, many knowledgeable commentators acknowledge that important constituencies

---

169. Robert A. Underwood, Guam Humanities Council "Thinking Out Loud Lecture Series," Lecture Number 3 (October 9, 2003)[hereafter Lecture No 3], 2; *Pacific Sunday News* (July 4, 2004).

in the community continue to question the need for, or practical utility of, such a plebiscite.[170]

In shaping an agenda for future discussions with the federal government Guam's leaders are able to learn from their past experiences. Careful review of the 1974 Guam study in light of the intervening decades may help shape consideration of the alternative courses of action open to Guam. Certain of the grievances emphasized in the report may have been addressed satisfactorily over the years; many may have been ignored; and new issues have probably developed that warrant attention. But the fundamental rationale for the study and for the presidential directive continues to provide a sound and convincing justification for addressing Guam's status aspirations. The national security interests of the United States and the sense of fairness underlying the study and directive are no less persuasive today than they were in 1975. By coincidence, reliance on this newly disclosed study might provide a basis for implementing a recent suggestion that Guam consider a new approach to dealing with the federal government, one that emphasized Guam's intrinsic value to the rest of the country and reflected a common understanding of fairness in dealing with the problems of U.S. citizens in a small Pacific territory.[171]

---

170. *Pacific Sunday News* (September 12, 2004). The experience over the years in Puerto Rico, the Virgin Islands, and Guam has demonstrated the range of problems that inevitably arise in connection with similar efforts to ascertain public opinion. The validity of such poll results is virtually certain to be challenged on one or more grounds: low voter turnout; the omission of certain status alternatives; inadequate definition of the status alternatives; insufficient public education; and the possible taint resulting from concurrent campaigns for office. It might be more effective and less expensive to employ a professional polling concern to conduct a thorough survey of public opinion on status issues among Guam's registered voters. As one aspect of such an effort, those voters meeting the requirements of the decolonization plebiscite could be asked initially to express their preference regarding the three alternatives specified by statute but then asked as well whether they personally favor other status alternatives, such as the status quo or commonwealth status similar to that enjoyed by the Northern Mariana Islands.

171. Underwood, Lecture No. 3, 2.

An effort might also be made to explore the lessons involved in the process of developing and pursuing the Commonwealth Act, which failed to get any significant support from federal officials in the late 1990s after years of frustrating negotiations with representatives of both the U. S. executive and legislative branches. Different interest groups, of course, may draw different conclusions from this experience. Those interested in self-determination for the Chamorros and the decolonization process might wish to consider whether the scheduled plebiscite, limited to a select group of voters, serves any important political or practical purpose in advancing the interests of all Guamanians. Those seeking Guamanian control over the applicability of federal laws in Guam should reflect on whether congressional rejection of the Commonwealth Act resulted from a view that the Northern Marianas Covenant more or less represented as far as Congress was willing to go with respect to special treatment for the insular areas. Those seeking a relationship with the federal government far beyond the Covenant will have to be candid in considering whether in fact they are willing to abandon their United States citizenship in order to achieve a status comparable to the free association status negotiated for the Marshall Islands, the Federated States of Micronesia, and Palau. Those convinced that only statehood provides the dignity and self-government to which all U.S. citizens are entitled should assess the effects of statehood on Guam's tax revenues and economic prosperity. Moreover, there are undoubtedly those in Guam who would prefer the status quo, because they have prospered under the current system and enjoy the legal and economic advantages that come with being an unincorporated territory of the United States.

One alternative that might emerge from such deliberations is for Guam to accept President Ford's directive as providing the basis for initial discussions with the federal government—looking forward to a commonwealth relationship as close as that in the Northern Marianas as possible. The directive certainly survived the Ford Administration; six months into the Carter Administration the newly appointed director of the Office of Territorial Affairs was advised by her staff that President Ford's directive had not been revoked or withdrawn. Such a limited strategy as a first step in addressing

Guam's status aspirations might not be acceptable to Guam's various constituencies, especially those who emphasize self-determination for Guam's Chamorro population rather than increased self-government for all Guamanians under a more traditional relationship with the federal government. But it would constitute an important advance in improving Guam's status, building on President Ford's 1975 directive while avoiding the very strong opposition faced a decade ago to many of the Commonwealth Act's most important provisions.[172]

Looking further into the future, the emphasis on possible reunification of Guam and the Northern Mariana Islands in both the 1974 study and the presidential directive may stimulate new thinking on this subject. Reunification, of course, has been on the agenda of federal officials, many members of Congress, and elected officials in Guam and the Northern Marianas for many decades since the rejection by Guamanian voters in 1969. Many members of Congress, lacking any knowledge of the history involved, are quick to complain about the illogic in having two separate U.S. insular areas so close together in the Western Pacific. During his second term in office in the 1980s, Governor Bordallo adopted a strategy directed toward reunification of the two political entities which guided the work of the new Commission on Self-Determination. He intended first to negotiate an agreement with the federal government to be implemented by the U.S. Congress that would replace the Organic Act of 1950 and provide commonwealth status for Guam. Then he envisaged a merger with the Northern Marianas into a single political entity which he hoped might enable the united archipelago realistically to seek a final political status, such as statehood, that would both protect U.S. national interests and satisfy the political aspirations of Guamanians.[173]

---

172. Memorandum, June 27, 1977, Scott to Van Cleve, 1. For a realistic assessment of the reaction of the U.S. Congress to the Commonwealth Act, see Leibowitz, "The Decline of Commonwealth," presented at the Conference on the Legacy of the Spanish-American War in the Pacific (Agana, Guam: June 17-18, 1998), 21-29.

173. Robert F. Rogers, "Guam's Search for Commonwealth Status," MARC Educational Series No. 4 (December 1984), 10-11; *Destiny's Landfall*, 271-72.

There are persuasive reasons for conducting a serious inquiry of this alternative, without any political commitment involved except to participate in the inquiry. Such an effort, regardless of its outcome, would help both entities in their future dealings with the U.S. Congress. Assessment of such a combination would be a prerequisite to any movement towards the possible goal of statehood. There are many who contend that the inability to vote for the president and members of Congress is more than offset by the retention of taxes paid under federal laws. But there are many others—laymen and political theorists alike—who are troubled by the concept of "second-class" U.S. citizens and maintain that the present scheme of American governance of U.S. citizens in its insular areas should be changed. Once such a study was conducted, both proponents and opponents of change would have a factual basis on which to make a judgment whether gradual movement towards this objective should be advocated. As the Guam study observed, it may be difficult to persuade the Northern Marianas to forego the benefits of its current status under the Covenant. It would be necessary to create significant financial or political arrangements that will enable reunification to be presented to the Northern Marianas people as protective of their current status and conducive to a more beneficial future relationship with the federal government.

A thorough study of reunification of Guam and the Northern Marianas could take at least two years and require the support of political leaders from both political entities. Its goal would be to produce a report analyzing the legal, political, economic, and social effects of combining the two areas, but not to make any recommendations on the subject. In each area major issues would have to be addressed:

Legal: The controlling documents for both jurisdictions, the Organic Act of 1950 and the Covenant, would be examined to see whether they might be reconciled and what kind of fundamental agreement would have to be approved by Congress if reunification were pursued by both political entities. The current application of federal laws, and proposed changes in same, would have to be explored. Some unique issues would be raised by the three express exceptions to the U.S. constitution contained in the Covenant and their possible continuation under a unified entity.

Political: Major problems would have to be addressed in this area, in light of the differences in population and the protection presently afforded the smaller islands in the Northern Marianas under the Covenant. The study group would have to identify the full range of issues that a constitutional convention for a combined entity would have to consider and what safeguards might have to be provided for "minorities"—ethnic or geographic. The structure of the two governments, the number of government employees and their compensation, and the current legislation in place would have to be examined and compared with respect to what changes would be required in a combined political entity.

Economic: Both Guam and the Northern Marianas have suffered from economic challenges different from those that affect the mainland—from typhoons to economic recessions in Japan. The federal programs available to both have helped deal with these economic disasters. The study would have to examine the economic statistics from both areas over the past decade, projections for the next decade, and analyze their respective economies and their projections. Does a combined entity exhibit more or less diversification, more or less susceptibility to foreign influences, more or less benefits from federal programs, or more or less promise of economic growth? What economies of scale, if any, would result from such a combination? Would the cost of government as a percentage of gross island product be more or less?

Social: In this area the very different populations in Guam and the Northern Marianas would be examined. Will the Carolinians in the Northern Marianas feel threatened by such a combination—a concern they expressed when the Northern Marianas pursued a separate status from the other districts of the Trust Territory of the Pacific Islands. How would the Chamorro, Filipino, and Statesider communities on Guam react to any combination of the two areas? What are the educational, public health, and law enforcement impacts of such a move to reunification?

Even this brief recital of the kind of questions that might be explored is intimidating. But an inquiry of this kind is certain to happen—if not now, then within the next twenty-five years. It provides a mechanism for looking at some of the critical issues that could illuminate for Guam—as well as for the Northern Marianas—an approach to reexamination of political status that would be responsive to the long-term needs of both insular areas. What the inquiry requires is the kind of forward-looking political leadership that both Guam and the Northern Mariana Islands want and deserve.

Bibliography

Clement, Michael R., Jr. 2002. *The Sella Bay Ammunition Wharf Controversy 1969-1975: Economic Development, Indigenous Rights and Colonialism in Guam.* Unpublished thesis, Micronesian Area Research Center, University of Guam.

Hofschneider, Penelope Bordallo. 2001. *A Campaign for Political Rights on the Island of Guam (1899-1950).* Saipan, MP: CNMI Division of Historic Preservation

Jacobs, John. 1995. *A Rage for Justice: The Passion and Politics of Phillip Burton.* Berkeley: University of California Press.

Leibowitz, Arnold H. 1989. *Defining Status: A Comprehensive Analysis of United States Territorial Relations.* Dordrecht: Martinus Nijhoff Publishers.

———. 1998. *The Decline of Commonwealth.* Paper presented at Conference on the Legacy of the Spanish-American War in the Pacific, Guam, June 17-18.

Micronesian Area Research Center. 1996. *MARC Working Papers #66: Inventory of the Papers of Antonio Borja Won Pat.* University of Guam.

Rogers, Robert F. 1984. "Guam's Search for Commonwealth Status." MARC Educational Series No. 4 (December).

———. 1995. *Destiny's Landfall: A History of Guam.* Honolulu: University of Hawaii Press.

Sanchez, Pedro C. 1989. *Guahan/Guam: The History of our Island.* Agana, Guam: Sanchez Publishing House.

Underwood, Robert A. 2003. *Thinking Out Loud Lecture Series*. Guam Humanities Council.

University of Guam and University of the Virgin Islands. 1994. *A Time of Change: Relations between the United States and American Samoa, Guam, the Northern Marianas, Puerto Rico and the United States Virgin Islands* (Conference Proceedings, February 8-11, 1993).

Willens, Howard P., and Deanne C. Siemer. 2000. *National Security and Self-Determination: United States Policy in Micronesia (1961-1972)*. Westport, CT: Praeger.

———. 2001. *An Honorable Accord: The Covenant between the Northern Mariana Islands and the United States*. Honolulu: University of Hawaii Press.

———. 2004. *Oral Histories of the Northern Mariana Islands: Political Life and Developments (1945-1995)*. Saipan, MP: CNMI Division of Historic Preservation.

Wyttenbach-Santos, Richard H.J. 1993. "Guam's Past, Present, and Future: Time Is on Whose Side?" 14th Annual Conference on Public Administration, November 18.

———. 1995. "Tricentennial of Guam's Loss of Freedom, July 1695 to July 1995," *Pacific Times Magazine* (January).

———. 1995. "Alternative Political Status Options for Guam," 16th Annual Conference on Public Administration, November 16.

———. 1996. "The Case for Chamorro Rights," 17th Annual Conference on Public Administration, November 14.

———. 1996. "The Status of Guam's Quest for Commonwealth Status." A speech delivered on December 10.

Appendix 1

The Presidential Approval Memorandum for Chairman,
Under Secretaries Committee, February 1, 1975
from Henry A. Kissinger

ADVANCE COPY

3433 **E2**

NATIONAL SECURITY COUNCIL
WASHINGTON, D.C. 20506

7502322

RELEASED IN FULL

SECRET

February 1, 1975

MEMORANDUM FOR

CHAIRMAN, UNDER SECRETARIES COMMITTEE

SUBJECT: Negotiations with Guam on a New Political Relationship

1. <u>General.</u> The President has reviewed the study conducted by the NSC Under Secretaries Committee and the recommendations contained therein for the negotiation of a new political relationship with Guam and has reached the decisions reflected below.

You are authorized to supervise, within the Executive Branch, implementation of the policies in this instruction, which are intended to give effect to the following objectives:

 -- To retain U.S. sovereignty over Guam, and, in particular, to maintain U.S. control over Guam's foreign affairs and defense and to preserve U.S. military basing rights to Guam.

 -- To enable Guam to move toward complete self-government in internal affairs under a self-drafted constitution consistent with the U.S. Constitution, in order to enhance prospects for Guam's continued close relationship with the Federal Government and for long-term stability on the island.

 -- To help promote the material well-being of Guamanians, in order to maintain stability on Guam.

 -- To enhance the prospects for the ultimate integration of Guam with the Northern Marianas, if this accords with the desires of the majority of Guamanians.

2. <u>Political Status</u>

 The U.S. negotiator should seek agreement with Guamanian representatives on a commonwealth arrangement no less favorable than that which we are negotiating with the Northern Marianas. If,

SECRET (XGDS)-3

S 0716

SECRET   - 2 -

however, Guamanian representatives prefer a modified unincorporated
territorial status, the U.S. would be willing to accept such an arrangement. Either arrangement should provide for full U.S. control of
Guam's foreign affairs and defense, for U.S. military basing rights
on Guam, for Guam's access to the Federal court system, and for
internal Guamanian self-government under a locally drafted constitution that would be consistent with the Federal Constitution.

3. International Status

       Trade Agreements and Membership in International Organizations.
The U.S. negotiator should seek clarification of the specific nature of
Guam's interest in entering into international trade agreements and
in participating in international organizations. Having done so, an attempt
should be made to satisfy Guam's reasonable, practical needs first
through means that would not lead to a separate international status
for the island. The U.S. position should take into consideration the
extent to which negotiation of a new political status and financial
support for Guam will indirectly satisfy Guam's putative need for an
enhanced international status. Basic U.S. policy will continue to be
to discourage membership for U.S. territories in international
organizations in order to avoid a separate international status for
these territories. This will not preclude the inclusion of Guamanian
representatives on U.S. delegations to international conferences and
organizations such as WHO and ESCAP when the questions involved
are directly relevant to Guam's reasonable, practical needs.

       Annual Reports to the United Nations. The United States will
continue to make annual reports to the United Nations on U.S.
administration of Guam pending our agreement with Guamanian
representatives on complete internal self-government.

4. Financial Assistance

       You are authorized to offer up to a total of $75 million in U.S.
financial assistance for Guam's capital improvement program, with
a maximum of one-half this amount to be in the form of a federal
grant. The precise level and composition of this assistance should
be determined by the Under Secretaries Committee. Federal loans,
which will constitute the remaining portion, will be repayable over
30 years, will bear interest equal to the average yield of outstanding

SECRET

PEL0184-0468

SECRET   - 3 -

marketable obligations of the U.S. of comparable maturities,
and will be repaid by withholdings from sums collected by the
U.S. to be rebated to Guam under Section 30 of the Organic Act.
The Secretary of the Interior, before requesting such loans in
the budgetary process, should determine that the maximum debt
service in any year during the life of these loans will not exceed
15 percent of the average annual revenues covered into the Guam
general fund during the two preceding years.

5. Congressional Consultations

The Congress should be kept informed of significant
developments in the negotiations with Guamanian representatives.

6. Negotiating Authority

Under your general supervision, the Assistant Secretary of
the Interior for Program Development and Budget should develop
and implement a negotiating approach that will give effect to the
above instructions, and should organize a U.S. negotiating team
that will include representation from the Departments of State and
Defense as well as the Department of the Interior.

Henry A. Kissinger

SECRET

Appendix 2

Memorandum for the President, August 9, 1974
from Robert S. Ingersoll,
Chairman of the Under Secretaries Committee

THE DEPUTY SECRETARY OF STATE

WASHINGTON

NSC UNDER SECRETARIES COMMITTEE

NSC-U/DM-127   August 9, 1974

MEMORANDUM FOR THE PRESIDENT

Subject: Guam

On August 14, 1973 the Deputy Secretary of Defense requested an Under Secretaries Committee study to examine the political, security, economic and social aspects of Guam, and to identify prospective courses of action by which US interests may be preserved. The enclosed study has been prepared under the chairmanship of the Department of the Interior.

To determine more precisely Guamanian aspirations politically, economically and socially, and to engender a sense of working together on common interests, the Secretary of the Interior invited Governor Camacho to participate in a joint review of the Guam-federal relationship. Due to internal Guamanian political considerations, it was not possible at this time for the Governor to engage in talks related even tangentially to political status. This study has been conducted with limited consultation with the Guamanians, however, and further consultation is planned.

A basic conclusion of the study is that Guam's strategic importance to the United States is such that its continued association in a federal relationship is essential. To satisfy Guamanians while maintaining this relationship, the study concludes that Federal Government attention in the near future is required to provide an improved political status for Guamanians and to address their economic and social aspirations -- including further diversification of the economy.

GDS

Dept. of State, RPS/IPS, Margaret P. Grafeld, Dir.
(7) Release ( ) Excise ( ) Deny (X) Declassify
Date 7-8-03 Exemption
DOD favors release. NSC concurs.

NSC DECLASSIFICATION REVIEW [E.O. 12958]
/X/ Declassify in full
by D.Sanborn Date 9/12/2003

INT-F01A-004-03

I 1015

149

-2-

The study recommendations have been divided
into two groups: those proposed for immediate
adoption and implementation; and those requiring
further study, consultation with Guamanians, or
action in the future. Agencies responsible for
implementation are listed after each recommendation, and, if the recommendation is approved,
will carry out that responsibility.

In cases where further study or consultation
with Guamanians is indicated before new courses
are adopted, the interagency study group will
coordinate the necessary effort, and action
agencies will thereafter follow procedures of
clearance and coordination in implementing follow-
on action.

Other than general approval, two recommendations in the study require your decision -- that
of a modified future political status for Guam,
and that of support for Guam's request for federal
assistance with respect to its capital improvements
programs. A decision on the status question is
desirable in August, if possible, because the status
negotiations we are conducting with the Northern
Marianas have already resulted in the promise of
commonwealth status for them, and the Guamanians
are anxious about their own future. The Committee
believes that the United States should be prepared
to work out a future political status with Guam
along commonwealth lines. We recommend your approval
of the several proposals in this regard.

The Committee favors Executive Branch support
for the Government of Guam's request for federal
assistance (it is asking for $56 million over a
five-year period for construction of schools and
improvement of the water supply and sewer system)
The Departments of Interior and Defense and the
Office of Micronesian Status Negotiations recommend
Administration support of a specific formula, while
the Department of State, though favoring support in
principle, suggests that recommendations on specific

-3-

levels require further investigation. OMB recommends that no position at all be adopted pending
further extensive study.

Guidance also is requested on two issues
concerning Guam's international role on which
there are divergent views:

-- The Department of Defense and the Office
   of Micronesian Status Negotiations advise
   against any special trade agreements for
   Guam and against its membership in the
   Asian Development Bank (ADB) or the UN's
   Economic Commission for Asia and the Far
   East (ECAFE), on the ground that any one
   of these might work against the US objective of a permanent federal relationship
   for Guam with the US.

-- The Departments of State and Interior,
   also with a view toward preserving
   Guamanian satisfaction with its US
   relationship, propose that we look for
   opportunities to include Guamanians on
   the US team in trade negotiations
   directly affecting their interests and,
   if there are advantages, that the US
   sponsor Guam's membership in ECAFE alone,
   or in both ECAFE and the ADB. The
   Treasury Department would have no objection
   to US sponsorship of Guamanian membership
   in either, if US interests are thereby
   served, but (like the Departments of State
   and Interior) Treasury considers Guam would
   hardly be a priority borrower from the ADB
   because of its relatively high per capita
   income.

The Office of Micronesian Status Negotiations
has participated in this study and concurs in its
recommendations, except as noted above. The
Central Intelligence Agency has not participated

GDS

—4—

because of the special status of Guam. All Departments and Agencies to which the study assigns
action or study responsibilities have reviewed the
study and have had an opportunity to comment.
Substantive comments have been incorporated in the
study where possible. In the case of OMB and the
Office of Micronesian Status Negotiations, memoranda
containing their full comments are appended.

Robert S. Ingersoll
Chairman

Attachment:

As stated

Appendix 3

The Guam Study
Table of Contents and Executive Summary
(August 1974)

SECRET

i

GUAM STUDY

C O N T E N T S

D 0717

~~SECRET~~

SECRET

The Secret Guam Study

SECRET

SECRET   v

EXECUTIVE SUMMARY

I. Introduction

The growing economic and political aspirations of the Guamanian people, and their discontent with their present status and circumstances has necessitated a review of U.S. national objectives, policies and programs in Guam to identify prospective courses of action by which Guamanian aspirations can be satisfied and U.S. interests most effectively fostered, enabling the U.S. to maintain its relationships in the area and an appropriate military posture in Guam.

Guam is an island territory of the United States about 30 miles long and from 4 1/2 to 9 miles wide located at the southern end of the Mariana Islands chain in the Western Pacific. It is strategically placed at the hub of a half circle formed by Japan, Taiwan, the Philippines, and New Guinea, and its distance from any of them is only half the distance from Hawaii to Guam. It has been American territory since the United States acquired it from Spain in 1898. There are some 30,000 American service personnel and their families on Guam, and about one-third of the land area is held by the Federal Government.

The original Chamorro population, numbering over 50,000 when Spain first took possession of the island in 1565, was reduced by warfare and disease over the next thirty years to some 5,000, and remained stable at about that level until the present century.

During Spanish rule, the Chamorros intermarried with Spaniards, Filipinos, Mexicans and in the present century with Chinese, Japanese and mainland Americans. The islanders now constitute a racial blend, and they have a mixed culture with strong Spanish and American elements. English is the official language and is spoken by everyone, but Chamorro is spoken in many homes and there is a resurgence of interest in Chamorro language and culture.

Guamanians have demonstrated that they are loyal American citizens during the Japanese occupation of the island, through service by many in the U.S. armed forces and through their generally strong sense of patriotism. However they feel entitled to more than they have received.

Guamanians would like to have more self-government. From 1898 until 1950, the U.S. Navy administered Guam. In 1950 an Organic Act by the U.S. Congress made Guam an "organized" territory under the responsibility of the Department of the Interior. The territory is also identified as "unincorporated" since the U.S. Constitution is not fully extended to Guam. The Governor was appointed by the President until amendment of the Organic Act in 1968 made the position elective. Guam's Legislature kept an elected representative in Washington after 1964, but he lacked official recognition until 1972 when an Act of Congress provided that Guam and the Virgin Islands should both have elected non-voting delegates in the House of Representatives. A Guam Constitutional Convention, called for by the Guam Legislature in 1968 and

SECRET

held in 1970, proposed extensive amendments to the Organic Act, including the changing of its name to "Constitution of the Territory of Guam." The proposed changes included but went beyond the amendments of 1968 and the Act of 1972. The U.S. Congress did not act on them. More recently, U.S. negotiations with the Trust Territory of the Pacific Islands (TTPI) and with the Northern Marianas regarding their future political status has sharpened Guamanian desire for greater political autonomy. Guamanians feel that they are second class citizens.

Guamanians are also afraid they may lose control of their own island to outsiders. Major construction projects – starting with military construction after World War II, continuing with reconstruction after the disastrous typhoon Karen in 1962 and with the construction of tourist hotels today – have brought in numerous Asian temporary workers and immigrants (many with families), numbering some 15,000. The native islanders, though having increased in numbers to around 60,000, are fearful of becoming dominated by non-native groups.

With the great population increase has come a need for more schools, and with both the population growth and urbanization has come a need for increased power and water and sewerage. Guam needs development capital and is seeking substantial federal subsidies for these capital improvements. It also, somewhat ambivalently, seeks more economic autonomy.

The Federal Government principally the Navy and Air Force, owns nearly a third of the land, but is faced with the need for some land exchanges with private individuals or the Government of Guam (GovGuam). Approximately one-third of the land is privately held, and the remaining third is held by GovGuam. GovGuam also needs certain lands now federally owned. Political tensions between the Democrat-controlled Legislature and the Republican Governor blocked arrangements for a package exchange of land between GovGuam and the U.S. Navy.

Against this background, the present study was undertaken.

II. U.S. Interest and Objectives Involving Guam.

U.S. interests in the Asia/Pacific area. As evidenced by three wars and numerous crises over the past thirty years the United States has essential national interests in the Pacific area. Our security interests involve protection of U.S. soil, assistance in the defense of our Asian allies, maintenance of regional stability and preservation of essential lines of communication. Our economic interests involve maintaining accessibility in the region for trade and investment.* Our political interests concern retaining diplomatic access to the region and obtaining support for U.S. Asian and worldwide policies. The future of the region will be largely determined by relations among Japan, China, the USSR and the United States. While the bipolar confrontation of the past has been muted, potential instability is inherent in the development of a new equilibrium. U.S. interests vis-a-vis the lesser powers of Asia are largely determined by their relationships with the major powers.

* The Department of State adds that a more relevant U.S. economic and political interest is the promotion of Guamanian economic development.

~~SECRET~~

U.S. National security objectives in Asia and the Pacific include deterrence of aggression, creation of an Asia-Pacific power balance in which no
single country or combination of countries can dominate the region, creation
of a stable environment for trade and development, and reassurance to our
allies of our continuing interest and ability to play a stabilizing role.

U.S. security policy is set forth in the Nixon Doctrine and in the
President's 1970-73 Foreign Policy Reports. Basically, it is that while
keeping our commitments and providing a shield if a nuclear power threatens
an ally or a nation whose survival we deem vital to our security, we look to
the nation threatened to assume primary responsibility for providing manpower for its defense.

We have commitments to assist, if they are overtly attacked, Japan, the
Republic of Korea (ROK), the Republic of China (ROC), the Philippines, Thailand,
Australia, and New Zealand.

The role of U.S. forces in the Pacific area is to deter nuclear and conventional attacks or threats to the U.S. itself, our allies and other nations
important to the security of the U.S. and of the region, and if deterrence
fails, to defeat such attacks.

Guam's role is to provide military bases and facilities to support the
capability of the U.S. forces. Its future role would grow if U.S. basing
options in Japan and/or the Philippines were significantly constrained.
Strategic forces, bombers and missile submarines, are currently based in Guam.
General operational missions, in the event of hostilities, would be operated
from and supported by military facilities on Guam. Logistic and staging
facilities there are required for peacetime operations and for contingency
use. Guam is the only major communications center in the Western Pacific.

U.S. Political and Economic Interests in Guam.

The U.S. has a political interest in ensuring that the Guamanian people
are fundamentally satisfied with their political status: we have an obligation to them as people, and preserving their loyalty ensures us a secure
base for discharging our defense requirements in the Western Pacific. Moreover, if they are not satisfied, there will be repercussions in the United
Nations to which, until Guam is acknowledged to have achieved self-government,
the United States has undertaken to report annually on Guam's situation.

It is in the United States interest to promote steady, rational and
broadly based economic development on Guam, with equitable distribution of
income. There is evidence that the unprecedented boom of the past decade
has introduced some distortion, but Guamanians are sensitive to outside
interference and initiatives for economic policy will have to flow from
Guamanian suggestions.

~~SECRET~~

III. Guam's Importance in Attaining U.S. Objectives

A. National Security Objectives

Guam has vital military importance. The strategic importance of Guam is not likely to decrease, nor is there any likelihood of a substantial reduction in its strategic military mission. Politically, moreover, the maintenance of military forces in Guam serves to remind Asian powers - allies and potential adversaries alike - that the U.S. is and intends to remain a resident Pacific power and a geographic neighbor to nations along the East Asian littoral. Current levels of military activity (approximately 12-14,000 personnel) will probably be maintained for the forseeable future.

Should a combination of foreign and domestic political pressures force the relocation of some military activities now forward based in Asia, a prospect that is not imminent but certainly possible, Guam and the TTPI would offer the nearest geographical relocation sites and it would be politically more reassuring to our Asian friends for us to place our transferred bases here rather than move them farther back to Hawaii or the U.S. mainland. In the event of base denial in Japan and the Philippines, according to CINCPAC and JCS studies, almost all the lands presently held by the military in Guam as well as substantial areas in the TTPI would be required.

Guamanians accept the continuation of Guam's historic role as a military bastion, but they also desire to develop their economy and the civilian community with more Guamanian identity and less dependence upon the military for their livelihood. Their goal of a multi-faceted, balanced economy is not yet attainable, however.

Current and potential areas of conflict.

General civilian/military relations are marked by three features involving ambivalent attitudes: (a) a public attitude that is favorably inclined in general toward the military presence because Guamanians are loyal, many of them have personally served in the military forces, and they recognize the economic benefits which flow from the military presence, (b) a social separation, generally, of the military and civilian (Guamanian) societies (though they have mutual working relationships and their children attend the same schools), and a feeling on the part of Guamanian civilians that they suffer discriminatory treatment, and (c) competition for land. There is inadequate rapport and understanding between the military and the local people, each side perhaps feeling privately the preeminence of its own rights in Guam. The problem is heightened by a press unsympathetic to the military position. Military reactions to such unfriendly commentaries reinforce the growing impression among many Guamanians that the military lacks sympathy with and understanding of local problems.

Land use problems constitute the most serious tangible issue between
the military and GovGuam. Land values have risen sharply in recent years
largely owing to the growth of tourism. Consequently because of location
or size, military land holdings are coming under greater criticism. Further
pressures on DOD-held lands may be anticipated due to population growth near
these lands and also because of their desirability. Generally Guamanians do
not understand why the military should continue to hold all these lands,
moreover, the majority of them either ignore the fact or are unaware that
Federal laws prohibit the transfer of federal land without full value
considerations (i.e. fair market value, or value for value exchange).

The Sella Bay Land Exchange Agreement, worked out between the Navy
and the Governor would have satisfied mutually several land needs on both
sides. However it was blocked by the Legislature. On the Navy side, a site
was required to build an ammunition pier to substitute for the inadequate
and dangerous location of the present unloading pier in Apra Harbor (Guam's
only port), and an optimum site on GovGuam and private land existed at
Sella Bay. On the GovGuam side, needed lands would be acquired from Navy
in exchange for the Sella Bay land, to build schools, to construct a power
plant on Cabras Island, to expand the Guam International Air Terminal which
shares the runways of the Naval Air Station (NAS) at Agana, to develop
facilities of the Port and establish recreation areas. The Navy, in good
faith and before the Legislature intervened, allowed GovGuam to start
construction of a steam power plant on Cabras Island and work is under way.
Though Navy was also willing for GovGuam to proceed with construction to
enlarge the Guam International Air Terminal, Federal Aviation Authority (FAA)
would not provide the necessary federal funds pending the final land exchange.

Two or three of the Legislators own land in Sella Bay, and their
desire to sell their land at a high profit for hotel and recreational purposes
(with which an ammunition pier might interfere) is presumed to have influenced
their decision to block the land exchange package. Radically separatist
attitudes on the part of the same Legislators - evidenced in talk of independence and of total exclusion of the U.S. military from Guam - is also
involved. The majority of Legislators were probably content simply to frustrate
the Governor (of the opposing political party) and make it appear in the
election campaigning later this year that the Governor is more interested
in looking after the military than taking care of the people of Guam.

NAS Agana - The runway and related facilities are currently used
jointly by civilian and military aircraft under a defacto arrangement. *
A Joint Use Agreement, which was contingent upon acquisition of a piece of
the land which the Navy had included in the Sella Bay land exchange package,
would formalize joint use, bring the facility up to FAA civilian standards,
and permit GovGuam to operate its portion. However, FAA has determined that
without title to the land needed for the expansion, GovGuam lacks sufficient
proprietary interest to meet the definition of a public airport under the
Airport and Airways Development Act of 1970. Furthermore, the source of
Gov Guam funding for additional maintenance, greater fire-fighting capability
and other improvements necessary for increased civilian aviation traffic
(the jumbo jets) has not been identified.

* A joint use agreement between the U.S. Navy and the Government of Guam
  was concluded on July 8, 1974.

x

Northwest Field - Northwest Field, an inactive USAF airfield
reserved for contingencies is coveted by Guamanians as a future site for
Guam's International Airport (when and if it outgrows the present shared
facilities at NAS Agana). But it is already the site of a vital satellite
tracking facility and adjacent to the site of the Naval Communication Station
(NAVCOMMSTA) Guam, the Navy's major communication station in the Western
Pacific. Increasing emphasis on these communication and intelligence
facilities is part of the Department of Defense's (DOD) world-wide planning
for facility consolidation. To protect the facilities' present requirements,
Navy is seeking to acquire 476 acres and to obtain restrictive easements on
2,090 more to complete the radio frequency interference(RFI) buffer zone
around the receiving antennas. Meanwhile, private landowners are seeking
easements through U.S. Government property at the field to allow for development of prime beach property. DOD is concerned that uncontrolled development
will cause serious electronic interference to neighboring installations.

Beaches - There is resentment among many Guamanians that the general
public is excluded from most military beaches (though about 40% of the total
population is eligible to use them). On the other hand the military feel
that GovGuam, which has developed about a third as much beach as the military,
should do more.

Won Pat's Proposal to Transfer all Unused Federal Land to GovGuam
Won Pat has proposed, in a bill introduced in the U.S. Congress, that
all unused USG land should be handed over if not reserved within a short
period by the President. DOD opposes this bill. The outlook is that the
Congress will pass another bill introduced by Congressman deLugo (which Won Pat
co-sponsored with others) providing for limited transfer of submerged lands
only.

Significant increase in the level of military activity, occasioned
by relocation of forces or outbreak of hostilities, is conceivably a source
of friction with Guamanians. It need not be. Guamanians are strong patriots
and will accept additional burdens readily if they understand the reasons;
a number of them have said they would donate their land in any national
emergency.

   B. Political Objectives
The basic political objective of the United States is to preserve
tranquility on Guam and to ensure conditions for continued Guamanian identification with the interests of the rest of the United States.

Future Political Status - Influenced by their long-standing desire
for greater self-government which no longer is satisfied by present arrangements, and looking askance at the progress of the Northern Marianas.toward
commonwealth status, politically articulate Guamanians are talking about
drafting their own constitution and acquiring more autonomy. A .large majority
of them are now believed to favor future union with the Northern Marianas.
Commonwealth seems to be the preferred future political status. There is
some support for statehood, present status and incorporated territory status,
respectively, with support for the last two being weak. There has also been
sporadic talk of independence, for which there is no real support. The status
commission appointed by the 12th Guam Legislature reportedly favors commonwealth,
but its report will not be made for several months. The Governor's Advisory
Council also reportedly favors commonwealth, though it is saying nothing
pending recommendation by the Legislature's status commission.

Appendix 3

 xi

Areas of Conflict

Virtually the entire range of the Federal/Guam relationship teems with potential sources of conflict. The problems reflect the ambivalence with which Guamanians regard their present status. On the one hand they want closer ties with the United States and greater representation in its councils. On the other hand they feel oppressed by the application of federal laws without regard for Guam's special circumstances, and seek greater autonomy. Greater autonomy is sought, for example with regard to wages, immigration, banking, and shipping. A higher debt ceiling is desired, and the right to borrow from international institutions. Such autonomy would be hard to accommodate substantially without change in status and even then could hardly be unlimited, except under independence, which Guamanians are not seeking.

C. Socio-Economic Objectives

The inequitable impact on Guam of Federal laws (which are, of course, intended to be for the benefit of all U.S. citizens) is a standard complaint of Guamanians.

While Guam has a minimum wage higher than that set by the Federal Government, by federal law the "prevailing wage" must be paid to alien workers temporarily admitted to Guam (as elsewhere in the U.S.). The Guamanian Department of Labor has determined for two years ahead a prevailing wage that rises semi-annually at a rate of about 17 percent a year. Guamanian employers feel it is too high and would like to be able to pay the minimum wage.

Federal immigration laws do not control where within the United States an immigrant may go. Guamanians feel too many Filipinos have settled in Guam and would like to have some control over the inflow of a culturally different group that could become a controlling element politically.

Though the Virgin Islands and American Samoa are exempted from the Intercoastal Shipping (Jones) Act, Guam, like Puerto Rico, is subject to it. All goods shipped to or from Hawaii or the mainland by Guamanians must be carried in U.S. ships. The Guamanians believe this increases their cost of living. They have asked for exemption from the Act when there are American shipping strikes and would like to be exempt altogether.

Guamanians would like to be able to exercise more influence on the determination of ship and aircraft routes and carriage rates.

U.S. banking laws are thought by some Guamanian officials to be potentially restrictive of economic expansion. In fact, U.S. laws governing operations by U.S. national banks abroad and in our territories are more liberal than those applied at home. The Guamanian desire to have anonymous bank accounts, as in Switzerland, neither accords with U.S. policy nor would be sufficient in itself to make Guam a major financial center as some have hoped.

Guamanians want more help from the Department of Housing and Urban Development (HUD) for urban renewal, more help from the Department of Health Education and Welfare for welfare.

They want more U.S. officials (FHA, HEW, and immigration) assigned to serve administratively the growing needs of Guam.

Foreign Investment

U.S. policy has allowed unlimited foreign investment in Guam. Tourism and Japanese hotels have created an alternative to economic dependence solely upon the federal and military establishment, but foreign acquisition of land and growing foreign economic power in Guam are matters of concern. The Government of Guam has employed the Stanford Research Institute to make a survey of alien investment in Guam. However, the current worry of Guamanians, induced by the world fuel shortage, is that tourism will fall off.

Federal/Territorial Financial Relationship

Beyond the general obligation of the United States to concern itself with the well-being of Guamanians as American citizens and beyond the national interest in ensuring satisfactory economic and social conditions on Guam, there is a legal obligation under the Organic Act for the Federal Government to rebate to the Government of Guam for use in its annual budget all Federal taxes collected on Guam. The bulk of these are income taxes collected from stateside personnel temporarily on Guam - mainly Federal employees. The Federal Government collects no income tax from Guamanians or from resident aliens; the Government of Guam collects income tax from them at the federal rate, but it is a Territorial tax. In 1973, the rebate of $11.7 million accounted for 20% of total income taxes collected on Guam. Federal financial support in 1973, in addition to the rebated income tax, included Federal grants-in-aid of various kinds ($10.6 million), typhoon rehabilitation grants and loans ($6.3 million), and Economic Development Fund grants ($1 million). Federal funds provided about 23% of the Government of Guam's combined budget. Recently (1971), the U.S. share of the burden was higher (29%), while back in 1953, when the budget was much smaller, it was as much as 40%. Guam's population increase and economic growth, with urban expansion, have created a need for extensive capital improvements in schools, water supply and sewer system, and the Government of Guam is now applying for Federal grants of $56 million over the next five years.

Role of the Military in the Economy

The economic impact of the U.S. military presence on Guam is indicated by the very large sector of the population constituted by the military (29% of the total) and by the size of military expenditures (about twice the Territorial budget). Military personnel and DOD employees constitute about 29% of the work force on the island and account for an even higher proportion of the total income. Military construction has been a major economic factor. While the military expenditures do not all directly affect the civilian economy, it might not be far from the mark to say that close to 50% of all economic activity on Guam is military-related. Federal programs to diversify the economy are largely lacking. The Guamanians are grateful for the contribution of the military to the economy though there is some jealousy regarding the more affluent living of military personnel.

International Agencies

Guam, as a Pacific territory of the United States, participates in the South Pacific Conference, a subsidiary organization of the South Pacific Commission organized by Pacific metropolitan powers in 1947 to advance the education, health, and economies of their Pacific territories through co-operation. Guam participates in regional World Health Organization activities. The Guamanians do not understand why they should not have membership in UN regional agencies that provide direct financial and technical assistance also. They also seek membership in the ADB. There is a need for a better definition of Guam's eligibility for membership in and assistance from international organizations.

IV. Options

A. Possible Military Changes

1. <u>Improvement in military/GovGuam relationships</u>, to develop rapport and understanding between the military and the local people, naturally suggests itself as a means of reducing or resolving controversies, facilitating solution to specific issues, and strengthening public support in Guam for U.S. military presence. There is, without doubt, misunderstanding on both sides. Some of the factors contributing to such misunderstanding are parts of history and cannot be reversed. But two immediate options to ameliorate the situation are available: (1) <u>to evaluate ongoing orientation and community relations programs in the military</u> to ascertain if they are effective in promoting good interpersonal relationships between the military and the Guamanians and to correct any possible deficiencies (this may help improve interpersonal relations in official as well as unofficial contacts without, however, resolving issues), and (2) <u>to broaden channels of communication</u> through the support and development of people-to-people programs (a course which has limitations and could be counterproductive if pushed beyond what people want to do but which can contribute to a better military image if pursued in moderation). Two other courses, if supported by GovGuam (the Governor and the Legislature), have potential to help but need to be approached carefully. (1) <u>We could establish a U.S. Government Liaison Office in Guam.</u> It could provide a central point on the scene for handling problems involving Federal agencies and the Guamanians and a communications-mediatory role between the Departments and GovGuam. But it would be another expense and it could on the one hand be resented by the Governor and Won Pat as undue Federal interference while on the other hand it could deteriorate into a one-way channel for complaints or result in excessive dependence on Federal agencies. (2) We could <u>contract for polls of Guamanian attitudes</u>, the results of which could justify U.S. actions. But cost would be involved and the results of polls would not necessarily be favorable. In any event, it is doubtful that the Legislature would take kindly to such a poll. Finally, we could <u>propose a referendum on the land exchange package in the 1974 election</u>. While public support of the land package could force key politicians to abandon their present opposition, existence of the referendum would intensify the issue politically, so complex an issue would be difficult for the general public to understand and the USG would be regarded as being bound by the results. It is RECOMMENDED (1) that the military review its orientation and community relations programs and seek to broaden channels of communication, (2) that the Governor be consulted with respect to the establishment of a liaison office and the conduct of public opinion polls.

2. <u>Land Adjustments</u>

The most pressing specific land issues concern relocation of the ammunition pier from Apra Harbor (where the Government of Guam is seeking to expand the commercial port), conflicting demands for aviation facilities at the Naval Air Station Agana, and access to and through DOD-held lands, including military beaches.

a. <u>Relocation of the Ammunition Pier</u>

Sella Bay, selected on the basis of engineering studies, is the ideal site (if available) to which to remove the ammunition handling operations now conducted in Apra Harbor. A package land exchange agreement reached by the Navy and the Governor and providing <u>inter alia</u> for this relocation was blocked by the Guam Legislature primarily because of opposition by certain politicians to the Sella Bay site, but also as a political rebuff to the Governor.

<u>To go on using the present pier for ammunition handling</u>
indefinitely would save funds and avoid some contention, but would continue to hazard the harbor area and hinder development of the commercial
port. <u>To press for Guamanian acceptance of relocation of the operations
to Sella Bay</u> is not politically feasible at this time. <u>To explore alternatives to Sella Bay as the location for a new ammunition handling pier</u>
would provide a fresh start and rethinking which might result in selecting
another site or alternatively might pave the way eventually to Guamanian
approval of the Sella Bay site. However, accepting in this manner the
Legislature's rebuff on Sella Bay could, on the other hand, encourage
Guamanians to further frustrate defense planning on Guam or to present new
demands, and alternative sites could cost more. <u>The exercise of eminent
domain</u> involves the risk of serious political repercussions that could complicate the military mission as well as Federal-Guam relations generally,
and DOD would not employ it except in outright national emergency.

It is RECOMMENDED (1) that the pier in Apra Harbor continue
to be used for the present, and (2) that alternatives to the Sella Bay site
be pursued (as DOD is already doing) since piecemeal solutions may be practicable where a "package deal" was not.

    b. <u>Conflicting demands for aviation facilities</u>

<u>Relocation of civil and/or military operations to Northwest
Field</u> is a suggestion that has frequently been made. Its advantages are
that it would solve the problem encountered by present air operations in an
area of growing urban congestion if both the military and civilian operations
moved and would provide some relief to congestion if either moved. Its dis-
advantages are the costs involved and interference with other facilities.
Support facilities (in which the Navy invested $110 million at NAS Agana) are
almost non-existent at Northwest Field and would have to be installed. Existing facilities at or near Northwest Field would have to be moved. Relocating
Naval Communication Station Guam would cost over $130 million (just its an-
tennas in excess of $20 million), while relocating the USAF Satellite Control
Facility would cost $20 million. If civilian air operations moved to North-
west Field, too, GovGuam might not be able to obtain adequate FAA funds to
share development costs, while the costs to GovGuam of running the Agana Air
Field alone would also be excessive. <u>To continue joint use of NAS Agana for
the present</u> would be more convenient to everyone and would involve much less
expense to the Government of Guam and less to the Navy, but it would make it
necessary <u>to improve and expand commercial aviation facilities at NAS Agana.</u>
A further possibility would be <u>to segregate military and civilian operations
into different and separate airfield complexes by transferring naval aviation
facilities from Agana to Andersen AFB and turning over completely the Agana
field to civilian use.</u> This would provide civilian aviation with a suitable
location with reduced air traffic congestion, but it would be very expensive
for GovGuam, and urban encroachment, if allowed to continue, would still pose
a problem. For the military, it would remove a source of friction with Guamanians and provide a less expensive relocation alternative to Northwest Field,
but it would nevertheless introduce a major unprogrammed expense and move
naval aviation units away from their munition and logistic support facilities.

It is RECOMMENDED (1) that Northwest Field not be developed
for aviation, (2) that joint military-civilian use of Agana Air Field continue for the next 8-10 years under formal agreement* and that the civilian
commercial aviation facilities there be improved, and (3) that urban encroachment at Agana Air Field must be reversed to preserve the field for permanent
civil aviation use. In order to best meet the long-term military and civilian requirements, a study will be made to investigate the feasibility and cost of eventual
transfer of naval activities from NAS Agana to Andersen AFB, as well as other
feasible options on Guam.

*An agreement was concluded July 8, 1

    c. <u>Guamanian access to beaches and other DOD-held lands</u>.
        Free Guamanian access to all Guam beaches is an issue which
some politicians have advanced and used in criticism of the military, though
"going to the beach" is not popular with Guamanians, and though the Government of Guam has more potential recreational beach frontage than the military.
A related issue concerns easements through Federal lands to individual private
properties and to areas envisioned for commercial tourist facility development.
        <u>To open all military beaches/conservation areas for joint use</u>
would go beyond what the general public is seeking and confront the Government of Guam with undesired joint maintenance costs. However, <u>to maintain
the status quo and deny Guamanians use of all military beaches and conserva-
tion areas</u> would be to ignore damaging criticism. An intermediate and preferred course would be <u>to open one or more beaches and conservation/recreation
areas to the public on a joint-use (and shared cost) basis as permitted by
security considerations</u>, if the Government of Guam is agreeable. This course
provides potential for defusing the issue though still confronting the Government of Guam with some costs and requiring attention to possible infringement
of security by foreign tourists.
        One of the reasons access or easement is sought is the
occasional isolation of private land (or government of Guam land) surrounded
by Federal land. <u>Purchase of Guamanian lands isolated by Federal land hold-
ings</u> would be theoretically fair, but there is political opposition to any
net increase in federal lands on Guam. <u>Exchange of lands isolated by Federal
land holdings</u> is equally fair and politically acceptable, but if not accomplished leaves the need for access.
        With respect to easements, <u>a liberal policy on easements per-
mitting access to private property as requested except in the most glaring
cases of interference</u> has the disadvantage of encouraging commercial encroachment that would seriously hamper military operations (e.g. NAVCOMMSTA) and
could violate security rules. A much more acceptable course would be to
<u>grant access easements on a case-by-case basis requiring as necessary restric-
tions or restrictive easements to make the development of private property
compatible with surrounding military operations</u>. While enforcement of restrictions could present opportunities for additional friction, restricted access
will be more acceptable than no access.
        RECOMMENDATIONS are: (1) Indicate willingness to open for
joint-use one or more beach areas and one or more potential park areas if
the Government of Guam is prepared to share costs, (2) Review posted lands,
and where possible, replace prohibitive type signs with the least restrictive
postings possible (e.g. danger warnings), (3) Consider access easements
through DOD lands to Government of Guam property and private property on a
case-by-case basis and replace prohibition of access with permission for
restrictive access where possible, and (4) With regard to land utilization
and acquisition, avoid activity consolidations or relocations that would
involve costs which the Congress would not accept without more compelling
strategic or political reasons than now apparent, give preference to exchange over purchase, and avoid condemnation except in outright national
emergency.
    3. <u>The Role of the Military in the Economy</u>
        The military presence is a major factor in the economy, account-
ing for perhaps 50% of the gross product of the Territory. While it would
be desirable and beneficial to have a more balanced and multifaceted economy,
the opportunities for the Federal Government to introduce economic changes
are limited. The best that can be done is to promote, advise and assist.

To stimulate the development of sectors such as farming, fishing, and small industry in Guam, RECOMMEND: (1) encouragement of private domestic investment, (2) consultation with the Government of Guam, offering it technical advice and assistance, (3) provision of federal aid funds as available, and (4) adoption of policies (e.g. with respect to wages where federally controlled) which will attract Guamanian labor into these economic activities. The Department of State also recommends that continuation of foreign investment be permitted in all sectors, including tourism.

    B. <u>Possible changes in socio-economic policy.</u>

The second major area in which problems with Guam need mutually satisfactory solution is that of socio-economic policy. Here the U.S. general interest and the asserted Guamanian interest (or interests) are by no means congruent, and the Guamanians have asked for a number of changes in Federal laws and policies.

        1. <u>Changes in Federal laws and programs.</u>

           <u>Wage rates</u>

Labor shortages on Guam have been met by the temporary importation of alien workers. Such importation is permitted by law and/or regulation provided (1) unemployed persons capable of performing the temporary service or labor cannot be found in this country and (2) the employment of a nonimmigrant temporary worker will not adversely affect the wages and working conditions of a worker in the United States similarly employed. The latter proviso has required that such alien workers not be paid less than the "prevailing wage." The prevailing wage schedule established by the Guam Department of Labor for skilled occupations in the construction industry (areas where wages generally are depressed compared to salaries of GovGuam employees, for example) runs between 40% and 45% above the corresponding Guamanian legal minimum wages (the difference between the minimum and prevailing wage is much higher elsewhere in the U.S.) but well below the prevailing wages in the Guamanian civil service. (In general, the Guamanian minimum wage is above the Federal minimum wage, as is true in many States, while the prevailing wage in Guam is about half the prevailing wage in the United States.) Guam's "prevailing journeyman wage schedule," governing wages to be paid temporary alien workers, initially provided for incremental wage increases in each trade every six months, rising at a rate of about 17% a year but the schedule was frozen early in 1974 pending impartial validation. Prior to its freezing, an active group of Guamanian businessmen were seeking modification of U.S. law to permit them to pay the Guamanian minimum wage rather than the "prevailing wage" to temporary alien workers. The GovGuam Executive has expressed its satisfaction with the payment of the "prevailing wage" to temporary alien workers but the Legislature was at least initially sympathetic to the businessmen (though recently the majority view is reported to have changed). The Labor Council of the Western Pacific (an AFL-CIO organ) supports continued insistence upon payment of the prevailing wage - and indeed would prefer an even higher wage - to encourage Guamanians to seek training in these trades and to protect American labor.

It is not possible to satisfy all Guamanian interests. <u>To permit Guamanian employers to pay temporary alien workers the legal minimum wage rather than the "prevailing wage" would satisfy certain Guamanian business interests</u> (the wage would be high enough to attract alien labor, low enough to hold labor costs on a par with those of foreign businessmen in Guam employing their own nationals as contract labor) but it would frustrate the development of an adequate indigenous labor pool and would perpetuate (and perhaps aggravate) the problem of a large alien sector in Guam's society.

The long-term U.S. and Guamanian interest would seem to lean on the side of a prevailing wage that accords with standard of living goals and which is obligatory to pay to temporary alien workers. Careful scrutiny should be given to the loophole through which treaty traders can bring in alien contract workers for a lesser wage. It is RECOMMENDED that further study be given to the problem of wage rates especially as it bears upon the question of temporary alien workers including those admitted as treaty traders.

Immigration
Temporary Admission of Aliens

Guamanian employers desire liberalization of the Immigration Act to permit temporary admission on nonimmigrant status (on H-2 visas) of aliens to perform work in permanent type jobs such as agriculture, fishing and tourism in which there are labor shortages but would like the Government of Guam to exercise the control. HR 981, if passed by the Senate, will permit temporary admission of alien workers for permanent type jobs where local labor is not available. It will also, as desired by Guamanians, limit the period of admission to one year with possible renewal of another 12 months at the end of the first year. The limitation should protect the growth of a pool of skilled Guamanian labor but unless enforced carefully it will fail to achieve its objective. Guamanians would also like to prohibit temporary alien workers from bringing in their families, but this appears contrary to existing law and could lead to social frustrations and frictions. It is RECOMMENDED (1) that the Administration, in any comments on HR 981, point out the dangers of over-reliance upon foreign labor and dangers of too rapid economic growth, either of which could occur if the measure is not administered very cautiously, and (2) that no administrative efforts be made to preclude families from accompanying H-2 workers.

Permanent Immigration

To guard against the growing Filipino population or other foreigners in Guam becoming the dominant element, Guamanians desire immigration to be more closely controlled, and would like to have their own hands on the controls.

The plenary power of Congress over the territories would, theoretically, provide authority for Congress to restrict immigration to Guam. To this end, Congress could restrict by federal law the number of immigrants who may settle on Guam. Such limitation would accord with Guamanian desires and there could be advisory input from the Government of Guam to the control. However, it would not satisfy Guamanians completely. It would reverse previous policy of trying to assimilate Guam into the United States as much as possible, and it might run counter to recent court decisions prohibiting discrimination against non-resident aliens. Congress could also render inapplicable to Guam certain immigrant visa preference categories. This would have parallel effect without interfering so much with the fabric of the Act. The Immigration and Naturalization Service could tighten existing loose practices which seem to facilitate the adjustment of the nonimmigrant status on Guam. (While present regulations do not permit an extension "which would result in an unbroken stay in the United States for more than three years," that stay may be broken by a short boat trip beyond the three-mile limit.) More rigid enforcement could only benefit Guam. To give Guam authority to control the movement of immigrants to Guam would doubtless lead to discriminatory laws which would be subject to testing in the courts like the laws of all of the States, but if the North Marianas should be given control over immigration in the current status negotiations, it would

be difficult and unwise to withhold the same control from Guam. It is RECOMMENDED (1) that loose practices permitting adjustment of status be tightened up, and (2) that unless over-riding reasons to the contrary are found, whatever autonomous control over immigration may be extended to the Northern Marianas also be extended to Guam.

Banking and Currency

Guamanians, in the hope of fostering greater economic development have thought of building Guam into a banking center and have asked about the possibilities of semiautonomous currency and anonymous accounts. To give Guam more local control over banks, whether U.S. or foreign, would meet their desire, but Guam already attempts to exercise more control over U.S. National Banks than that exercised by any State, and its oppressive supervision has threatened to drive those banks out of Guam.   To permit anonymous bank accounts would not attract funds unless Guam were a major financial, transportation and communication center, which it is not, and would violate the U.S. international position of discouraging secrecy on disclosure of ownership. It is RECOMMENDED that the status quo be maintained.

Shipping laws and Regulations

The coastwise or intercoastal provisions of the Merchant Marine Act of 1920, as amended, require all cargoes carried between American ports to travel in American-flag ships. Though the Act was made applicable to American insular territories in principle, its application could be deferred by the President and was so deferred with respect to the Virgin Islands by annual Presidential action until 1936 when its amendment by Congress permanently exempted the Virgin Islands until the President should issue a proclamation applying it. The Act was applied to Puerto Rico, Guam and American Samoa. However, in 1934 when the British claimed that its application to American Samoa was in contravention of the Tripartite treaty of 1899 which gave equal commercial rights to the U.K., the U.S. and Germany in the entire Samoan group, the Congress made the restrictive provisions permanently inapplicable to American Samoa; both Puerto Rico and Guam feel that the restrictive provisions are detrimental to their economies. Guamanians have requested suspension of the provisions at least during American shipping strikes, but would prefer to be exempted all together like the Virgin Islands and American Samoa.

To obtain Congressional legislation exempting Guam from application of the coastwise shipping laws of the United States would satisfy Guam and put it in the same basis as the Virgin Islands and American Samoa. But it would probably require extending similar exemption to Puerto Rico (and raise questions about Hawaii and Alaska), and it would have a harmful effect on American shipping. To seek standby legislation to exempt Guam during American shipping strikes would help keep supplies moving to Guam when there are strikes but would be considered anti-labor. It is RECOMMENDED that further study be made.

Supplying Guam's Energy Requirements

Guam's civilian economy and military capability are particularly vulnerable to interruptions in fuel imports. No specific options are proposed since it is likely they would be overtaken by events. However, it is RECOMMENDED that decisions made by those developing fuel policy take into consideration Guam's needs and ensure that Guam gets its proper share of allocations.

Number of Federal Officers assigned to Guam

Guamanians have asked for the assignment of additional immigration, FHA, and HEW officers. They have also asked that Guamanians

be assigned as federal officers. It is RECOMMENDED (1) that Federal Departments represented in Guam review their existing positions with a view to authorizing and assigning on a priority basis to Guam any additional personnel for which the review indicates a need, (2) that efforts be made to train and utilize Guamanian personnel, and (3) continued study be given to the establishment of a Federal Office Building in Guam.

2. Changes in Foreign Investment Policy

The Government of Guam, uncertain about the social and economic consequences of a continuation of the foreign investment which has blossomed in Guam in the past decade has sought to contract for a professional study of alien investment in Guam. Some Congressmen and the Department of Defense are also concerned about large foreign investment and eventual foreign dominance of the economy and its potential for adverse impact on future military presence. State and Interior believe that foreign investment can be beneficial. Interior believes effective control of this investment can be maintained. There is general concurrence on the insufficiency of economic data. It is RECOMMENDED (1) that a study of the entire Guamanian economy in all its aspects be conducted (by the Federal Reserve Board if its services are available) and that in it attention be paid to the matter of foreign investment including the extent and dangers of land alienation, (2) that access to the proposed Stanford Research study be requested, (3) that appropriate actions be recommended upon completion of such studies, and meanwhile, (4) that Guamanians should be advised that action by their own legislature is the best means of forestalling land alienation. (The Department of State believes that the USG should not recommend to the Guamanian legislature that it take legal action to discourage foreign ownership of lands since this would not be in Guam's economic interest, and is contrary to U.S. policy on the international free flow of capital.)

3. Changes in Federal/territorial financial arrangements

Guam is faced with growing social and infrastructure needs beyond its own means. The Government of Guam's capital improvement requirements for badly need school construction and equally necessary expansion of the water supply and sewage disposal systems is estimated at $125.7 million, of which Guam itself can provide $55.4 million. It is anticipating the availability of $14.2 million in Environmental Protection Agency funds, but is asking for a special Congressional authorization of $56 million in grants. It is not possible in this study to justify in detail the precise capital improvements planned, nor the precise federal support requested. But on solid political grounds Guam is entitled to equal treatment with the Northern Marianas. Guam's present per capita support from the United States, reckoned in terms both of budgetary help to the Government of Guam and Federal expenditures in non-military programs in Guam, as an estimated $672 in 1973. Guamanian average per capita income was an estimated $2,691, about half the U.S. average. Should the Congress authorize the capital improvement assistance requested by Guam ($56 million, or $11.7 million for each of five years), the average per capita aid to Guamanians (the 66,500 permanent residents) would be $744. This would compare to $1,430 per capita for the Northern Marianas and $544 for the five other districts of Micronesia which can be expected if future financial arrangements now envisaged for these areas following their attainment of new political status go into effect. The assistance requested by Guam, an American territory of long-standing, is not out of line with our intentions regarding the Northern Marianas and the rest of Micronesia whose people are not yet American citizens. Whether or not Guam could make do with less than the $56 million requested, it would be contrary to our

objective of giving Guam as favorable treatment as the Northern Marianas to be unresponsive.

If it is decided to accede to the Guamanian request <u>the viable options</u> appear to be:

1. <u>A federal grant of $56 million.</u>
2. <u>A federal grant of $32.37 million for schools and authorization for water and sewers of:</u>
    (a) <u>$23.7 million in loans</u>
    (b) <u>$11.85 million in grants and $11.85 million in loans, or</u>
    (c) <u>a $23.7 million federally-guaranteed bond issue</u>
3. <u>Any of the foregoing conditioned on a set annual increase in local revenues.</u>

Since schools are not self-amortizing, it would be reasonable to extend the entire $32 million asked for school construction in grant form. As for the utilities, to make the entire $23.7 million a repayable loan when Guam itself is providing $26.5 million for them does not seem as reasonable as extending 50% as grant and 50% as loan. Utilization of a Federally guaranteed bond issue for the utilities is not responsive to the Guamanian request and could have strong opposition in Congress because it involves commitment of future unappropriated funds. To make the disbursements of aid conditional upon increasing local revenues would encourage fiscal responsibility in Guam but it also could make future disbursements subject to factors outside control of the Guamanian authorities (e.g. a Japanese recession), and this seems inadvisable. It is RECOMMENDED: (1) that Congressional support be sought for a special authorization of $56 million fund for the construction of schools, water supply and sewers over the five-year period FY 1975-79, the entire $32.37 million for schools to be a grant, but only 50% of the $23.7 million for water supply and sewers ($11.85 million) to be a grant, the remaining 50% ($11.85 million) to be a loan repayable at moderate interest over a 30 year period*, (2) that all Federal Agencies having programs in Guam look for opportunities to increase their programs wherever inadequacies may exist, (3) that Congressional support be sought, when the time comes, to extend the Guam Economic Development Fund upon its expiration, and (4) that the economic study recommended in the preceding section assess the directions in which the economy has the best potential for development to meet the aspirations of Guamanians and to reckon the capital requirements for such development, suggesting where financing might most suitably be provided by the Federal Government and where by other sources.

---

* The Department of State does not associate itself with this recommendation which it believes is insufficiently substantiated by available data. Nevertheless, it believes that on political grounds, the request for capital development assistance should be supported in principle by the Executive Branch, details to be worked out in the normal budgetary process. The Office of Management and Budget believes there is insufficient evidence, at least pending further study, to justify a posture of support even in principle.

C. Possible changes in Guam's international role.
    1. Implications for Other U.S. Territories

An Ad Hoc Advisory Group is examining aspects of Puerto Rico's relationship with the U.S., including an as yet unspecified Puerto Rican desire for participation in international affairs. The Puerto Rican Government has begun steps to join the Caribbean Development Bank as a contributing member, and prospects for USG approval appear to be good. Although Puerto Rico has so far demonstrated little interest in membership in the UN Economic Commission for Latin America, there is little doubt that it could join, and Guam membership in ECAFE could stimulate interest in that direction. Puerto Rico has in the past made separate trade agreements, which have resulted in little apparent benefit to the U.S. or to Puerto Rico. Virgin Islands and American Samoan involvement or interest in foreign affairs is essentially non-existent at this time but likewise could be stimulated. A federal decision to extend Guam's international role could have important implications for the future international role of other U.S. territories.

    2. Separate Trade Agreements for Guam

Governor Camacho has proposed that, in addition to having its present free port status, Guam be authorized to enter into trade agreements with neighboring islands. Congress could delegate this authority to Guam but matters of commercial importance to the U.S. might get involved in negotiations, constitutional questions might arise relating to the President's responsibility for the conduct of U.S. foreign policy, and Guamanian separation could needlessly be encouraged. To avoid these problems and still provide reasonable satisfaction to Guam, the U.S. could negotiate agreements for Guam, perhaps using a Guamanian on its trade delegation. It is RECOMMENDED by Interior and State (1) that in the context of a general dialogue with Guam's Governor or Legislators, the U.S. should explore what Guamanians have in mind as advantages to be achieved and ascertain whether mutual benefits exist in such a course, and if they do (2) that the U.S. carry out trade negotiations for Guam, using a Guamanian representative designated by the Secretary of State after consultation with the Governor of Guam. They also recommend (3) that opportunities be explored to put Guamanians on U.S. trade delegations as advisors in negotiations directly affecting Guam. (OSD and the Joint Staff demur to (2) and (3) on grounds that they would conflict with our objective of preserving a permanent federal relationship.)

    3. Guamanian membership in international organizations, viz., ECAFE

Guamanian interest in joining international organizations stems less from status considerations than from expectation of tangible benefits, but it is also affected by the desire of Guamanians to have equal status with other Pacific islanders. The Governor of Guam is exploring the possibility of securing loans from the Asian Development Bank (ADB); a prior requirement is membership in the Economic Commission for Asia and the Far East (ECAFE). To achieve associate membership in ECAFE, Guam must be sponsored by the U.S. ECAFE's terms of reference would permit associate membership (and some British territories have it). However, the U.S. has long been opposed to

The Secret Guam Study

the use of any UN developmental funds for territories of developed countries.
Moreover, ECAFE associate membership for territories is informally regarded
by most ECAFE members as a step toward independence. To encourage Guam to
join international organizations is contrary to the principle of federalism
and should be avoided. To refuse to sponsor Guam for associate membership
in ECAFE, however, is politically touchy since it may have the effect of
encouraging separatist sentiment. To sponsor membership with the proviso
that Guam not be eligible for any concessional aid and that technical aid
be reimbursed is feasible but superfluous unless Guam is to belong to the ADB.
It is RECOMMENDED (1) that in general, Guamanian membership in international
organizations be discouraged but (2) that exceptions be allowed where it is
mutually advantageous and the primacy of the Federal Government is not
challenged, (3) that a decision on associate membership in ECAFE be treated
as a reasonable exception if it appears after further investigation that
Guamanian membership in the ADB is possible and would be advantageous or
that Guam would derive other compelling advantages from ECAFE membership
without harm to the U.S., and (4) that because of possible Puerto Rican
interest in ECLA membership, the two questions be considered in conjunction
with one another. (Defense and the Joint Staff disconcur in the suggestion
that exception be made on these grounds, but believe that the main issue
is ADB membership. The Office of Micronesian Status Negotiations (OMSN) opposes
any exception.)

4. Guamanian membership in the Asian Development Bank (ADB)

        Guam has capital investment plans exceeding its resources and
anticipated Federal support. Since March 1973, it has been requesting USG
sponsorship of Guamanian membership. However, Guam's per capita income of
over $2,000 renders it seemingly ineligible for Special Funds Loans and
Ordinary Capital loans from the Bank, and the ADB interest rate is 7 1/2%.
If the U.S. sponsored Guam, it would have to guarantee the Guamanian capital
subscription and repayment of any loans. It is against U.S. policy to
support concessional assistance to countries on Guam's economic level, but
we would not object to reimbursable technical assistance. Refusing to
sponsor Guam could cause a deterioration in Federal–Guam relations.
Sponsoring Guam would be good public relations for us and might help Guam,
but more information is required. (OSD and the Joint Staff believe it
would be contrary to U.S. objectives on Guam; it could stimulate Guam's
appetite for an increased role in international affairs and for greater
autonomy.) It is RECOMMENDED (1) that further inquiries be directed to
the ADB to determine with certainty Guam's eligibility for loans and
technical assistance and to determine the possible level of its capital
subscription, (2) that the information obtained be reviewed and Congressional
reaction to authorizing the requisite capital subscription and requisite
guarantee of loan repayment be solicited before any commitment is made to
Guam to sponsor its membership, (3) that discussions then be pursued
with Guam officials and if benefits to Guam appear worthwhile and justify
costs to the U.S., the U.S. should sponsor Guam. (OSD, the Joint Staff and OMSN
recommend (1) that Guam's ineligibility, if substantiated, should be
fully discussed with Guamanians to avoid misrepresentation of the U.S.
position by Guamanian radicals, and (2) they recommend a broad policy of
discouraging U.S. states and territories from participation directly in
international organizations, though bona fide exceptions should be considered on a case-by-case basis. Treasury, while not objecting to U.S. sponsorship of Guam for ECAFE or ADB membership if there are political or other reasons
in the U.S. interest, believes, like State and Interior, that Guam would not be
a priority borrower because of its relatively high per capital income.)

5. __Annual reports to the United Nations__

Some Guamanians would like to have the annual reports on
Guam made by the United States discontinued at once. Others would
regard that as an effort to frustrate their aspirations, and UN members of
the Afro-Asian group would seek to embarrass the United States. The
Committee of 24 wants to send a mission to Guam and would at all events
insist upon sending a visiting mission before relieving the U.S. of
its obligation to report. Reporting can be discontinued when "self-government"
is achieved. Either independence or permanent association with another
State, freely adopted, is considered self-government. It is RECOMMENDED
(1) that the United States for the present continue reporting, (2) that a
visiting mission from the UN be fended off until at least after the Guamanian
elections late in 1974, and (3) that the United States seek termination of
its reporting requirement to the UN when the question of Guam's status
has been resolved.

D. __Alternatives for Future Political Status__
Politically articulate Guamanians, determined to have more self-
government and more say about what happens to them, probably cannot be
satisfied short of drafting their own constitution and moving ahead in
either of two directions: (1) toward greater autonomy from the United
States, or (2) toward greater integration with the United States while
gaining a larger voice in U.S. policies affecting Guam. The first path
leads from a modified territorial status to commonwealth (or permanent
free association) status. The second path leads from modified territorial
status (with the optional step of "incorporated territory") to statehood.
Statehood is not being sought, though it is a possible ultimate goal.
Any future status which will prove satisfactory must serve both
essential U.S. and Guamanian interests, and it should also serve these
interests on both sides which are regarded as only slightly short of
essential. It is, therefore, the U.S. objective to work out with the
Guamanians a future political status which to serve their requirements
would involve them in drafting the basic organ or constitution and be no
less favorable than the arrangement for the Northern Marianas; and which
to serve U.S. requirement would be consistent with the U.S. Constitution,
preserve U.S. control over defense and foreign affairs, create no obstacles
to the unification of Guam and the Northern Marianas, and preserve a close
political relationship with the United States. The following three options
appear feasible, though #1(a) and #3 are somewhat marginal, the former because
it would have trouble meeting the Guamanian desire for a self-drafted
constitution, and the latter for absence of either strong Guamanian or
Congressional support. Each option, if strongly supported by Guamanians,
would enable the U.S. to terminate future reporting to the United Nations.
Under each option U.S. sovereignty would remain, Guam's policy and system
would be consistent with the U.S. Constitution, and Guamanians would remain
American citizens.
1(a). __Modified territorial status (unincorporated in fact but
not so designated) with greater self-government achieved through revision
of the Organic Act along lines to be drafted by the Guamanians.__ The
Guamanian Constitutional Convention of 1970 sponsored by the Guam Legislature, but not recognized by the Congress, proposed revision of the
Organic Act, to retitle it "Constitution of the Territory of Guam" and
to provide for somewhat more self-government (e.g. an elected governor).

The Congressional revision of the Organic Act in 1972 has already provided for an elected governor, and in view of the future status prospects for the Northern Marianas, Guamanians are not very likely to be satisfied with this option now. Also, it might not be the best option to preserve the possibility of future union of Guam and the Northern Marianas, though it would otherwise serve our interests very well.

    1(b). <u>The same status achieved through prior Congressional authorization and subsequent Congressional approval of a Guamanian-drafted constitution for the "Territory of Guam."</u> This would amply serve both U.S. and Guamanian objectives if regarded by Guamanians and Northern Marianas as equal to what the latter achieve. Though it would, in fact, be the same thing with a different name, the title "Commonwealth" is currently highly regarded and if the title makes a difference, to deny it will not serve our interests.

    2. <u>Incorporated territorial status with further self-government (similar to Hawaii and Alaska before Statehood except that the Governor would be elected rather than appointed),</u>

        (a) <u>to be achieved through passage of a new Organic Act along lines to be drafted by Guamanians, or</u>

        (b) <u>to be achieved through Congressional enabling legislation authorizing and accepting a Guamanian-drafted constitution.</u>

While this option would meet most of the U.S. interests and would satisfy international public opinion if accompanied by some form of referendum, it lacks appeal for the Guamanians because it would deprive them of currently rebated taxes and Guam would lose its free port status, and Congress would probably not support it.

    3. <u>Commonwealth</u>. This option would meet all U.S. objectives. It would be a better way to preserve the option of ultimate Guam/Northern Marianas union than would modified territorial status. It would serve Guam's essential and important interests as well as <u>Option 1(b)</u> and has the advantage of presenting a more attractive image. It will probably be Guam's option. It will satisfy international opinion. It is the recommended option for the U.S.

    <u>Recommendations are:</u>

    (a) That the U.S. be prepared to accept commonwealth or modified territorial status for Guam with terms as good as those for the Northern Marianas.

    (b) That Guamanians draft their own constitution subject to Congressional acceptance.

    (c) That key Congressmen be informed of this policy.

    (d) That to forestall problems vis-a-vis our negotiations with the Northern Marianas, the Governor and key Senators of Guam be informed of our preparedness, when Guamanians are ready, to see Guam have a status and arrangement no less favorable than the Northern Marianas.

<u>NOTE:</u> The preparation of a negotiating scenario at this time is considered premature.

RECAPITULATION OF RECOMMENDATIONS *

IMMEDIATE ACTIONS

MILITARY-GUAMANIAN RELATIONSHIPS

1. To the extent that proves effective, broaden channels of communication through support and development of people-to-people programs such as scouting, sports clubs, women's clubs, etc. (DEFENSE)

2. Continue, for the present, to use the pier in Apra Harbor for ammunition handling, under waiver procedure. (DEFENSE)

3. Conclude with the Government of Guam a formal agreement for the joint military-civilian use of Naval Air Station Agana. For the next 8-10 years improve and expand the civilian commercial aviation facilities at the Agana Air Field without moving the Naval air activities. (DEFENSE)
   (NOTE: A joint use agreement was concluded July 8, 1974, subsequent to the preparation of this study.)

4. Indicate willingness to open for joint-use one or more beach areas and one or more potential park/recreation areas if the Government of Guam is prepared to share costs. (DEFENSE)

ACTIONS INVOLVING FURTHER STUDY OR CONSULTATION

1. Discuss with the Governor of Guam, and, if he reacts favorably, with the Legislature, the establishment of a Federal Liaison Office in Guam. (INTERIOR)

2. Ascertain whether the Governor and the Legislature would be willing to have public opinion polls conducted periodically by contract for the Federal Government. (INTERIOR)

3. Evaluate ongoing orientation and community relations programs in the military to ascertain if they are effective in promoting good interpersonal relationships between the military and the Guamanians and to correct any possible dificiencies. (DEFENSE)

MILITARY LAND ADJUSTMENTS

4. Continue to explore alternatives to Sella Bay as the site for a new ammunition pier. (DEFENSE)

5. Consult with Government of Guam to ensure that necessary actions are taken to reverse the process of encroachment at Agana Air Field so that the long-term commercial use of this field can be preserved. (INTERIOR, FAA, DEFENSE)

6. In order to best meet the long-term military and civilian requirements, a study will be made to investigate the feasibility and cost of eventual transfer of naval activities from NAS Agana to Andersen AFB, as well as other feasible options on Guam. (DEFENSE)

7. Review posted lands and where possible replace prohibitive type signs with danger warnings. (DEFENSE)

8. Consider access easements through DOD lands to Government of Guam property and private property on a case-by-case basis and replace prohibition of access with permission for restrictive access where possible. (DEFENSE)

---

* Agencies responsible for actions are listed after each recommendation. Where several agencies are listed, the first has primary responsibility unless other arrangements are made. Studies and consultation listed on right hand side will be coordinated by Inter-Agency Study Group.

MILITARY ROLE IN THE ECONOMY

5. Promote private investment in farming, fishing and small industry with a view to developing a multi-faceted civilian economy on Guam less dependent economically on the military presence. (INTERIOR, COMMERCE, AGRICULTURE)

5a. Additional recommendation by State. Continue to accept foreign investment in all sectors.

9. Consult with Government of Guam, offering technical advice and assistance for the development of farming, fishing and small industry, and provide federal financial assistance for these areas as available, consulting with the Congress to get its support therefor. (AGRICULTURE, COMMERCE, INTERIOR, LABOR)

IMMIGRATION AND WAGES OF ALIENS

6. Make no administrative efforts to preclude families from accompanying temporary alien workers (H-2 visas) to Guam. (JUSTICE, STATE)

10. Give additional study to the wages paid to aliens in Guam. The long-term U.S. and Guamanian interest would seem to lean on the side of a prevailing wage that accords with standards of living goals and which is obligatory to pay to temporary alien workers whatever their specific non-immigrant status. Careful scrutiny should be given to the existing loophole through which treaty traders can bring in alien contract workers for a wage less than the prevailing wage. (LABOR, JUSTICE)

7. Have immigration authorities tighten existing loose practices including devices by which time limitations on the stay of H-2 workers are evaded and which, taken together, seem to help non-immigrants on Guam adjust their status to that of immigrants. (JUSTICE)

11. The Administration should, in any comments to the Congress concerning HR 981, point out the dangers of over-reliance upon foreign labor and the dangers of too rapid economic growth either of which could occur if the measure is not administered cautiously. (JUSTICE, COMMERCE, LABOR)

12. Unless over-riding reasons to the contrary are found, whatever autonomous control over immigration is in future extended to the Northern Marianas should also be extended to Guam. (INTERIOR, JUSTICE, STATE)

8. Maintain the status quo. (TREASURY)

BANKING AND CURRENCY

(None)

(None)

SHIPPING

13. Give additional study to placing Guam in the same status as the Virgin Islands and American Samoa with respect to the Jones Act (coastwise shipping). (INTERIOR, TRANSPORTATION, LABOR, COMMERCE)

NUMBER OF FEDERAL OFFICERS ASSIGNED TO GUAM

(None)

14. Federal Departments represented in Guam should conduct a comprehensive survey of Guam's requirements compared to Departmental representation on Guam and to the extent that a need for a larger number of federal officers is indicated, authorize positions and assign personnel on a priority basis. (INTERIOR AND ALL AGENCIES INVOLVED)

15. Foster training of Guamanians to perform Federal service in Guam. (IMMIGRATION, HUD, HEW, LABOR)

16. Study the possibility of establishing a Federal office building in Guam. (INTERIOR)

SUPPLYING GUAM'S ENERGY REQUIREMENTS

9. Ensure that Guam gets its proper share of fuel allocations. (FEDERAL ENERGY OFFICE, DEFENSE)

17. Any decisions made by those developing fuel policy should take into consideration Guam's needs and provide for adequate allocation to Guam. (FEO, INTERIOR)

FOREIGN INVESTMENT POLICY

(None)

18. Conduct a thorough economic study of Guam giving attention inter alia to development potential and financing resources, including federal assistance and domestic and foreign investment. Also, obtain results of Stanford Research Institute's study of alien investment in Guam. (FEDERAL RESERVE BOARD, INTERIOR, COMMERCE, TREASURY)

19. In conjunction with land alienation, advise the Government of Guam that it is in a better position than the Federal Government to deal with this problem, and encourage it to legislate appropriate safeguards. (INTERIOR)

19b. State recommends against encouragement of such legislation.

FEDERAL-TERRITORIAL FINANCIAL ARRANGEMENTS

10. Interior, OSD, the Joint Staff and OMB recommend a special Congressional authorization of $56 million for the construction of schools, water supply and sewers over the five year period FY 1974-79, the entire $32.37 million for schools to be a grant, but the $23.7 million for water and sewers to be 50% grant, 50% loan (30 years, moderate interest). State agrees in principle on offering support, but recommends further study on specifics. OMB recommends more study before any decision is made. (INTERIOR, OMB)

20. Study the possibility of providing matching funds or otherwise tying federal subsidy to local performance and effort, possible increase in Guam Development Fund, and possible increase in allocations from the several federal agencies. (INTERIOR)

INTERNATIONAL TRADE AGREEMENTS FOR GUAM

11. Recommendation by Interior and State:
Look for opportunities in trade negotiations that directly concern Guam to place Guamanians on U.S. trade delegations as advisers or consultants or, in appropriate circumstances, as principals. Commerce, while not objecting, believes present practices suffice. (OSD and the Joint Staff demur on principle.) (STR, STATE, COMMERCE)

21a. Recommendation by Interior and State (Commerce concurring):
In the context of general dialogue with Guam's Governor or his representatives (and Legislators if the occasion arises) explore what Guamanians may have in mind as advantages to be achieved from separate trade agreements with neighboring or other areas if they choose to introduce the subject. If separate trade agreements do appear to be beneficial to both Guam and the rest of the United States, suggest to Guam officials a procedure whereby these agreements would be negotiated for Guam by a negotiator designated by the Secretary of State upon nomination by the Governor. If mutual benefits do not appear, discourage Guamanian initiative toward special agreements. (INTERIOR, STATE)

21b. Recommendation by OSD and the Joint Staff:
Discourage separate or direct Guamanian trade agreements, if clear benefit to the U.S. does not exist, in view of the U.S. objective of preserving the permanence of a Federal relationship and the erosion of that relationship which separate trade agreements might induce. (INTERIOR, STATE)

GUAMANIAN MEMBERSHIP IN INTERNATIONAL ORGANIZATIONS (ECAFE, ADB)

12. In general, discourage Guamanian membership in international organizations since the federal principle is that the Federal Government shall represent the entire United States internationally and since membership could contribute to separatist trends. However, exceptions to the general principle of keeping Guam out of international organizations can continue to be made (as in the case of the World Health Organization)where it is mutually advantageous to Guam and to the United States as a whole, where the primacy of the Federal Government is not challenged, where refusal to sponsor membership appears likely to induce separatist sentiment, and where by utilization of appropriate provisos the U.S. can preserve its established policy stance on a world basis. (INTERIOR, STATE AND OTHERS AS APPROPRIATE)

22a. Recommendation by Interior and State (Commerce & Treasury concur): Treat the question of associate membership for Guam in ECAFE as a reasonable exception to the general principle of keeping Guam out of international organizations if it appears after further investigation (a)that Guamanian membership in the Asia Development Bank (for which ECAFE membership is prerequisite) is possible and would be advantageous, or (b) that membership in ECAFE would of itself be advantageous to Guam. The question should be considered in conjunction with the related question of ECLA membership for Puerto Rico. (STATE, TREASURY, COMMERCE)

22b. Recommendation by OSD, the Joint Staff, and OMSN: Treat the question of sponsoring Guamanian associate membership in ECAFE in conjunction with and subsidiary to the questions of Guamanian membership in the ADB. (STATE, TREASURY, COMMERCE)

23a. Recommendation by Interior and State (Commerce & Treasury concur): After making further inquiries of the ADB to ascertain Guam's eligibility for loans and technical assistance and to determine the possible level of its capital subscription, and if favorable Congressional reaction is obtained, review the question of costs and benefits of ADB membership with Guam officials. If the benefits appear worthwhile, the U.S. should sponsor Guam's membership. If they do not appear worthwhile, declining to sponsor will be reasonable. (TREASURY, STATE, COMMERCE)

23b. Recommendation by OSD, the Joint Staff, and OMSN:
The United States should not sponsor Guam for membership in
the ADB because such activity appears to be inconsistent
with U.S. security objectives on Guam and the goal of
insuring the permanence of a Federal relationship with
Guam. (TREASURY, STATE, COMMERCE)

GUAM AND THE UNITED NATIONS

24. The United States should seek termination of its requirement
to make annual reports on Guam to the United Nations when the
question of Guam's status is resolved, but not sooner. (STATE)

FUTURE POLITICAL STATUS

25. In order to avoid misunderstandings and efforts at cross-
purposes, key Congressmen should be informed that the
adjacent recommendations (15,16,17) embody the preferred
policy of the Executive Branch.(WHITE HOUSE)

26. In order to forestall Guamanian jealousy of the Northern
Marianas and to avoid unnecessary frustration or confusion
which might affect U.S. negotiations in Saipan, the Governor
and key Legislators in Guam should, after the foregoing
Congressional consultations, be informed promptly though informally that the United States wants Guam to have a status
and arrangements no less favorable than those which will obtain in the Northern Marianas and that the Federal Government
will be ready to entertain Guamanian views regarding future
arrangements as soon as Guam is prepared to present them.
(INTERIOR, OFFICE OF MICRONESIAN STATUS NEGOTIATIONS)

13. For the present, continue annual reporting to the United
Nations. (INTERIOR, STATE)

14. A visiting mission from the UN to Guam should be fended off
at least until after the Guamanian elections late in 1974.
(STATE)

15. Be prepared to accept a commonwealth or modified territorial status for Guam as selected by Guam itself. This
status and its specific arrangements should be as good
as what is worked out for the Northern Marianas.
(EXECUTIVE OFFICE OF THE PRESIDENT)

16. Permit the Guamanians to draft their own constitution
subject to the acceptance of the United States.
(EXECUTIVE OFFICE OF THE PRESIDENT)

17. Be prepared to establish with Guam a Joint Status Commission or some other forum that is mutually agreeable
in which to discuss Guam's future as soon as the Political
Status Commission appointed by the 12th Guam Legislature
has submitted its report to the Legislature and the
Governor has had an opportunity to present his views.
(EXECUTIVE OFFICE OF THE PRESIDENT)

Appendix 4

Memorandum, March 25, 1975,
from Staff Director Gathright to
Members of the Under Secretaries Committee

DEPARTMENT OF STATE

Washington, D.C. 20520

V137577/
TA 3255
(91)

NSC UNDER SECRETARIES COMMITTEE

March 25, 1975

TO: Interior - Royston C. Hughes
                 - Emmett Rice
                 - Kurt Herge
                 - James Wilson, Jr.
       Defense   - Morton I. Abramowitz
       JCS   - Brig. Gen. James Keefe, Jr.
       NSC   - John A. Froebe, Jr.
       State   - EA - William Gleysteen
                      - Leo Moser
                 - IO - Robert Blake
                 - H - Alexander Schnee
                 - L - Oliver T. Johnson

SUBJECT: Meeting of Special Committee on Guam
         March 11, 1975

         Attached for your information is a record of
the topics discussed and the actions taken· at the
meeting of the Special Committee on Guam.

                        Wreatham E. Gathright
                        Staff Director

       Attachment:

         As stated

<u>NSC UNDER SECRETARIES COMMITTEE</u>

MEETING OF
SPECIAL COMMITTEE ON GUAM
MARCH 11, 1975*

    1. The Special Committee discussed steps to
implement the President's directive of February 1,
1975 concerning "Negotiations with Guam on a New
Political Relationship."

    2. It was noted that the policy role of the
NSC system involves in particular the US strategic
interest in Guam; the relationship of negotiations
with Guam to negotiations involving the TTPI, and
Guam's apparent desire for an enhanced international
political status through associate membership in
certain international organizations.

    3. Consistent with the President's directive
and in view of domestic and Congressional considerations, Interior will take the lead in operational
aspects of the negotiations. In this regard:

    -- Interior expects to complete internal
       organizational and staffing arrange-
       ments within two-to-four weeks;

    -- Interior does not anticipate any
       special budgetary requirements for
       these purposes; and

    -- Interior plans to establish an inter-
       agency backstopping group which will
       include as core members the departments
       and agencies having a primary interest
       in these matters. Departments and
       agencies having a more specialized interest
       are to be called on as necessary.

---

*A list of participants is attached.

GDS

-2-

4. The special Constitutional responsibility of the Congress for matters affecting US territories was recognized, and it was noted that present arrangements respecting Guam (the Organic Act of 1950) are the creation of the Congress. The possibility that the Guamanians might seek to deal directly with the Congress was discussed. While there has been some contact by the Executive Branch with members of the Congress (in particular, Senator Jackson) on the possibility of a new political status for Guam, there was general agreement that an early approach to the Congress would be desirable. Interior will take the lead vis-a-vis the Congress.

5. Respecting the possibility that the Congress might request a copy of the President's directive, it was pointed out that a decision on such a request would involve consideration of the question of executive privilege.

6. It was noted that the President's directive provides clear guidance concerning our approach to dealing with Guam's interest in participating in international organizations. Concern was expressed that adverse precedents might be set by our handling of similar problems involving Puerto Rico. (The NSC Staff representative stated that an interagency study might be requested.)

7. The Chairman noted that within the Department of State, he would look to the Bureau of East Asian Affairs as the central point of contact and that he would also call on, in particular, the Bureau of International Organization Affairs, the Office of the Legal Adviser, and the Congressional Relations Staff.

Actions

-- The Chairman requested that Interior provide an options paper concerning

-3-

our negotiating approach for consideration by the Special Committee.
This is to be done as soon as Interior
has completed its internal organization and staffing arrangements.

-- It was agreed that any inquiries from
the press or the Congress should be
referred to Interior (Office of Territorial Affairs). It was also agreed
that Interior would develop contingency
questions and answers for use in connection with such inquiries and would
circulate them to members of the Special
Committee.

Attachment:

List of Participants

NSC UNDER SECRETARIES COMMITTEE

SPECIAL COMMITTEE

MEETING ON GUAM

March 11, 1975

Participants

The Chairman	Robert S. Ingersoll
Interior	Royston C. Hughes
	Emmett Rice
	Kurt Herge
	James Wilson, Jr.
Defense	Captain Edward Whelan, OSD/ISA
	Colonel James Diddle, JCS
NSC Staff	John A. Froebe, Jr.
State	William Gleysteen
	Robert Blake
	Leo Moser
	Oliver T. Johnson
NSC/USC	Wreatham E. Gathright

Appendix 5

Memorandum, April 23, 1975, from Emmett M. Rice,
Acting Director of the Office of Territorial Affairs,
to Assistant Secretary of the Interior Royston C. Hughes

United States Department of the Interior

OFFICE OF THE SECRETARY
WASHINGTON, D.C. 20240

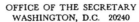 APR 23 1975

Memorandum

To: Assistant Secretary, Program Development and Budget

From: Acting Director of Territorial Affairs

Subject: Guam Future Political Status and Federal Relationship

Contained in this memorandum are alternative courses of action together with the recommendations of this Office concerning decisions to be taken in the short term relating to the Guam-Federal Government discussions. As the person immediately responsible to the Chairman of the Under Secretaries Committee for the development and implementation of a coordinated Federal approach to these discussions, your decision on the four following matters will set in motion the necessary machinery of the Executive Branch for these talks.

Role of the United States Congress in These Discussions

Both the Under Secretaries Committee Guam Study and the Memorandum of February 5, 1975, from the Assistant to the President for National Security Affairs call attention to the necessity for the involvement of and continuing Executive Branch consultation with the Congress in the Guam-Federal discussions. This is an area where the negotiations with the Trust Territory (Micronesia and the Marianas) and the discussions regarding Puerto Rico have diverged in policy and practice and in which neither provide a suitable model for the Guam discussions. Since the Congress is the final authority for any alterations in the Guam Organic Act and for any Federal grants or loans which may result from the Guam discussions, authoritative Congressional involvement from the outset should have the effect of fashioning with the Guamanians programs and agreements which Members of Congress will have an interest in seeing fully approved. Further, a United States team which is representative of both the Executive and Legislative Branches will encourage the Guamanians to represent themselves similarly thereby preventing a one-branch or one-party domination of the discussions.

 CONSERVE AMERICA'S ENERGY

Save Energy and You Serve America!

I 0808

-2-

The following three options are presented for consideration:

A. Direct Congressional Involvement

A letter from the Secretary of the Interior to the Chairmen of
the Senate and House Committees on Interior and Insular Affairs would
apprise the Congress of all actions taken to date and offer (under appropriate security considerations) to make available for study and background
the USC Guam study and related documents. The letter would request that
each Chairman appoint one or two Committee members and appropriate staff
to serve on the Federal delegation for the discussions. The Senators and
Representatives selected would participate fully in any discussions held
with the Guamanians and the Congressional staff would work with the Interior
Department and Executive Branch personnel when desirable.

B. Congressional Consultation

A letter from the Secretary of the Interior to appropriate Committee Chairmen or the Congressional leadership informing them of actions
taken to date and of proposed Executive Branch actions with regard to
Guam's future Federal relationship would be sent immediately. This letter
would also request the addressees' thoughts as to the nature and extent of
Congressional involvement in the discussions and state Executive Branch
desire to keep appropriate Members of Congress fully informed as the discussions proceed. Members of Congress in this situation would not likely
be involved directly in the discussions and continuing contact with them
would be through staff channels.

C. Congressional Consultation (Minimal)

A letter from the Secretary of the Interior would inform the
leadership of the Congress regarding Executive Branch action and intent
concerning Guam's future Federal relationship and state further its intent
to fully consult from time to time with the Congress as the discussions
proceed.

RECOMMENDATION:

This Office recommends the first approach (A.) for the reasons listed
above and for the additional reason that the Congress will then be able to
determine in its own way the involvement of the Guam non-voting delegate
(Honorable Antonio Won Pat). The actual implementation of this approach
will warrant discussion with Under Secretary Ingersoll and eventually
with Congress.

-3-

Organization of Interior Department Staffing for Guam Discussions

This Office recommends that there be established within the Office of
Territorial Affairs a two or three person staff contingent for the Guam
discussions. These persons could be employed by contract in the short-term
as adequate position slots do not exist at present in this Office. They
would report through the Director of Territorial Affairs to the Assistant
Secretary for Program Development and Budget and would comprise his personal
staff for this exercise. Coordination with other Federal agencies,
Congressional staff and other parties would be handled through the senior
member of this staff and through the Assistant Secretary when appropriate.
The present resources and expertise of the Office of Territorial Affairs
will be available to complement the work of this proposed contingent. Coordination as necessary with the Staff Director of the Under Secretaries Committee would be effected through the Director of Territorial Affairs and
the Assistant Secretary.

Depending upon the role of the U.S. Congress, the U.S. delegation for the
Guam discussions would function most efficiently if comprised of less than
ten members, one of whom should be the senior staff person mentioned above.

Involvement of Other Federal Agencies

The model used in the TTPI negotiations for involvement of other Federal
Agencies should prove applicable to the Guam discussions. This Office,
therefore, recommends that letters over your signature be sent to each of
the principals of the Under Secretaries Committee requesting that he forward to this Department the name(s) of those to be involved at the working
level in this exercise. In most cases, the other Federal Agencies involved
will be the Departments of State and Defense although, since budgetary
concerns will likely plan an important role in the discussions, representation from OMB and perhaps from the Treasury will prove necessary at times.

The makeup of the Executive Branch members of the U.S. delegation to the
discussions should be a decision of the Assistant Secretary of the Interior
as a recommendation to the Chairman of the Under Secretaries Committee. Each
Department called upon to furnish a delegate should be prepared to provide
representation commensurate in rank with that from the Congress.

Contact With the Guamanians

Initial contact regarding the Guam-Federal relationship discussions was
made by the Interior Department with former Governor Camacho. Mr. Camacho
felt that a delay in Guam's response would be necessary due to the pending
election. The Camacho administration defeat has had the effect of negating
the life of the Executive Branch invitation to the Guamanians and new action
is now necessary. The invitation should come from the Secretary of the
Interior.

This Office recommends, however, that the invitation to the discussions be
delayed until after the question of U.S. Congressional involvement is

-4-

settled. It is likely that the Guamanians will desire that the Executive/
Legislative representation in their delegation mirror the U.S. mixture and
the Secretary should be able to indicate the nature of the U.S. delegation
in his invitation. Further, precipitous action by the Executive Branch in
this area may have an adverse effect on the Congress. We finally recommend
that, in his letter of invitation, the Secretary be joined by the leadership or the Interior Committee Chairmen of the Congress if possible.

If you approve the above recommendations, this Office will furnish for
your approval and, when appropriate, the Secretary's signature, drafts
of the letters called for above. I am further able to make staffing
recommendations for the personnel additions recommended above should
you so desire.

Emmett M. Rice

Appendix 6

Letter, August 22, 1975, from Frank F. Blas,
Chairman of Guam's Special Commission on the Political Status of Guam,
to President Gerald R. Ford

THIRTEENTH GUAM LEGISLATURE

P. O. BOX 373
AGANA, TERRITORY OF GUAM
U. S. A. 96910

Collaj
RELEASE

August 22, 19

1975

on General Governmental Operations

ank F. Blas — Chairman
rd R. Duenas — Vice Chairman

e D. Ada
d T. Charfauros
. Duenas
o M. Palomo
ardo Salas

The President,
The White House,
Washington D.C.

Dear Mr. President:

As Chairman, I wish to inform you of the organization of the
Special Commission on the Political Status of Guam.   The
thirteen members of the Commission include representatives
of the general public and representatives of the Executive
and Legislative branches of the Guam government.

The Guam law creating the Special Commission states that "a
resolution of some of Guam's basic economic, social and political questions should be sought within the framework of
political status negotiations with the federal government with
all due speed."

Accordingly, the Commission has formally approved a timetable
for accomplishing its purposes, among which are identifying
points of discussion for inclusion in any status negotiations,
and drafting a plebiscite for submission to the voters during
next year's Primary Election in September.

In a March 3, 1975 meeting between Mr. Norman Ross, former
Assistant Director to the President's Domestic Council, and
the Governor of Guam, Ricardo J. Bordallo, Guam's relationship
with the United States was discussed and a Presidential Task
Force was mentioned by Mr. Ross as one method of studying all
aspects of Guam's political status.

The recently concluded and successful status talks with the
Northern Marianas were conducted by Ambassador Haydn Williams,
appointed to represent the President of the United States, and
the Political Status Commission of the Northern Marianas.

The Commission believes its mission can be accomplished much
quicker if liaison were established as soon as possible between
the office of the President and itself.

D 0717

201

Therefore, the Commission, by this letter, respectfully requests that a representative of your office be appointed for the purpose of establishing initial dialogue with the Special Commission on the Political Status of Guam in order that proper coordination can be maintained throughout our efforts to resolve the important question of the future relationship of Guam to the United States of America.

Sincerely yours,

FRANK F. BLAS
Chairman
Special Commission
on the Political
Status of Guam

Appendix 7

Letter, August 27, 1975, from Assistant Secretary of the Interior
Royston C. Hughes to Robert S. Ingersoll, Chairman of the
Under Secretaries Committee

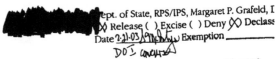

AUG 2 7 1975

Dear Mr. Ingersoll:

At our last meeting relative to Guam Future Political Status and
Federal relationship, I was requested to study the matter of U.S.
Congressional participation, develop alternative approaches, and
transmit recommendations for review and decision prior to any
further action.

Alternative courses of action together with my recommendations
concerning decisions to be taken in the short term relating to
the Guam-Federal Government discussions follow.

<u>Role of the United States Congress in These Discussions</u>

Both the Under Secretaries Committee Guam Study and the Memorandum
of February 5, 1975, from the Assistant to the President for National
Security Affairs call attention to the necessity for the involvement
of and continuing Executive Branch consultation with the Congress in
the Guam-Federal discussions. This is an area where the negotiations
with the Trust Territory (Micronesia and the Marianas) and the discussions regarding Puerto Rico have diverged in policy and practice
and in which neither provide a suitable model for the Guam discussions.
Since the Congress is the final authority for any alterations in the
Guam Organic Act and for any Federal grants or loans which may result
from the Guam discussions, authoritative Congressional involvement
from the outset should have the effect of fashioning with the Guamanians
programs and agreements which Members of Congress will have an interest
in seeing fully approved. Further, a United States team which is representative of both the Executive and Legislative Branches will encourage
the Guamanians to represent themselves similarly thereby preventing a
one-branch or one-party domination of the discussions.

The following three options are presented for consideration:

    A.   <u>Direct Congressional Involvement</u>

       A letter from the Secretary of the Interior to the Chairman
of the Senate and House Committees on Interior and Insular Affairs
would apprise the Congress of all actions taken to date and offer
(under appropriate security considerations) to make available for

Classified by NSC
GDS

I 0808

-2-

study and background the USC Guam study and related documents. The letter would request that each Chairman appoint one or two Committee members and appropriate staff to serve on the Federal delegation for the discussions. The Senators and Representatives selected would participate fully in any discussions held with the Guamanians and the Congressional staff would work with the Interior Department and Executive Branch personnel when desirable.

B. Congressional Consultation

A letter from the Secretary of the Interior to appropriate Committee Chairmen or the Congressional leadership informing them of actions taken to date and of proposed Executive Branch actions with regard to Guam's future Federal relationship would be sent immediately. This letter would also request the addressees' thoughts as to the nature and extent of Congressional involvement in the discussions and state Executive Branch desire to keep appropriate Members of Congress fully informed as the discussions proceed. Members of Congress in this situation would not likely be involved directly in the discussions and continuing contact with them would be through staff channels.

C. Congressional Consultation (Minimal)

A letter from the Secretary of the Interior would inform the leadership of the Congress regarding Executive Branch action and intent concerning Guam's future Federal relationship and state further its intent to fully consult from time to time with the Congress as the discussions proceed.

RECOMMENDATION:

This Office recommends the first approach (A.) for the reasons listed above and for the additional reason that the Congress will then be able to determine in its own way the involvement of the Guam non-voting delegate (Honorable Antonio Won Pat).

Organization of Interior Department Staffing for Guam Discussions

If the Assistant Secretary - Program Development and Budget, Department of the Interior, is to continue to take the lead role in this exercise, I recommend that there be established within the Office of Territorial Affairs a two or three person staff contingent for the Guam discussions. They would report through the Director of Territorial Affairs to the Assistant Secretary - Program Development and Budget and would comprise his personal staff for this exercise. Coordination with other Federal agencies, Congressional staff and other parties would be handled through the senior member of this staff and through the Assistant Secretary when appropriate. The present resources and expertise of the Office of Territorial Affairs will be available to complement the work of this proposed contingent. Coordination as necessary with the Staff Director of the Under S████████████ Committee would be effected through the Director of Terr████████████ the Assistant Secretary.

-3-

Depending upon the role of the U.S. Congress, the U.S. delegation for the Guam discussions would function most efficiently if comprised of less than ten members, one of whom should be the senior staff person mentioned above.

It is, however, my personal recommendation that the instructions of the Under Secretaries Committee be modified so as to substitute the Director, Office of Territorial Affairs, Department of the Interior, for the Assistant Secretary - Program Development and Budget, Department of the Interior as the individual to assume the lead role in the exercise. Such a substitution would not only be economic of time and effort, but practical as well in that the Director of Territorial Affairs could devote greater personal attention to the exercise. Additionally, his present staff has already had considerable status negotiations experience in the Marianas negotiations which has from time to time involved in-depth studies for comparison purposes of the Guam structure as it presently exists.

Involvement of Other Federal Agencies

The model used in the TTPI negotiations for involvement of other Federal Agencies should prove applicable to the Guam discussions. I therefore recommend that letters over your signature be sent to each of the principals of the Under Secretaries Committee requesting that he forward the name(s) of those to be involved at the working level in this exercise. In most cases, the other Federal Agencies involved will be the Departments of State and Defense although, since budgetary concerns will likely play an important role in the discussions, representation from OMB and perhaps from the Treasury will prove necessary at times.

The makeup of the Executive Branch members of the U.S. delegation to the discussions should be a decision of the Assistant Secretary or Director of Territorial Affairs, Department of the Interior, as a recommendation to the Chairman of the Under Secretaries Committee. Each Department called upon to furnish a delegate should be prepared to provide representation of appropriate rank.

Contact with the Guamanians

Initial contact regarding the Guam-Federal relationship discussions was made by the Interior Department with former Governor Camacho. Mr. Camacho felt that a delay in Guam's response would be necessary due to the pending election. The Camacho administration defeat has had the effect of negating the life of the Executive Branch invitation to the Guamanians and new action is now necessary. The invitation should come from the Secretary of the Interior.

I recommend, however, that the invitation to the discussions be delayed until after the question of U.S. Congressional involvement is

-4-

settled. It is likely that the Guamanians will desire that the Executive/Legislative representation in their delegation mirror the U.S. mixture and the Secretary should be able to indicate the nature of the U.S. delegation in his invitation. Further, precipitous action by the Executive Branch in this area may have an adverse effect on the Congress. I finally recommend that, in his letter of invitation, the Secretary be joined by the leadership or the Interior Committee Chairmen of the Congress if possible.

I am attaching a draft proposed letter to be sent to the Speaker of the House and the President of the Senate of the U.S. Congress.

Other issues of significance are:

1. **The Under Secretaries Committee Study on Guam.** This document is classified **SECRET** and also contains Inter-Agency Group appraisals of Guamanian positions and the positions of some members. We need to determine how much, if any, of this report should be shared with any Members of Congress who may participate in the Federal Delegation to these talks. I recommend that only the summary and other public-source background material be made available.

2. **The nature of Executive Branch membership on the Federal Delegation to the Task Force.** Depending upon Congressional responses to the enclosed draft, I recommend that Executive Branch representation on the Task Force be numerically equivalent to that of the Congress. The three Agencies immediately concerned are Interior, State, and Defense, with the latter possibly desiring dual representation from the Office of the Secretary and from the services. OMB and the Domestic Council are additional alternatives. It further appears advisable for the Administration group to meet internally prior to any organizational meeting of the full Federal Delegation.

3. **Agenda for organizational meeting of the Federal Delegation.** If the Congress chooses to appoint Members to the Federal Delegation, the following points may arise at the organizational meeting:

- chairmanship of the Federal Delegation;

- coordination of Administration and Congressional staff work;

- the Guam Organic Act;

- the role of the military on Guam;

- the situation regarding Guam's request for a $56 million, one time capital improvements grant; and

- the political status situation in the Trust Territory, particularly the Marianas.

4/27/75

-5-

While the last four of these points will not need to be addressed substantively, we will need to solicit Congressional viewpoints. It is my recommendation that the Department of Interior participant become either chairman or co-chairman with a Member of Congress of the Federal Delegation.

4. Another issue is the pending Won Pat Bill and Government of Guam's separate request for $56 million for school, water and sewer projects. A decision is necessary as to whether the administration should support this request and, if so, whether it is a part of the $75 million negotiating authority contained in the Guam Study instructions.

There appears to be no record of detailed justification independently of that transmitted by Guam. The following language regarding the $56 million request appears on page 136 of the Guam Study: "Validating their (Guam's) request in detail is not possible in this study." A footnote on page 147 of the study says "(The Department of) State favors an executive branch commitment to support 'in principle' this Guam request for capital development assistance, with detailed investigation of the request to be left to the normal budgetary process involving the Government of Guam, Interior, and the Congress. The Office of Management and Budget (OMB) shares similar doubts and believes that no position should be recommended until its own review has been completed."

We have asked Mr. Floyd Fagg, Comptroller for Guam, for his analysis and justification of Guam's needs. We hope to have the necessary justification at an early date.

Sincerely yours,

(sgd) Royston C. Hughes

Royston C. Hughes
Assistant Secretary

Honorable Robert S. Ingersoll
Deputy Secretary of State
Washington, D.C. 20520

cc:
Secy. Surname File

EMRICE:ckr   8/27/75
OTA

I 0808

Appendix 8

Memorandum for the Record, October 7, 1975,
prepared by Richard Y. Scott of the Office of Territorial Affairs

UNCLASSIFIED

(PE5.0184-0684 (

RELEASED IN FULL

MEMORANDUM FOR THE RECORD

Subj: Meeting with Congressman Phillip Burton, October 7, 1975

Participants: Emmett Rice, Deputy DOTA
                 Stephen Sander, Staff Ass't DOTA
                 Richard Scott, Staff Ass't DOTA

                 Congressman Phillip Burton
                 Adrian Winkel, Interior Committee Staff

Met with Burton on October 7, 1975 to get his views on extent of
Congressional involvement in future Guam-Federal relations discussions.
Before getting into substance of our meeting, Burton made point
emphatically that no action or discussion on Guam's political
status would take place until after Marianas Covenant Bill was passed
by Congress. Burton indicated he planned to visit Saipan incident
to installation of new Marianas government and would visit Guam
immediately thereafter to assess situation there.

At this point Rice summarized Guam Political Status Commission
(GPSC) scenario which has the GPSC or successor commission entering into
negotiations with Federal Government, culminating in a basic political agreement with the United States. The Constitutional Convention
would follow the agreement. Before hearing our plan for the talks,
Burton's response to the GPSC scenario was quick and to the point.
There should be no negotiations. He wants to push Won Pat's Constitutional
Convention Bill through Congress as first order of business. (House
passed Bill October 6. No action contemplated by Senate until after
Marianas Covenant vote). Burton's idea of changing Guam-Federal
relations is for Guam to first adopt a constitution; then he would make
some changes in the Organic Act and broaden scope of Federal
programs and services applicable to Guam. On applicability of Federal
laws, Burton saw little chance of exempting Guam from Jones Act.
He was sympathetic to Guam's desire to control immigration. He
supports Won Pat on the subject of inventorying military land
holdings to determine what lands are in excess. Burton also talked
about replacing the Guam Federal Comptroller with GAO and the
GAO could then monitor Guam by sending a few people out to Guam
for several months a year. This should reduce the costs of the
operation. He noted that the people of Guam, including Won Pat,
are opposed to the fact of the Federal Comptroller.

Rice brought conversation back to Administration involvement in talks
with Guam and Congressional involvement. He mentioned GPSC letter to

UNCLASSIFIED

S 0716

(P950184-0685)

the President, of which Burton was aware, and said that we did not have
in mind establishing a U.S. Commission for political status talks but
rather a presidentially designated representative who would open
a dialogue with Guamanians. This seemed to ease his mind but he
said that the Director of Territorial Affairs had the authority
now to work with Guam and that is the way it should continue.
Burton does not like the idea of working through a commission. He
cited major problems confronting his sub-committee as a result of
the Puerto Rico-US Commission. He has not yet figured out a way to handle
this and it may take a lot of time. (Footnote: He gave impression
that his sub-committee would act on Puerto Rico legislation
before taking up Guam or the Virgin Islands). Burton did say he liked
the flexibility afforded by Executive Branch conducting talks
with Congressional consultations along the way.

Burton covered several other subjects besides Guam. (See Sander
MEMCON for details). Subjects included Virgin Islands financial
plight, Sections 2 and 3 of the Marianas Covenant Bill, future
plans for his sub-committee.

Richard M. Scott

Appendix 9

Letter, March 25, 1976, from Under Secretary of the Interior
Kent Frizzell to the Chairman of the Under Secretaries Committee

 United States Department of the Interior

OFFICE OF THE SECRETARY
WASHINGTON, D.C. 20240

C0216
RELEASE
C-INTERIOR
=-NSC
C-STATE

MAR 2 5 1976

Memorandum

To: Chairman, Under Secretaries Committee

From: Under Secretary of the Interior

Subject: Approach to Guam-Federal Relations Discussions

Enclosures: (1) Chronology of Events
            (2) Draft Letter to President of the Senate and Speaker
                 of the House of Representatives

Pursuant to the President's decisions transmitted by the National
Security Council (NSC) Memorandum of February 1, 1975, and follow
on directive of the NSC Under Secretaries Committee's Special Committee on Guam of March 11, 1975, the Assistant Secretary of the
Interior for Program Development and Budget (PD&B) was directed to
"develop and implement a negotiating approach" to effect the Presidential decisions on the Guam Study. Subsequently, you agreed to a
request of the Acting Secretary of the Interior, that as a practical
matter but without amending the President's directive, responsibility
and authority for developing and implementing this approach be transferred to Fred M. Zeder, Director, Office of Territorial Affairs
(DOTA). This transfer has taken place and Mr. Zeder now represents
this Department on the Special Committee on Guam in place of the
Assistant Secretary (PD&B). Also, as reported in the Assistant
Secretary of the Interior letter of November 3, 1975, an Inter
Agency Working Group for Guam-Federal Relations has been established.

By way of background to this proposal, I am enclosing a brief chronology of events from 1973 to date which have to do with Guam-Federal
relations discussions. You will note that Guam's Executive and
Legislative Branches have both expressed interest in the subject and
have already committed both time and money in preparation for possible
discussions with the Federal Government. The most recent indication
of Guamanian interest is a letter to the President from the Governor
of Guam requesting the initiation of discussions with the Federal
Government on the important question of the future relationship of

 Classified by NSC
SUBJECT TO GDS XX EO 11652
AUTOMATICALLY DOWNGRADED AT TWO-YEAR INTERVALS
DECLASSIFIED ON DECEMBER 31, 1982 (year)

D 0717

217

-2-

Guam to the United States of America. An interim reply to this
letter and to the one from the Chairman, Special Commission on the
Political Status of Guam indicated a general receptiveness to the
Guamanian request but deferred answering the substance of the request
until the U.S. Senate had voted on the Marianas Covenant.

It is readily apparent from the activities on Guam over the past
three years that there is a desire to upgrade the Guam-Federal relationship. However, the pressures for change are not so much aimed
at a modified or revised political arrangement as they are at restrictive Federal statutes and regulations that in Guam's view inhibit economic development and financial self-sufficiency. The
prevalent view on Guam is that they need more control over the
application of Federal laws and regulations affecting economic
development. They feel that some of these laws and regulations
should not apply to Guam or in some instances are inconsistently
applied. Most of the principal ones are well known and have been
explored before without success. Included is the issue of the
Merchant Marine Act of 1920 (Jones Act) where Guam is "domestic"
and must use American bottoms in shipping; whereas, regulations
affecting air transport for the island of Guam are "foreign."
More recent regulations of air pollution control have caused an
expensive situation requiring the use of low sulfur oil by the
Guam Power Authority when many Guamanians feel the island has an
open air basin in the Pacific where Continental U.S. environmental
standards should not apply. Another long standing issue is immigration where Guam has little, if any control. These laws and
regulations intended for the mainland are considered by the
Guamanians to be major obstacles in Guam's development, particularly in transhipping and private sector expansion. This view
was recently substantiated in a poll on political status conducted by the University of Guam. Status quo with increased
control over immigration, trade and airlines was the preferred
choice of thirty-five percent of those polled from a list of
options including commonwealth, separate statehood, union with
Hawaii or the Northern Marianas or independence. An additional
ten percent chose status quo without any additional control
over matters affecting Guam.

In the past, the amount of land used for military purposes has
been an issue in Guam-Federal relations. However, two developments
have tended to defuse this issue during the past two years: (1) U.S.
military presence on Guam has had a dampening effect on the economic
recession there; and (2) substantial progress has been made to
resolve outstanding land issues. The latter includes the Join Use
Agreement which has made Guam eligible for FAA Airport Development

-3-

Aid Funds at the International Airport/Naval Air Station, general
agreement between GOVGUAM and the Navy concerning future steps to
relocate the ammunition pier at Apra Harbor and efforts by the
Navy to declare excess various parcels of land no longer required
for military operations or activities.

Looking to the future, the following civil-military issues can
be anticipated:
    - Differing views on how to transfer excess military land, the
Government of Guam (GOVGUAM) preferring to modify existing federal
statutes to permit direct transfer without having to pay fair market
value; Department of Defense preferring to enter into a land exchange agreement which would round out existing base areas.

    - Some friction and problems due to the interlocking relation-
ship which exists between GOVGUAM and the Military Services in the
management of public utilities, e.g. water, sewers, electricity and
telephones.

    - Increasing concern in the military community about the qual-
ity of public services provided by GOVGUAM, particularly in the
field of dependent children education.

Another factor that has commanded more immediate attention amongst
the people of Guam than changing Guam's basic relationship with the
Federal Government is the Territory's financial plight. For the
past eighteen months, Guam has experienced severe financial problems
caused by an over-expansion of its economy (tourist industry) in
the period 1968-1973, the current recession, an exaggerated inflation rate and poor planning, management and control of finances at
the GOVGUAM level. The Department of the Interior is fully aware
of Guam's financial problems and will continue to work with GOVGUAM
to find ways of easing the situation.

Even though pressures for change in the Guam-Federal relationship
have been temporarily diverted by the more immediate need to improve
Guam's economy, there remain some nagging problems in the Guam-Federal
relationship. These problems will continue to grow unless the relationship is clarified.

As a starting point in developing options for a "negotiating approach,"
we have established the premise that we treat Guam as a domestic
matter. Presidential decision on the Guam Study specifically states
that U.S. sovereignty over Guam will be retained. Basic U.S. interests
in Guam, i.e. control over foreign affairs and defense, are not considered negotiable. Therefore, it is important at the outset to

establish that the United States Government is not entering into
unlimited political status negotiations with Guam. Instead, the
Executive Branch of the Federal Government will enter into discussions with the appropriate entity on Guam, now identified as
the Special Commission on the Political Status of Guam, for the
purpose of perfecting the Guam-Federal relationship to the extent
possible.

It is our intention to move ahead with these discussions as soon
as possible after receiving Congressional acquiesence of the
approach recommended in this memorandum. However, progress in the
discussions with the Guamanians may hinge on resolution of Guam's
domestic political problems. Several events have occurred over
the past eight months which many have some effect on the progress
of our discussions with Guam.

The introduction by Congressman Won Pat of a bill in the House of
Representatives last September authorizing Guam to convene a constitutional convention has somewhat complicated the sequence of
events leading to discussions on Guam-Federal relations as viewed
by the Guamanians. The Special Commission on the Political Status
of Guam undertook last August the responsibility of determining
what the people of Guam hoped to accomplish with a change in
political status. They established a timetable and work program
to culminate in a plebiscite in September 1976 which would determine
officially the people's political status preference, i.e. commonwealth,
statehood, county of Hawaii, status quo. Following this determination, the Commission (or its successor since the Commission's
charter expires December 31, 1976, with the ending of the Thirteenth
Guam Legislature) would determine and recommend to the Legislature
and the Governor what steps should be taken to get the best benefits for Guam within the framework of the U.S. Constitution. The
Commission does not consider that Won Pat's bill calling for a constitutional convention is necessarily in conflict with the Commission's
objectives, but that it is premature to draft a constitution until it
is known what status is desired by the people.

Congressman Won Pat has met with the Commission to discuss the
timing of the Constitutional Convention but the discussions apparently
did not result in a compromise solution. Won Pat, with the full
support of Congressman Phillip Burton, is certain that Congress will
pass his constitutional convention bill and he envisions an election
of delegates to the convention in September 1976.

-5-

This is an election year for the Republican-controlled Guam Legislature and Congressman Won Pat. Although Won Pat is a popular politician in Guam and apparently not in danger of being defeated in the election next November, he looks upon the Commission as a challenge to his stature as the advocate for improving Guam's relationship with the Federal Government. If he could delay any substantive work of the Commission until after the 1976 elections, he feels the Commission may cease to exist. Seven members of the Commission (4 Republican, 3 Democrat) are also Senators in the Legislature and it is possible that the composition of the Commission will change or that a successor commission would not be created. However, since we intend to begin discussions with the Commission in May, and both the Governor and Speaker of the Legislature are ex-officio members of the Commission, it appears doubtful that the Guamanians would for political reasons fail to keep the momentum going for an improved relationship with the Federal Government.

Recommended Approach to Guam-Federal Relations Discussions

Several elements make up the recommended approach submitted herein for your approval, namely: (1) Overall U.S. objectives and the Presidential directive on the Guam Study; (2) Organization of an Executive Branch delegation by Mr. Zeder to represent the Federal Government in these discussions; (3) Communication with Congress to apprise the minority members and Chairmen of the Senate and House Committees on Interior and Insular Affairs of the Administration's plans relative to these discussions, and assuming no serious objections to the proposal, Presidential letters to the President of the Senate and the Speaker of the House (enclosure (2)) informing them of our plans; (4) Initial communication with Guam, consisting of letters from the President to the Governor of Guam, Speaker of the Guam Legislature and Chairman of the Special Commission on the Political Status of Guam to be followed by an initial series of meetings with the Commission on Guam in May 1976.

Overall U.S. Objectives and the Presidential Directive (NSC Memorandum of February 1, 1975)

The overall U.S. objectives in any Guam-Federal relations discussions remain those stated in the Presidential directive. There are, however, several areas in the directive which if read literally are inaccurate, undesirable or require some clarification due to changed circumstances.

-6-

I would like to consider it as within Mr. Zeder's discretion to interpret these passages in the spirit of the directive without requesting NSC modification of the directives. However, if the Chairman of the Under Secretaries Committee believes a formal request is necessary, I would ask Mr. Zeder to draft one for USC use. Specifically, in paragraph 2, the directive states that the Federal side "should seek a commonwealth arrangement no less favorable than that which we are negotiating with the Northern Marianas." "Commonwealth" is an imprecise term which strictly speaking might require further definition. If "no less favorable" were deemed to include the financial provisions of the Marianas Covenant, the financial assistance due Guam would be difficult to define comparably and would be potentially exorbitant in amount. There also may be a problem in defining the phrase "modified unincorporated territorial status," and the statement that the agreement should provide "for U.S. military basing rights on Guam" seemingly ignores the fact that the U.S. already has military base rights which it simply wishes to continue as they now exist and which the Federal side may not wish to include explicitly in the negotiations.

Paragraph 4 in the NSC directive authorizes the Federal negotiators to offer "up to a total of $75 million in U.S. financial assistance for Guam's capital improvement program..."

A Guamanian financial crisis unforeseen at the time of the Presidential decision may force Federal assistance to the Guam capital improvement program prior to the commencement of these discussions. Such assistance may diminish the potential leverage of the Presidential decision's authorization to the head of the Federal Delegation to offer Guam up to $75 million in financial assistance.

Interior is currently working with GOVGUAM to ease Guam's financial dilemma and will inform the Chairman of the Under Secretaries Committee (USC) and the USC Special Committee on Guam of financial assistance authorized or given Guam prior to discussions. At the time of Guam-Federal discussions, it may be necessary to seek an NSC determination as to whether the amount of prior assistance should be deducted from the $75 million authorized maximum. In submitting financial assistance proposals to the Office of Management and Budget (OMB), Interior will remind OMB that a $75 million authorization is contained in the Presidential decision on the Guam Study.

-7-

In paragraph 6, the Presidential directive states that under the general supervision of the Chairman of the Under Secretaries Committee "the Assistant Secretary of the Interior for Program Development and Budget should develop and implement a negotiating approach that will give effect to the above instructions, and should organize a U.S. negotiating team that will include representation from the Departments of State and Defense as well as the Department of the Interior."

At the time of the Presidential directive, the position of Director, Office of Territorial Affairs, Department of the Interior, was vacant, and the background of the then Assistant Secretary of the Interior for Program Development and Budget made it logical to designate him the action official. Now, however, the Director, Office of Territorial Affairs, is the concerned official; his chain of command to the Secretary of the Interior does not lead through the Assistant Secretary for Program Development and Budget.

Accordingly, it is appropriate to substitute in the Presidential directive the words "Director, Office of Territorial Affairs, Department of the Interior" for the words "Assistant Secretary of the Interior for Program Development and Budget." The NSC staff has indicated that this change can be effected by a letter of notification, with explanation of the rationale, from the Under Secretaries Committee to the NSC. Inasmuch as no NSC approval is required, it is recommended that the USC send such a letter forward.

Organization of Federal Delegation

Fred M. Zeder, Director, Office of Territorial Affairs (DOTA), Department of the Interior, will head the Federal delegation involved in discussions with Guam on its relationship to the Federal Government. He derives his authority from the Presidential directive on the Guam Study dated February 1, 1975, your letter to me of September 25, 1975, and any subsequent instructions that issue from the President. He will report to you as Chairman, NSC Under Secretaries Committee, on the progress of the discussions.

The Federal Delegation headed by Mr. Zeder will include representation from the Departments of State, Defense and Interior pursuant to the Presidential directive. Inasmuch as these discussions will involve questions of constitutional law and applicability of Federal laws, a representative of the Department of Justice should be included

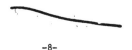

-8-

as a member of the Delegation. At Mr. Zeder's discretion, other
departments/agencies having specialized interests in the Guam-
Federal Relations Discussions will be requested to provide representation on the Delegation.

There has been no special provision in the Interior Department
budget for funding administrative and logistics costs that will
necessarily be incurred in the course of these discussions. Unlike the Office for Micronesian Status Negotiations which receives
special funding for the operation of the office and conduct of
Micronesian status negotiations, the Director, Office of Territorial
Affairs, is expected to undertake this new obligation without additional budgetary support. Therefore, it will be necessary for those
Executive Branch Departments/Agencies having representation on the
Federal Delegation to fund travel and per diem for their representatives involved in these discussions on Guam. Interior will provide
the necessary conference facilities for any discussions held in
Washington, D. C.

Although the foregoing organizational concept is in line with the
Presidential directive on the Guam Study, I would like to propose
an alternative for your consideration. Since the Governor of Guam
requested that the President appoint a Personal Representative and
Guam's Special Commission asked that the President designate a
representative from the White House, it may be appropriate for the
President to consider such appointment. Appointment of a President's
Personal Representative would have the advantage of elevating the
importance, in the eyes of the Guamanians, the Federal Government
attaches to these discussions. Under this alternative, the President would be requested to appoint Mr. Zeder as his personal representative to open and carry on discussions with the Special Commission
relative to the Guam-Federal relationship. The announcement of this
appointment would be made in the Presidential response to the Governor
and Special Commission.

Terms of Reference for the President's Representative should specify
that the scope of his authority in these discussions emanates from
Presidential decisions on the NSC Under Secretaries Committee's
study on Guam and from any subsequent instructions issued by the
President. His authority should extend to include tactics, composition of the Executive Branch delegation involved in discussions with
the Guamanians, determination of frequency and site of meetings with
the Guamanian entity, and procedural matters. He should have broad
authority and full responsibility for consultation with all
Congressional committees having an interest in the outcome of these
discussions. He would also be the focal point for all incoming and
outgoing communications concerning or connected with these discussions.

-9-

The Under Secretaries Committee would establish an Inter Agency
Group for Guam-Federal Relations to be chaired by the President's
Representative which would supersede the existing USC Special Com-
mittee on Guam. The Inter Agency Working Group for Guam-Federal
Relations is already in being and would continue to function in
support of the IAG.

The foregoing differs only in degree from the organizational arrangement in the Presidential directive on the NSC USC Guam Study. The
main strength of this approach is the effect such appointment would
have on Guamanian U.S. citizens of placing these discussions on a
par with the recent Northern Marianas negotiations.

Communication with the U.S. Congress

In view of the special Constitutional responsibility of the U.S.
Congress in matters affecting the status of Guam as an unincorporated
U.S. Territory, perhaps the most important aspect of the Administration's initiative to enter into discussions with Guam is to make a
prior determination that the Congress has no serious reservations or
objections to our recommended approach. Furthermore, since we intend to treat these discussions as a domestic matter, it may be
desirable to obtain the specific concurrence of the Domestic
Council on our approach as described in the following paragraphs
prior to communicating with the Congress.

Scenario for Communication with Congress

After an appropriate time interval following Senate action on House
Joint Resolution 549 (Marianas Covenant), Mr. Fred M. Zeder, Director,
Office of Territorial Affairs, will meet with selected members of
Congress to obtain their views on the Administration's proposal to
meet with Guamanians in the near term to work out improvements in
the Guam-Federal relationship. The Domestic Council last fall
recommended that Interior first apprise minority leaders of Congress
and the ranking minority members of the Senate and House Committees
on Interior and Insular Affairs of the Administration's plans for
Guam-Federal relations discussions, and after that the chairmen of
these committees and the chairman of the House Subcommittee on
Territorial and Insular Affairs. Once the discussions with Guam
have begun, however, it will be necessary to expand our contacts
to other committees such as Armed Services, Judiciary, Commerce,
and Labor and Public Welfare. Interior will coordinate this effort
through the Domestic Council with the assistance of the appropriate
Department/Agency Offices of Congressional Liaison/Relations.

-10-

In each of his meetings with the Members of Congress, Mr. Zeder will first acknowledge the special Constitutional responsibility of the Congress in matters affecting the status of Guam as an unincorporated territory of the United States, and that it is not the Administration's intent to change the basic relationship. He will inform them, however, that both the Governor of Guam and the Chairman, Special Commission on the Political Status of Guam have requested the President to appoint a representative of his office to work with Guamanian representatives on the resolution of some of the imperfections of Guam's relationship to the Federal Government. At this point, he would note that the President's preference is for the Director, Office of Territorial Affairs, to head up an Executive Branch delegation for these talks. Although it is not envisioned that Congress would participate directly in these Guam-Federal relations discussions, Mr. Zeder would emphasize the point that he would establish and maintain close coordination in all aspects of the Guam-Federal relations discussions with those members of Congress and Congressional Committees designated by the leadership.

Mr. Zeder would then outline to the Members the Administration's general approach to the Guamanians as follows: In April letters would be sent from the White House to the Governor of Guam and the Speaker of the Guam Legislature, both of whom are ex-officio members of the Special Commission on the Political Status of Guam (hereafter referred to as Commission) that Mr. Zeder, DOTA, will represent the Federal Government in discussions with the Commission in a review and possible modification of the current relationship. The letters will suggest a meeting of the two delegations in May 1976 to exchange views on the nature of the future political relationship, to review progress made thus far in resolving many of the contentious issues, to discuss parameters for the content of a Guam Constitution (assuming Congress authorizes a Constitutional Convention) and a general discussion of the applicability of Federal laws to Guam.

Agreement would be reached during the May meetings on the substance, frequency and locale of future meetings, agenda and channels of communication. A joint communique for public release would issue from this initial series of talks in order to demonstrate publicly that the Federal Government is officially and actively responding to the Guamanian's desire for the resolution of some of the problems in the Guam-Federal relationship.

Mr. Zeder would set forth to the Members of Congress the overall objectives of these discussions. First, the Administration considers

226

-11-

our relationship to Guam to be a domestic matter. There is no
question of giving up U.S. sovereignty over Guam. The U.S. will
maintain control over Guam's foreign affairs and defense, including
U.S. military basing rights to Guam. Secondly, we support Guam's
move toward complete self-government in internal affairs under a
self-drafted constitution consistent with the U.S. Constitution.
Efforts will continue to promote the material well-being of Guamanians, and over the long term, the Federal Government's actions
should enhance the prospects for the ultimate integration of Guam
with the Northern Marianas.

The vehicle for presenting the changes in the Guam-Federal relationship to the U.S. Congress involves several factors. The Guam Commission may seek to enter into negotiations with the Federal Government similar to the Northern Marianas political status negotiations
with the objective of concluding an agreement similar to the Northern
Marianas Covenant. In the Administration's view this is not desirable
since we are talking about changes in the relationship between the
U.S. and one of its Territories and not creating a new political
entity, as is the case with the Northern Marianas. It is anticipated
that Guam's Constitutional Convention will treat several of the
issues of the Organic Act relationship. Other proposals such as
amendments to the Organic Act as well as changes to existing legislation affecting commerce, immigration and naturalization, labor,
taxation, banking, customs, duties and Federal programs and services
would result in either a series of legislative proposals or an
omnibus bill being submitted to Congress by the Secretary of the
Interior. The development of such a legislative package would be
accomplished in full consultation and cooperation with the Congress.

Mr. Zeder will report to you the results of his meetings with
designated Members of Congress. One or more of those Members
initially contacted may object to the Administration's plan and
propose a significant modification. For instance, Congressman
Won Pat last June introduced House Joint Resolution 489 calling for
the creation of a Commission on the Political Status of Guam to be
composed of seven Members of Congress and a representative to be
appointed by each of the following: the President; Governor of
Guam; and Speaker of the Guam Legislature. The House has not
acted on HJR 489 but Won Pat currently is trying to revive it.
There is also the precedent of the Ad Hoc Advisory Committee on
Puerto Rico whose report is now being considered by the Congress.
Should one or more Members seriously object to the proposal as
outlined by Mr. Zeder and propose a joint Congressional/Executive
Branch approach similar to those mentioned above, and persist in
their objections after attempts by Mr. Zeder to dissuade them,
Mr. Zeder will make recommendations to you as to how next to pro-
ceed. However, in the more likely event that these particular
Members of Congress do not raise serious objections, the President

out of the U.N. Trusteeship,

-12-

would be requested to send letters to the President of the Senate
and the Speaker of the House of Representatives (enclosure (2))
officially informing them of the Administration's plan to begin a
series of discussions with the Special Commission on the Political
Status of Guam in full coordination with the Congress.

Initial Communication with Guam Following Congressional Sanction
of Administration Proposal.

In order to add prestige to these discussions and recognize the
importance the Federal Government attaches to Guam, the President
would send letters to the Governor of Guam, Speaker of the Guam
Legislature and Chairman, Special Commission on the Political
Status of Guam notifying them of the Federal Government's interest
in discussing with the Commission Guam's relationship with the
Federal Government. The letter would include the designation of
Fred M. Zeder, Director, Office of Territorial Affairs, as the head
of the Federal Delegation for these discussions. The theme of the
letters would stress the view that the Federal Government is entering into these discussions in order to strengthen and enhance Guam's
position as a member of the United States political family. The
letter would suggest an early meeting of both delegations but leave
the detailed arrangements to the heads of the respective delegations.

Mr. Zeder would then communicate with the Chairman, Special Commission
on the Political Status of Guam and suggest a series of meetings on
Guam in mid-May 1976. In his communication, Mr. Zeder would suggest
that these meetings result in an exchange of views on the nature of
the future political relationship, progress made thus far in resolving many contentious issues, Guam's plans for a Constitutional Convention and identification of specific issues related to Federal laws
and regulations applicable to Guam. He would also indicate that he
hoped for agreement during this initial series of meetings on the
substance, frequency and locale of future Delegation meetings.

The specific objectives of the Federal Delegation during the initial
series of meetings would be:

    - to indicate publicly to the officials and people of Guam that
recent Federal Government attention to the political status of the
Trust Territory of the Pacific Islands, Northern Marianas and Puerto
Rico is paralleled by a concern for Guam;

    - to attempt to forestall any possibility that a Guam Constitu-
tional Convention or other Guamanian action might cause the Federal

-13-

Government embarrassment or difficulty by acting outside limits the Federal Government considered appropriate.

After the initial series, Mr. Zeder would consider how best to proceed and make recommendations to you in June. It may seem desirable to move quickly into full-scale substantive discussions, either because Won Pat's proposal for a Constitutional Convention has been rejected or postponed or because the Federal side sees advantage in holding discussions concurrently with the Convention process or in persuading the Guamanians to postpone the Convention until the Guam-Federal relations discussions have resulted in delineating an improved relationship. Also, if the Guam Political Status Commission proceeds to hold a September 1976 plebiscite on political status preferences, it would also be a factor affecting this decision.

Even if the recommended approach is followed, i.e. initial series of meetings in May, a second series of meetings would probably be needed in July, and could probably be announced in the May meeting communique.

CHRONOLOGY OF EVENTS REGARDING DISCUSSIONS OF THE GUAM-FEDERAL RELATIONSHIP

1973

- The Twelfth Guam Legislature established a Political Status Commission comprising nine of its members.

- Secretary of the Interior Rogers Morton invited the Governor of Guam to establish a representative group to begin discussions with the Federal Government.

1974

- Governor Camacho of Guam requested a postponement of the discussions in view of the pending gubernatorial and legislature elections.

- / ᵕ Executive Branch Inter Agency Group met in Washington to review internally the Guam-Federal relationship and consolidate positions for possible future discussions with Guam.

- The Political Status Commission of the Twelfth Guam Legislature issued a preliminary report and was dissolved in September.

- The November elections seated a new governor, the Honorable Ricardo Bordallo, and shifted the partisan majority of the Legislature.

1975

- Secretary Morton appeared before the House Committee on Interior and Insular Affairs and, as the Executive Branch Secretary charged with the primary responsibility for supervision of Guam affairs, reaffirmed Administration support for a review of the Guam-Federal relationship.

- Governor Bordallo of Guam met with Secretary Morton and the White House Domestic Council to express his interest in a task force to study Guam's relationship with the Federal Government.

UNCLASSIFIED

DRAFT

LETTER FROM THE PRESIDENT TO THE SPEAKER OF THE HOUSE OF REPRESENTATIVES
AND PRESIDENT OF THE SENATE ON SUBJECT OF GUAM-FEDERAL RELATIONS DISCUSSIONS.

Dear Mr. Speaker (or Mr. President):

I am writing you now to propose that a review take place concerning the relationship of Guam and the Federal Government. What I believe we seek is a newly refined definition of the Guam-Federal bond which gives full weight to the views of Americans on both sides of the Pacific. My proposal is not an uninvited initiative on the part of this Administration. Rather, as you are aware, the past two years have witnessed a growing and considerable interest in many quarters about the course of the Guam-Federal relationship. On Guam, I believe this interest is generated out of the fact that Guamanians are intensely proud of their American citizenship and hope to continue to seek assistance and growth through the Federal Government. This Administration strongly supports Guam in this viewpoint. It further supports, with the Congress, efforts in furtherance of our joint interests in a strengthened and durable relationship with Guam.

By way of background to this proposal, I am enclosing a brief chronology of events occuring since 1973 which have to do with Guam-Federal discussions. You will note that Guam's Executive and

-2-

Legislative Branches have already committed both time and money in preparation for possible discussions with the Federal Government. Given, however, that both branches changed significantly in Guam's 1974 elections, I feel that former Secretary of the Interior Rogers Morton's 1973 invitation to former Governor Carlos Camacho to initiate Guam-Federal discussions has lapsed.

The Governor of Guam recently requested me to designate a representative of the Federal Government who would work with Guamanian officials in a review of the Guam-Federal relationship. With this in mind, I believe it advisable for the Federal Government to indicate its receptivity to the idea of a review of the Guam-Federal relationship and to invite the Guamanians to join with us in this important mission. I have designated Fred M. Zeder, Director, Office of Territorial Affairs, Department of the Interior, acting on my behalf, as the Federal Government representative to coordinate Executive Branch involvement in this effort. He will be joined by representatives of an appropriate level from the Departments of State, Defense and Justice in this review of the Guam-Federal relationship. Other Federal agencies concerned with Guam will be called upon as the need arises.

Our best political judgment at this time indicates that, while the question of Guam's political status will be subsumed in the broader scope of such talks, the subject of the Guam Organic Act

-3-

will and should undoubtedly be considered. Congressman Antonio Won Pat has called attention to the fact that this Act, which defines Guam's political status, has been in force twenty-five years as of August 1, 1975. He also has introduced legislation subsequently passed by the House which would authorize Guam to convene a constitutional convention for the purpose of drafting a constitution for self-government.

Since Congress is the final authority for any alterations of the Organic Act and for legislation affecting Guam, it seems both beneficial and necessary that the Executive Branch discussions with Guamanians on Guam-Federal Relations and its review of the Guam Constitution be fully coordinated with the Congress. In order to effect this coordination, I request that you designate Members of the House (Senate) from appropriate Committees with whom the Executive Branch representative will consult on a regular basis.

In order to insure that the effective coordination and consultation is accomplished, may I suggest a meeting of the Executive Branch representatives for the Guam discussions with the designated Members of Congress on or about _____. At that time, we would like to share with you our thoughts on the direction and preliminary goals of Guam-Federal discussions and, more importantly, to benefit from the views of the Congress.

It is the firm opinion of this administration that, working with and guided by the views and aspirations of our fellow citizens

-4-

on Guam, we together can fashion a future for this Pacific gate-
way to America which is truly reflective of the creativity of our
great nation.

Sincerely yours,

President of the United States

Appendix 10

Letter, May 17, 1976, from the
Chairman of the Under Secretaries Committee
to the Under Secretary of the Interior

THE DEPUTY SECRETARY OF STATE
WASHINGTON

CU24.a
Recommend
RELEASE
T-STATE

UNCLASSIFIED

NSC UNDER SECRETARIES COMMITTEE

May 17, 1976

TO: The Under Secretary of the Interior

SUBJECT: Approach to Guam-Federal Relations
         Discussions

     The approach to Guam-Federal relations dis-
cussions recommended in your memorandum of
March 25, 1976, is approved subject to the
following modifications and comments:

     1. Overall US Objectives and the Presidential
Directive - The interpretations proposed in your
memorandum regarding paragraph 2 of the Presidential
directive are approved on the understanding that
the United States is willing to discuss a commonwealth status or a modified unincorporated territorial status for Guam if Guamanian representatives
so desire. Regarding paragraph 4 of the directive,
authority is contained therein for federal negotiators to offer up to a total of $75 million in US
financial assistance for Guam's capital improvement
program with the precise level and composition of
this assistance to be determined by the Under
Secretaries Committee. The US negotiators should
discuss possible US assistance along these lines
during the course of the negotiations with the
Guamanian representatives and should refer tentative understandings to the Under Secretaries
Committee for approval.

     2. Federal Delegation - The Director of the
Office of Territorial Affairs of the Department of
the Interior should head the federal delegation.

UNCLASSIFIED

S0701

-2-   UNCLASSIFIED

His authority should be based on the Presidential
directive of February 1, 1975, and the letter of
September 25, 1975, from the Chairman of the NSC
Under Secretaries Committee. It is believed that
this authority is adequate for the purposes of
the discussions with Guam and will ensure effective
coordination of the views of the interested US
agencies.

    3. <u>Consultation with the Congress</u> - The
general approach outlined in your memorandum is
approved. On the basis of these consultations,
and assuming that no unforeseen objections are
raised, the President would officially advise the
President of the Senate and the Speaker of the
House of the Administration's plans for the
discussions with Guam. An appropriate memorandum
attaching draft letters should be prepared and
sent to the Special Committee on Guam for approval.

    4. <u>Initial Communication with Guam</u> - The
approach set forth in your memorandum is approved.
Presidential letters to the Guamanian officials
should be drafted and sent to the Special Committee
on Guam along with the draft letters to the
President and the Speaker.

Charles W. Robinson
Chairman

cc: Members, Special
Committee on Guam

UNCLASSIFIED